COMING HOME TO NEZ PERCE COUNTRY

COMING HOME TO NEZ PERCE COUNTRY

THE NIIMÍIPUU CAMPAIGN TO REPATRIATE THEIR EXPLOITED HERITAGE

TREVOR JAMES BOND

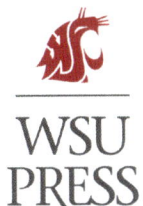

WSU
PRESS

Washington State University Press
Pullman, Washington

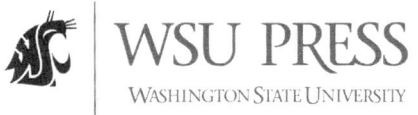

Washington State University Press
PO Box 645910
Pullman, Washington 99164-5910
Phone: 800-354-7360
Fax: 509-335-8568
Email: wsupress@wsu.edu
Website: wsupress.wsu.edu

Library of Congress Cataloging-in-Publication Data

Names: Bond, Trevor James, 1970- author.
Title: Coming home to Nez Perce country : the Niimiipuu campaign to
   repatriate their exploited heritage / by Trevor James Bond.
Description: Pullman, Washington : Washington State University Press,
   [2021] | Includes bibliographical references and index.
Identifiers: LCCN 2021058762 | ISBN 9780874224054 (trade paperback)
Subjects: LCSH: Spalding, Henry Harmon, 1803-1874--Ethnological
   collections. | United States. Native American Graves Protection and
   Repatriation Act. | Nez Percé Indians--Material culture. | Cultural
   property--Repatriation.
Classification: LCC E99.N5 B64 2021 | DDC 979.5004/974124--dc23
LC record available at https://lccn.loc.gov/2021058762

On the cover: Nez Perce crupper (used to prevent a horse's saddle from slipping forward) from the Spalding-Allen Collection. Design by TG Design.

Images and Niimíipuu cultural interpretation of the Spalding-Allen Collection, curated by the Nez Perce Tribe in collaboration with Washington State University's Center for Digital Scholarship and Curation, may be found on the Plateau Peoples' Web Portal: https://plateauportal.libraries.wsu.edu/collection/spalding-allen-collection-nez-perce.

The Washington State University Pullman campus is located on the homelands of the Niimíipuu (Nez Perce) Tribe and the Palus people. We acknowledge their presence here since time immemorial and recognize their continuing connection to the land, to the water, and to their ancestors. WSU Press is committed to publishing works that foster a deeper understanding of the Pacific Northwest and the contributions of its Native peoples.

For Nakia, Josiah, and Robin

Contents

List of Figures

Introduction

On April 27, 1846, writing from Lapwai, beyond the borders of the United States on the Clear Water River, the first missionary to the Nez Perce (Niimíipuu) Tribe, Henry Harmon Spalding, addressed a letter to his "Dear Brother" and former Western Reserve classmate, Dr. Dudley Allen, in Ohio.[1] Spalding noted in his fine handwriting that covered all available space on the paper, "after many promises & a long delay I have started the boxes containing a small collection of articles of Indian manufacture with some specimens of stone &c, all designed for yourself."[2]

Spalding did not ship everything that he had collected for Allen. He regretted that the two "Grey Bear skins & a pack saddle" were not shipped because "it was thought they would be destroyed on Board ship by rats." Who knew that bear skins are a rat delicacy? Fortunately, this letter and the boxes that Spalding sent to Allen stuffed with priceless Nez Perce and Plateau Indian artifacts survived the journey to Ohio. It was a long trip: some 465 miles west down the Columbia River to Fort Vancouver. From there, they travelled across the Pacific to the Sandwich Islands (Hawai'i), then south around the cape of South America to Boston, followed by an overland journey west to Ohio.

Roughly 150 years later, in an ironic turn, the collection that Spalding assembled became the focus of a major struggle over ownership between the Nez Perce Tribe and the National Park Service on one side and the Ohio Historical Society on the other. The Spalding-Allen Collection, the context of its creation, its subsequent survival, and the prolonged efforts of the Nez Perce and the National Park Service to acquire and keep the objects in the Nez Perce homeland will be the focus of this book, the first extended treatment of this story.

The act of collecting is a topic of increasing scholarly interest. As the scholar Curtis Hinsley observed, collecting is "an expression of desire through the exercise of power over others."[3] This "exercise of power" includes the acquisition of selected items and the act of describing the items in new ways. Unfortunately, we do not know the exact details of how Spalding acquired his collection or from whom, but there are clues to the context present in Spalding's surviving correspondence, the judgement of scholars, and importantly, Nez Perce oral traditions. These issues comprise the early chapters.

1

Connected to the notions of power and description, collecting is also associated with place. The curator and scholar Christian Feest defined collecting as "a process by which samples of a complex whole are removed from their meaningful and functional context in order to be preserved under artificial conditions and within a new frame of reference."[4] When Spalding shipped the collection around the world to Allen, and Allen's descendants in turn donated the collection to Oberlin College, this Nez Perce material culture was far removed from its "meaningful and functional context." I argue that place and context matters when interpreting material culture. The shirts and dresses in the Spalding-Allen Collection, for example, come from a specific place, were created from resources present there, and made by people whose decedents still live there. These objects, therefore, inform a specific place and way of life. These powerful connections are lost when the items are stored away from public view in a far distant repository. The story of the "lost" years of the Spalding-Allen Collection during its residence in Ohio is the subject of chapter four in part two.

Henry Spalding's collecting was also closely linked to colonialism, westward expansion, and the American domination of the Oregon Country. Spalding sought to change the Nez Perce so that they could assimilate into the dominant culture. In this way, he was at the vanguard of more than a century of concerted efforts by the United States government to seize resources and change Nez Perce culture and the cultures of Native peoples across the United States.

This is a tale of survivance—the resilience and enduring presence of the Nez Perce people advocating for justice and the repatriation of their cultural heritage. It is also an example of the contested ownership of a collection by an institution, the Ohio Historical Society, of the material culture of a far distant people, the Nez Perce. However, in this case, the American public sided with the Nez Perce and their supporters. Their success drew upon a close collaboration with the National Park Service, persuasion, and a sophisticated media campaign. In the end, the Nez Perce Tribe repatriated the earliest documented collection of artifacts of their people and the largest and best documented surviving collection of Plateau material culture.[5]

While the roots of this story—the origins of the collection and the activities of Henry Spalding—date to the nineteenth century, much of the story, including the contested ownership of the Spalding-Allen Collection and its eventual return to the Nez Perce homeland, takes place during the late twentieth century. This is the subject of parts two and three of the book. With few exceptions, historians have largely ignored contemporary Nez Perce history and instead continue to write primarily about nineteenth-century topics, such as Chief Joseph and the war of 1877.[6]

Stepping back, this research also centers on the very enterprise of history: how primary sources are created, preserved, and ultimately made available for researchers. For the survival and accessibility of primary sources is never neutral, and their preservation—among collectors and families and over time in institutions—is never assured. This book explores the making of a collection, informed by an archive of documents whose ownership was contested, tangled in the legacy of colonialism. Archivists, curators, and scholars refer to the origins of collections, their creation and the history of their care as "provenance." Provenance is critical to all historical research because it informs the interpretation of all primary sources. However, many scholars do not ask basic questions regarding the provenance of the collections they rely upon for their research. Why is a particular collection located in Washington, DC, or New Haven, or London? How was it acquired and under what circumstances? Do other communities have a vested interest or a claim to it? What barriers are in place that hinder access to the materials?

For curators at museums, libraries, and other cultural institutions, the provenance of their early acquired collections is often murky. Generally, the names of the collectors are known but not always how they acquired their collections. The circumstances through which collections are acquired are often unrecorded by the collectors, leaving museum curators to fill in the missing pieces with incomplete evidence. My research seeks to answer these and other questions related to the provenance of the Spalding-Allen Collection.

This story is much broader than one tribe's efforts to reclaim a portion of their cultural heritage. The ultimate success of the Nez Perce reclaiming the Spalding-Allen Collection is one example in a larger struggle of Indigenous communities around the world to reclaim their cultural heritage—heritage that was, in many cases, extracted and shipped great distances from source communities.

On another level, these events mark the start of a shift in relationships between collecting institutions (museums, archives, and libraries) and Native peoples. The passage of the Native American Graves Protection and Repatriation Act (NAGPRA) on November 16, 1990, mandated that any institution in the United States that received federal funds must report to the federal government their holdings of Native American (and Native Hawaiian) remains and associated funeral and sacred objects. NAGPRA also compelled repositories to contact representatives of the Native communities regarding these materials—the descendants of the peoples whose physical remains and funeral and sacred objects were collected by non-native people. These affected communities would then determine the final disposition of these objects based on a "reasonable" conclusion derived from a "preponderance" of available evidence.

In 1993, the American Alliance of Museums (AAM) adopted a Code of Ethics for Museums which states, among other points, that collections in a museum are "accounted for and documented" and that "competing claims of ownership that may be asserted in connection with objects in its custody should be handled openly, seriously, responsively and with respect for the dignity of all parties involved."[7]

The spirit of NAGPRA, that native communities should have legal protections over categories of their material culture, led to discussions in 2006 among museum officials to define what constituted "sacred" objects, as well as conversations in the archives community over protocols for Native American archival materials.[8] At its August 13, 2018, meeting in Washington, DC, the Society of American Archivists (SAA) formally endorsed the Protocols for Native American Archival Materials. According to the American Archivists website, "when presented with the Protocols in 2008, the SAA Council declined to endorse them, opting instead to solicit feedback and discussion over a multi-year period." The SAA admitted that many of the original criticisms of the protocols were based in the "language of cultural insensitivity and white supremacy" and after more feedback and discussion the council again declined to endorse the protocols in 2012. However, six years later, "the SAA Council acknowledges that endorsement of these Protocols is long overdue. We regret and apologize that SAA did not take action to endorse the Protocols sooner and engage in more appropriate discussion."[9]

NAGPRA and its legal requirements marked a major change in the relationship between institutions, such as museums, and Native communities. However, in the years after the passage of NAGPRA not all curators, anthropologists, collectors, and scientists embraced the law. The most controversial case of NAPGRA centered on the disposition of the remains of Kennewick Man or the Ancient One whose skeleton two college students found in 1996 in the shallows of the Columbia River near the city of Kennewick, Washington. Local police initially opened a murder investigation, but scientists determined that the bones were very old: over 8,500 years old.

The Confederated Tribes of the Colville Reservation and four other tribes sued the US Army Corps of Engineers (who managed the land where the skeleton was found) to repatriate Kennewick Man and rebury him. Before the bones were returned, a group of scientists led by Doug Owsley, a forensic anthropologist at the Smithsonian Institution, filed another lawsuit to halt the repatriation so that the remains could be studied. The scientists argued in court that the bones were so old they could not be linked to living Native Americans. Owsley based his opinion on evidence that Kennewick Man consumed a marine diet, indicating that he lived near the coast, but had travelled up the Columbia River only to hunt. Some scientists, drawing on skull measurements reminiscent of nineteenth-century methodologies, claimed that Kennewick Man's skull had "Caucasoid" features and that he was European. Others joined the fray, including a group in California, modern day pagans who sued for the bones to bury them in a pre-Christian Norse ceremony.

Recent evidence bolstered the arguments of the Native groups that Kennewick man was indeed a distant relative. In 2015, a group of Danish scientists published a paper in *Nature* proving that Kennewick Man's DNA did not belong to a European but rather most closely resembled the DNA of members of the Confederated Tribes of the Colville Reservation.[10] Other Plateau communities objected to the Colville participation in the study, as it required further samples taken from the "Ancient One." After the publication of the DNA findings and proof of the close connection with Plateau Indians, which came as no surprise to Native American groups, powerful political allies sought to repatriate the remains. Recovering the remains was more complicated than simply receiving the remains stored in the Burke Museum. According to Nakia

Williamson-Cloud, director for the Nez Perce Tribe Cultural Resource Program, several researchers held on to samples of the Ancient One and were reluctant to return them for reburial.

In August 2015, Senator Patty Murray of Washington state introduced legislation to return Kennewick Man's skeleton to the Colville and the coalition of Columbia Basin tribes. Washington governor Jay Inslee and Representative Dan Newhouse lent public support to Murray's legislation. Murray's legislation was attached to the 2016 Water Resources Act, a bill that had strong bipartisan support. President Obama signed the bill on December 16, 2016. After the passage of her amendment, Senator Murray said, "After more than 20 years of debate, it's time to return the Ancient One to his rightful resting place."[11] Just upriver from the site of the discovery of Kennewick Man's remains, Wanapum elder Rex Buck articulated the view of many Native Americans that it was time to honor Kennewick Man, the Ancient One, by reburial. "We need to put him back so he can rest," Buck said.[12]

As the litigation over Kennewick Man demonstrated, NAGPRA remains a slow and at times controversial process. For the first few years after 1990 and the passage of the law, this was especially true. Today, NAGPRA claims generally follow a routine, bureaucratic process. In the early 1990s, some in the scientific and museum community saw the law as a potential threat that would force the return of collections and disrupt scholarship. However, decades later, most view the law as having a very positive effect on the relations between Native American communities, curators, and academics. Anthropologist Max Carocci observed in a 2018 essay that NAGPRA covers more than burials, exhumations, and repatriations. According to Carocci, the legislation "was meant to provide a framework for re-assessing power imbalances between museum and Indigenous North American communities, which for many decades were left out of even the most basic decisions about the fate of their cultural heritage lying in museums, storage facilities, and research laboratories."[13] A generation after the passage of NAGPRA, dialog and consultation around the management of cultural heritage between Native American groups and museums is part of the ethos of curating Native American collections at most major American museums. NAGPRA has also led in some cases to a sense of healing. According to curator Chip Colwell, "repatriation may also heal by restoring broken relationships between the living and the dead, as much as between the scientific and Indigenous communities. Repatriation heals by visibly shifting power; it symbolizes freedom from colonialism."[14]

NAGPRA has had an impact. After three decades, Native Americans and Native Hawaiians have reclaimed more than 50,000 sets of human remains, 1.4 million funerary objects, and 14,000 sacred objects and objects of cultural patrimony.[15] However, the greatest obstacle in returning bodies and sacred burial goods (estimated at 200,000 sets of remains and more than one million funerary objects) held in federal repositories and museums nationwide is the lack of documentation (provenance) of where collections came from. Centuries of collecting and poor record keeping, and more recently, decades of dam and road construction preceded by hasty archaeological digs, resulted in millions of poorly documented Native American collections (bodies, grave goods, and other objects) in museums. According to a 2010 Government Accountability Office report, the vast numbers of unidentified collections was a result of "poor curation practices by agencies and repositories, along with poor historical records and documentation."[16] These "vast numbers" represent roughly 75 percent of all bones labeled as Native American, comprising some 122,736 sets of remains. These bodies remain in limbo because according to the institutions that hold the bones, they do not have the documentation to return the bodies to the culturally affiliated tribes.[17] The Spalding-Allen Collection differs dramatically from many early Native American collections because Spalding wrote a detailed letter describing the objects and their relative value. The letter also dates and situates the items in the collection.

In the struggle over the Spalding-Allen Collection, the Ohio Historical Society resisted NAGPRA. They were slow to report on their holdings to the federal government and their relationship with Native American history centered on curating historical collections, not engaging with contemporary Native communities. On the other extreme, the Nez Perce National Historical Park, founded by a series of cooperative agreements and an extremely close working relationship with the Nez Perce Tribe, exceed the spirit of NAGPRA. Frank Walker, superintendent of the Nez Perce National Historical Park, characterized the nature of this partnership: "our relationship had built a level of trust and respect rarely seen between a Native Nation and the National Park Service."[18] Although

NAGPRA is part of this story and an important legal development in the changing relationships between Native American groups and museums, the Nez Perce decided not to pursue a NAGPRA claim against the Ohio Historical Society. Such claims generally take years to resolve and many NPS officials and Nez Perce feared the Spalding-Allen Collection would be sold on the open market before a resolution.

The Spalding-Allen Collection is at the center of this research. To keep it there, I draw upon an anthropological framework for collecting and curating collections—what anthropologists Amy Margaris and Linda Grimm call a "life history" approach for collections. Meaning is not inherent in objects, and by extension archives, but "is imparted and revealed through their interactions with human agents."[19] Collections require human interaction to be meaningful. And when collections are removed from the cultural settings and the people that best understand the artifacts, the collections further lose cultural context. By drawing upon a life history approach for the Spalding-Allen Collection, we see that the curation and meaning associated with it, depending on the individuals associated with it and where the collection was held, is an ongoing process: a process that changes over time. This research demonstrates that the "life history" of this particular collection remains most vibrant after the collection returned to its "meaningful and functional" context in Nez Perce country.[20]

This "life history" approach is appropriate in another sense, for it is a methodology employed by oral historians. In oral history, a "life history" refers to an expansive interview, generally recorded in multiple lengthy sessions, in which the interviewee can relate their whole life, "from childhood to the present."[21] This book is a "life history" of a collection. I consulted texts and interviewed individuals to tease out the context in which the Nez Perce created the objects in the Spalding-Allen Collection, its journey across the United States, and its story until its return to Nez Perce country. My research therefore draws upon the expertise of curators, dealers, conservators, and most importantly the Nez Perce, who preserve the traditions of their material culture, passed down many generations. The prominence of Nez Perce voices in this work seeks to put their voices on an equal footing with those written sources that, starting with Spalding and his fellow missionaries, reflect the views of the dominant culture.

Prior to conducting any interviews, I completed a Washington State University (WSU) Institutional Review Board (IRB) Exemption Determination Application. On February 5, 2015, the WSU IRB notified me that IRB oversight was not required for my research. The IRB determination, however, did not constitute permission to recruit members of the Nez Perce Tribe for interviews or conduct my research on their reserved lands. I then completed a Nez Perce research permit to interview enrolled members of the Nez Perce Tribe.[22]

A professor had described to me his visit before a different tribal research board as a grilling worse than any graduate exam. I prepared for my visit and, after scheduling my appointment with help from Josiah Pinkham, I arrived at the Nez Perce Tribal Executive Committee (NPTEC) headquarters early and practiced my brief speech describing my research project. Nakia Williamson-Cloud advised me to be quiet and then he succinctly and eloquently summarized my project and indicated his support. After the presentation, a few of the NPTEC members asked questions and it was then that I met Bill Picard who later recorded an amazing interview. They approved my research permit on April 21, 2015. After this meeting, I reflected on one of the key questions included on the Nez Perce Tribe's Research Permit application. How does this research benefit the Nez Perce Tribe?

To start to answer this question, I wanted to ensure that the research I conducted would be easily available to the Tribe, so I changed the release forms that I had planned to use for the interviews from those of the WSU Libraries to those of the National Park Service. After I conducted the interviews, I sent my interviewees copies of the transcripts of our interviews. Upon completing my dissertation on which this book is based, I donated the releases, audio files, and transcripts from the oral histories to the Nez Perce National Historical Park in Idaho so that the interviews would be with the Spading-Allen Collection. If any royalties result from this book, I will make donations to the Nez Perce Tribe and to Washington State University in support of programs that benefit the Niimíipuu people.

In addition to generously sharing their cultural expertise, several of the Nez Perce I interviewed, including Nakia Williamson-Cloud, Josiah Pinkham, and Kevin Peters, also brought their knowledge of Nez Perce material culture. These men intimately know how their ancestors made the items in the Spalding-Allen Collection because they continue these same traditions. Between the three of them, they fashion a wide range of traditional Nez Perce items such as head dresses, beaded gun cases, carved flutes, men's shirts, cradleboards, and other objects.[23]

For this methodology of conducting interviews and listening to Indian perspectives, I am indebted to Lucullus V. McWhorter, whose papers are held in the archives at Washington State University, where I work. McWhorter was a rancher and an advocate for Native issues. In his youth, McWhorter found the outdoors more compelling than the classroom. Though he ended his formal education when he was twelve, McWhorter became a passionate amateur archaeologist, a collector of arrow points, and eventually an ethnographer and historian. McWhorter began forming his archive in earnest in 1906, when he assisted the Yakama people in their struggle against legislation proposed by Washington Senator Wesley Jones that every Yakama Indian give up three fourths of his or her land allotment in exchange for irrigation rights.[24] To win public support for his position, McWhorter collected documents from Indian agents, Yakama sources, and conducted interviews with Indians and non-Indians for a series of pamphlets—*The Crime Against the Yakimas* (1913), *The Continued Crime Against the Yakimas* (1916), *The Discards* (1920)—that he published on behalf of Yakama rights. The Yakama Tribe prevailed and kept their water. Because of these efforts in 1909, the Yakama adopted McWhorter with the name "Old Wolf" and invited him to tribal deliberations, where he listened and took notes.

In these pamphlets and his later books, McWhorter became a close friend and trusted advocate to many Plateau peoples. His writings provided Native perspectives on historical events decades before historians began to include Native American voices in their work.[25] According to Nez Perce Tribe member and park ranger/cultural interpreter, Diane Mallikan, the only books the Nez Perce would read of their history were *Yellow Wolf: His Own Story* and *Hear Me My Chiefs!* by McWhorter. The other histories of the Nez Perce, according to Mallikan, "contained so many lies because historians depended almost exclusively on military reports as the foundation of their research."[26] McWhorter is an instructive model not only for what he wrote, but also for how he wrote.

In addition to my training as a historian, I bring to this research a background in archives and libraries. I oversee the department of

Manuscripts, Archives, and Special Collections at Washington State University located in Pullman, Washington, on traditional Nez Perce and Palouse lands. In my work at WSU and collaboration with colleagues, I have learned that many of the significant collections that document the early culture of this region's Native American communities no longer reside in this region. Important collections gathered by early Euro-American colonizers now grace the storage vaults of museums and research institutions across the United States, Canada, and Europe. Often these collections are poorly documented and inaccessible to the very communities that are particularly interested in them. This pattern of acquisition continues today where the wealthiest of private (and some public) institutions can afford to acquire collections offered by specialized dealers while regional institutions and Tribes, archives, libraries, and museums simply cannot compete in this marketplace.

My work at WSU includes codirecting the Center for Digital Scholarship and Curation (CDSC), established in 2015 as a collaboration between the WSU Libraries and the College of Arts and Sciences. Our work involves the ethical curation of digital cultural heritage. My colleague and CDSC director, Dr. Kimberly Christen, developed the Mukurtu Content Management System in collaboration with Alex Merrill, the CDSC's director of technology.[27] Mukurtu is an Australian aboriginal term for a dilly bag or a safe keeping place. Created as a safe keeping place for digital cultural objects, Mukurtu was designed with Indigenous protocols for circulating and sharing information. For instance, Mukurtu provides communities with options for circulating digital heritage at a granular level. As an example, a Tribe managing their Mukurtu site may determine that access to particular images or recordings should be for women only, or restricted by family, clan, or other kin group or at certain times of the year. Site administrators can assign these nuanced protocols to individual digital objects. Mukurtu also rebalances the control and authority over categorizing and describing collections by putting Native/Indigenous knowledge on par with archival or library description. Our current work with Mukurtu seeks to develop models for the shared curation of Native American cultural heritage between major American collecting institutions such as the Smithsonian, the Library of Congress, and sovereign Native American Tribes.

A highly visible example of Mukurtu available online is the Plateau Peoples' Web Portal, a collaboration between WSU and eight tribes from the Columbia Plateau, including the Niimíipuu. In 2020, as the Nez Perce National Historical Park completed the final stages of consultation for a new long-term exhibit, the Spalding-Allen Collection moved from the exhibit area (where most of the collection has remained since 1978) to rest in the temperature-controlled collections storage vault at the park. But the Spalding-Allen Collection is still be available to the public online. The photographs and research materials developed as part of this book are now part of the Niimíipuu section of the portal.[28] This book is another answer for how this research benefits the Nez Perce Tribe.

Grunge and the Spalding-Allen Collection Campaign

I first learned of the Spalding-Allen Collection at the start of my graduate history program at WSU. The events had taken place less than a decade before I came to work at the university. Initially, I had planned to write about the Spalding-Allen Collection as the fourth chapter in a dissertation about collectors whose collections founded archival repositories in the region. After writing the first three chapters, I realized that the planned chapter on Henry Spalding and the Spalding-Allen Collection should be the entire research project.[29]

As I learned more about the collection, I found it surprising the Nez Perce Tribe had raised the staggering sum of more than $608,000 to purchase it from the Ohio Historical Society. And I wondered, why did they have to pay for it in the first place? The fact that one of my favorite bands, Pearl Jam, played a small role in the fundraising for the return of the collections was also intriguing. As I began my research, I discovered the Spalding-Allen Collection was the largest and earliest documented surviving collection of Nez Perce material culture. The collection included beautifully made dresses and shirts with elaborate decorative elements. Not only was it in exquisite condition and extremely rare but also the collection itself served as an important bridge between contemporary Nez Perce culture and the lifeways of the Nez Perce during early contact.

In conducting my research, I realized that I saw the collection differently from the Niimíipuu experts I interviewed. Like them, I admired the designs and condition of the artifacts and their documented age. However, when as we dug deeper during interviews with curators and members of the Nez Perce Tribe, I came to appreciate that they viewed these items not only as museum pieces, but as examples of techniques, providing an opportunity for the repatriation of skills and life ways. In particular, the use of decorative porcupine quillwork—present in the collection—was replaced by beads after sustained Euro-American exchange when beads could be readily attained. The collection's examples of quill decorations allow contemporary Nez Perce to see how these materials were processed and sewn onto the garments, thereby providing inspiration to contemporary Nez Perce artists. These objects also represent a rich opportunity to revitalize the Nez Perce language, for the technical vocabulary of garments and horse regalia include words uncommon in everyday Nez Perce speech.

Place matters for this story. The items in the Spalding-Allen Collection came from a particular place on the Columbia Plateau, and were made by people who fashioned them from local plants and animals. One can simply walk outside the Nez Perce National Historical Park gallery in Spalding, Idaho, and see the plants and (if one is lucky) the animals used to fashion the objects in the collection. The descendants of the Niimíipuu people who made the items in the collection work at the park site and live nearby.

The Spalding-Allen Collection, once removed from the Columbia Plateau, lost much of its connection with the people who understood, used, and appreciated the objects in it. According to Nakia Williamson-Cloud, "the problem with collecting in general in terms of the museum environment today is you kind of strip these items out of their natural context." And in doing so this creates, Williamson-Cloud continued, a "gap between the knowledge and understanding of how these items… were utilized and how they were worn and [on] what occasions… who this item was originally made for and how it was used and all the knowledge that went with it. And it puts it in a kind of relatively inert environment."[30]

Furthermore, something is lost when artifacts are removed from their cultural setting and placed in a distant, inert environment. The objects that comprise the Spalding-Allen Collection are not only beautiful to see but also engage multiple senses: touch, smell, and sound, particularly when the Nez Perce language is spoken. The scholars Constance Classen and David Howes argue, "the sensory values of an artifact, furthermore, do not reside in the artifact alone but in its social use and environmental context. This dynamic web of sensuous and social meaning is broken when an artifact is removed from its cultural setting and inserted within the visual symbol system of the museum."[31] The return of the Spalding-Allen Collection to the Nez Perce and its "natural context," and the healing of its "dynamic web of sensuous and social meaning," represented an important milestone in a broader Nez Perce effort to retain and reclaim their cultural heritage. Collections, I argue, are best curated by individuals knowledgeable about the local context of the items.

This research explores one collection and one community's struggle to regain its cultural heritage. However, this story is important on a much broader level because museums and other collecting institutions hold vast and poorly documented collections related to Indigenous peoples around the world. By piecing together the provenance of these collections—when they were acquired, under what circumstances, how the institutions came to own them—affected communities can begin a dialog with museum curators around the ethical, shared curation of these collections.

This book examines the dynamics of a Native American Nation seeking to preserve its culture by repatriating a collection from the ownership of a museum that claimed title under dubious circumstances. In this sense, this research transcends the efforts of one tribe on the Columbian Plateau, and speaks to communities across the globe who wish to see their material culture held by museums and private collectors return home.

Part 1

Collecting

Chapter 1

The Nez Perce and the Missionary Collector

I want more [Native American collections]. They are all worth the having!
I will try and pay for them all in due course of time. If you see proper you
will oblige me by any different curiosities, that you can send me.

—Dudley Allen, letter to Henry Spalding

Henry and Eliza Spalding served as the first missionaries to the Nez
Perce Tribe on the Columbia Plateau near Lewiston, Idaho, arriving
in 1836 and staying through 1847. To supplement the operating funds
provided by the American Board of Commissioners for Foreign Missions
(ABCFM), Henry Spalding collected Nez Perce and Plateau Indian
material culture and shipped these objects in two barrels to his friend
and benefactor Dudley Allen in Ohio. Spalding was not the first collector
in the Northwest: he followed a tradition that had begun a century before
with early contacts by Euro-American explorers and fur traders.

Importantly, the Spalding-Allen Collection survived the two-year
journey, as did the letter that Spalding mailed to Allen with details of
the shipment. The circumstances by which Spalding acquired the collection became a factor in the Nez Perce Tribe's efforts to repatriate the
collection owned by the Ohio Historical Society. I argue based in part on
Niimíipuu oral tradition that Spalding did not purchase the collection
from the Nez Perce people but instead listed what he thought to be the
value of the items in exchange for trade goods sent by Allen. Spalding's
collecting on behalf of his friend and financial supporter Allen is one key
example of an early missionary removing important items of cultural heritage that later came under the custody of a distant museum, a pattern
that was repeated by other missionaries and colonialists.

Beyond Spalding's collecting, his missionary methods left enduring divisions among the Nez Perce that continue to the present day. His legacy as a trader, collector, and stern missionary later influenced questions over the ownership of the Spalding-Allen Collection. To his supporters, Spalding was a driven, industrious, and devout missionary. His fellow missionaries found Spalding difficult, quarrelsome, and quick-tempered. The historian Alvin Josephy described Henry Spalding as "a severe and bitter man of 33, with a thin-skinned, jealous nature and a sudden, furious temper."[1] According to Nez Perce oral histories, Spalding suppressed Native culture, including the wearing of regalia and participation in the seasonal journeys to gather food in specific places at the correct time of year. He wanted the Nez Perce people to become sedentary farmers, dress as Euro-Americans, and adopt Christianity, abandoning their traditional beliefs. Spalding also employed harsh punishment of the Niimíipuu people in the form of public whippings and he developed a reputation as more of a trader than a religious teacher.

The Niimíipuu (Nez Perce)

In the early nineteenth century, the Nez Perce was one of the largest and most powerful tribes of the Northwest, with a population in 1805 of roughly six thousand individuals.[2] It was also the most influential tribe of the inland Columbia Plateau. Situated in the hilly plateau country of modern Washington, Oregon, and Idaho, the Nez Perce located their camps and villages beneath the steep hills on the Columbia, Snake, and Clearwater Rivers. At the start of the nineteenth century, scholars estimate there were more than seventy permanent Nez Perce villages ranging from thirty to two hundred individuals depending on the season and social groups. Archaeologists have identified three hundred total sites including seasonal camps, located near available food sources.[3] Generally a headman united several villages into a band. A chief sometimes led a group of bands on activities, such as war parties or buffalo hunts. However, the Nez Perce preferred temporary local leadership to permanent leaders. They expected their leaders to make good decisions, live in a morally exemplary manner, and to be generous with their supporters.[4]

According to tradition, the Nez Perce trace their origins to a monster whose body once filled the upper Clearwater River in north central Idaho. After the monster ate most of the people and animals living on the land, the trickster hero, Coyote, armed with five stone knives, pitch, and fire-making tools, challenged the monster to a contest: each would try to inhale the other. Coyote went first and could not inhale the monster, but the monster easily inhaled Coyote. Once the monster swallowed Coyote whole, Coyote lit a fire inside the monster and used his knives to cut out the monster's heart. Coyote then sliced up the monster's body and threw the pieces across the land. From these bloody pieces of the monster formed many Native peoples: the Coeur d'Alene, Cayuse, Pend d'Oreille (Kalispel), Flathead, Blackfeet, Crow, Sioux, and other Indian tribes. Coyote then washed the monster's blood off his hands, thus forming the Nez Perce.[5]

The Nez Perce did not practice agriculture but strategically migrated to locations where food was most seasonally abundant. With the introduction of the horse after 1700, the Nez Perce dramatically increased the distances they travelled as part of these migrations. The spring snow melts brought enormous salmon runs up the rivers beside their villages and camps. Scholars estimate that per capita, the Nez Perce consumed over five hundred pounds of fish per year. The Nez Perce joined other Plateau Indian groups at places such as Celilo Falls where they would fish and trade for a range of goods including beads, dentalium shells, and other ornaments to decorate their shirts, dresses, and leggings. After the fishing season, the Nez Perce gathered roots and berries from the higher valleys in late spring and early summer.[6]

In mid-summer, they gathered roots, such as camas, and berries, including thornberries, huckleberries, currants, and chokecherries. They stored portions of this bounty in woven bags and placed the preserved food in winter storage pits. At the appropriate time, they would gather bear grass and the other materials they used in their basketry. During the summer, the Nez Perce joined with neighboring tribes including the Umatilla, Cayuse, and Yakama to form large hunting parties that crossed the Lolo Pass into Montana to find buffalo. After the hunt, in addition to preserving the meat for sustenance and trade, they tanned the skins and wove the hair into rope and made clothes and other household goods.[7] By November, the Nez Perce would settle into their winter quarters until the following spring. These lifeways were disrupted as the Nez Perce people engaged with Euro-Americans.

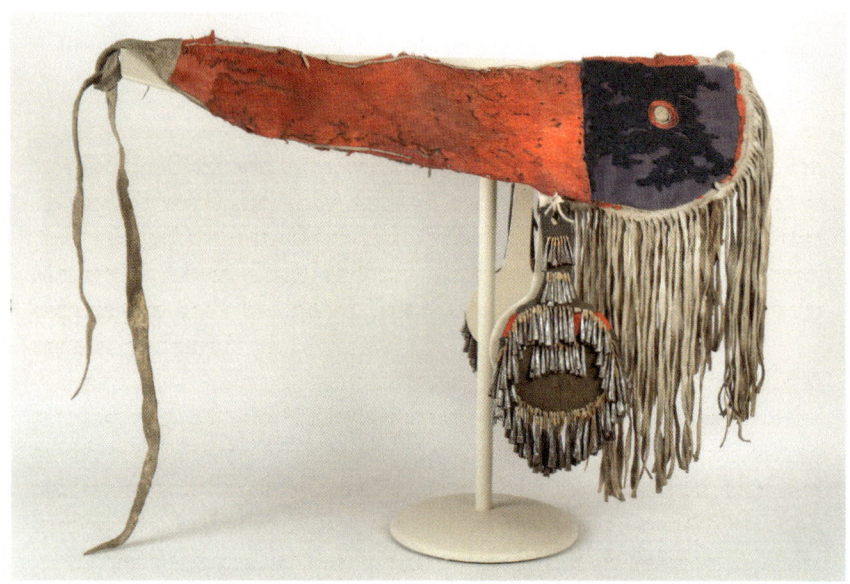

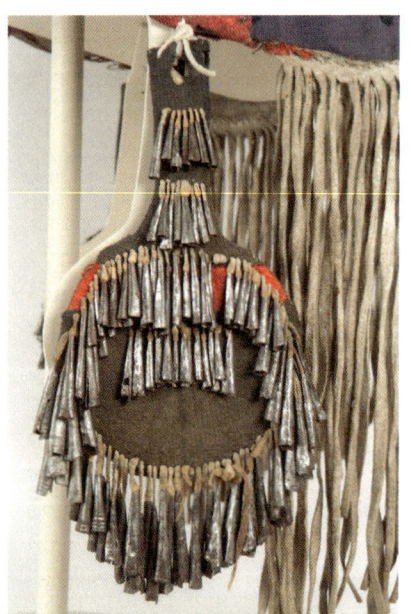
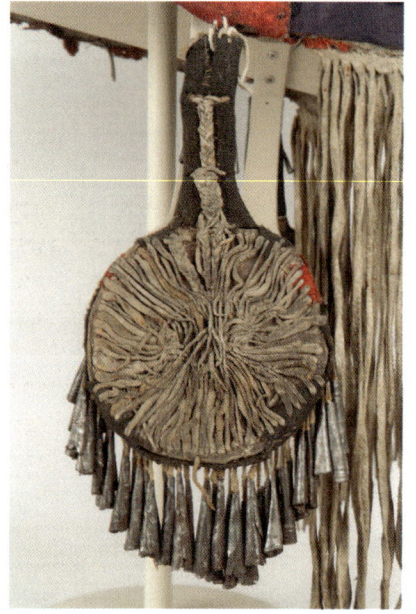

Horse crupper from the Spalding-Allen Collection made of bison hide, wool, red-and-blue trade cloth (heavily soiled from cultural use and insect damage), and cut and hand-rolled tin cone jingles. Photographs by Zach Mazur. Courtesy of the Nez Perce National Historical Park. NEPE 8756.

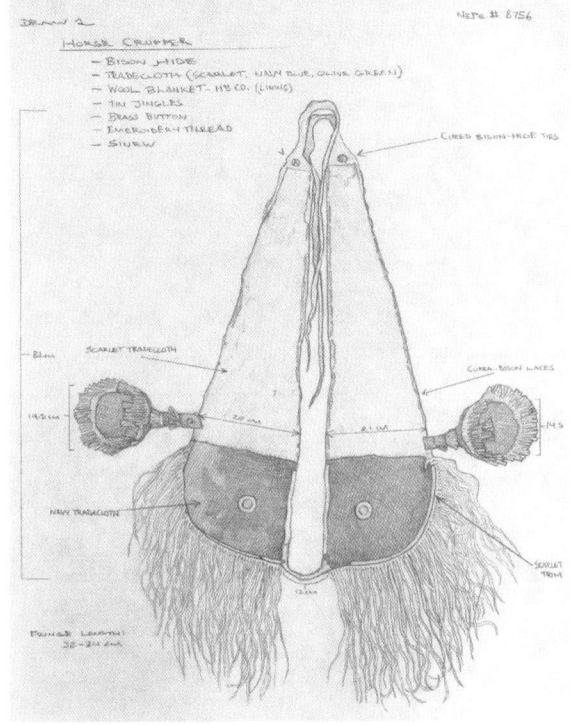

Drawings of the horse crupper by Nakia Williamson-Cloud.

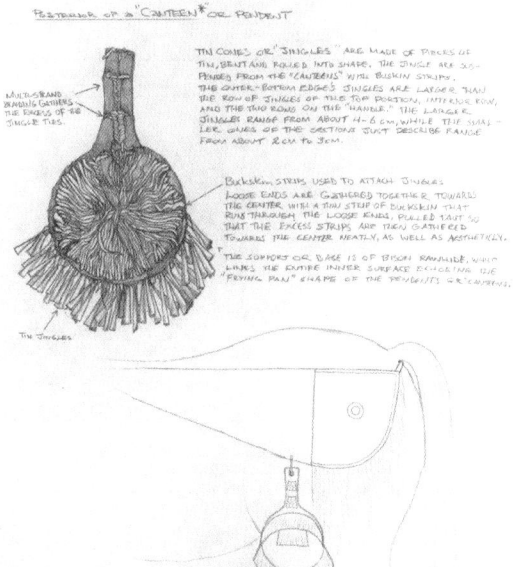

The Arrival of the Euro-Americans

In September 1805, the Lewis and Clark Expedition arrived in Nez Perce country on their journey west to the Pacific Ocean. A hunting party led by William Clark was initially spotted in the Weippe Prairie by the son of Chief Twisted Hair Aleiya and two companions. The boys reported to their village that the intruders had glassy, fishlike eyes and speculated that Meriwether Lewis, Clark, and their party were related to dogs or bears because they had a bad odor.[8] Twisted Hair's brother Al-We-Yas met the party and offered food.

Lewis and Clark and their party were starving after a long and difficult crossing over the Lolo Pass. After some initial unease, the Nez Perce fed members of the expedition, provided them with horses, and served as their guides down a portion of the Columbia River. The Niimíipuu remained friendly when Lewis and Clark and their party returned in 1806.

Between this contact and the arrival of Spalding's mission in 1836, the Nez Perce enjoyed a period of relative prosperity fueled in part by their engagement with the fur trade. They served as brokers in an extensive trade network that extended from the plains of Montana to Celilo Falls on the Columbia River.[9]

Hearing of the power of Euro-American technology, as witnessed by neighboring tribes—and perhaps inspired by the teachings of Spokane Garry, a Plateau spiritual leader who attended an Anglican school—the Nez Perce and Flathead Tribes sent a delegation of four men to St. Louis, Missouri, the exact purpose of which is still debated.[10] There, in 1831, they met the superintendent of Indian Affairs, William Clark, famous for his journey across the continent with Meriwether Lewis. A newspaper report of the meeting characterized the nature of the visit as the Indians' spiritual quest seeking the book of heaven.[11] Some Nez Perce do not agree with this interpretation. Nakia Williamson-Cloud remarked that the Nez Perce already had religious traditions and that that they were not "waiting for religion." Rather in the missionary era of the mid-nineteenth century, "the academics and those people that taught" were "missionaries...especially out in the west."[12] Subsequent events and Protestant propaganda have led some scholars to surmise that the purpose of the trip was to request missionary teachers to gain new spiritual power.[13] One year later, the Reverend Samuel Parker visited Nez Perce lands and wrote to his missionary colleagues to send reinforcements.

In 1836, Henry Spalding and his wife Eliza joined Marcus and Narcissa Whitman and William Gray on a mission to bring Christianity to the Indians of the Oregon Country (present-day Oregon, Washington, and Idaho), then a contested region under joint occupation by Britain and the United States. On their way to meet the Whitmans, Henry and Eliza Spalding visited the mansion of Dudley Allen in Kinsman, Ohio. There Spalding had a wagon prepared for their overland journey west. Spalding and Allen had met five years earlier in 1831, when Spalding enrolled at Ohio's Western Reserve College, and the two men became lifelong friends and correspondents. Allen was a noted physician and remained a steadfast supporter of Spalding and his missionary activities.[14] Spalding repaid Allen for the goods Allen had shipped to him and Allen's cash donations to the American Board of Commissioners for Foreign Missions (ABCFM) by writing letters to his friend and sending "Indian curiosities" back to Ohio. It would be another thirty-five years before Spalding and Allen met again in person, but in the intervening decades they maintained an active correspondence.[15]

Spalding, Whitman, and the other Oregon Country missionaries received support for their activities from the ABCFM, an enterprise with a global reach. Established in 1810 by graduates of Williams College, in the midst of the Second Great Awakening, the ABCFM sent its first missionaries to India in 1812. In addition to ministries abroad, the organization sponsored missions to American Indian tribes, both within the United States and, in the case of the Spaldings and Whitmans, to regions that would later become incorporated into the continental United States.[16]

After the ABCFM established the Whitmans and Spaldings in the Oregon Country in 1838, the organization sent reinforcements. This second wave of missionaries included Elkanah and Mary Walker, Cushing and Myra Eells, Asa and Sarah Gray, and Cornelius Rogers. During their journeys across the continent, the missionaries bickered and quarreled with each other about differences in personalities and missionary practices. This dissension led to their decision to establish multiple mission stations at Tshimikain (near Spokane), Waiilatpu (near Walla Walla), Lapwai (near Lewiston), and Kamiah (farther from Lewiston). These missionaries were among the first American, non-Indian permanent residents of the Oregon Country. Henry and Eliza Spalding served as the first missionaries to the Nez Perce. Except for a brief period between 1847 and 1862, Presbyterian missionaries maintained a presence among the Nez Perce until 1932.[17]

In the 1830s, the Columbia Plateau was home to powerful bands of Cayuse, Nez Perce, and Spokans, who had less contact with whites than neighboring tribes to the west and east. While these communities maintained their traditions through oral and material culture, the ABCFM missionaries were excessively literate. The letters, diaries, and other publications of these missionaries provide much of the early documentation of the Plateau tribes to whom they ministered. Asa Smith, Spalding's colleague and fierce critic, who established another mission to the Nez Perce at Kamiah between 1839 and 1841, studied the Nez Perce language and wrote in detail about their seasonal rounds, while Spalding and Whitman met and mentioned Nez Perce leaders in their letters. Spalding also kept detailed climatic data and botanical samples of the region.[18]

According to Nakia Williamson-Cloud many "Nez Perce people initially were fairly responsive to his [Henry Spalding] coming to this area. Not necessarily just for the fact that we…somehow…didn't know who God was or…didn't have any religion and we were waiting for religion. That's how sometimes the history books sort of characterize it." Instead, the Nez Perce sought the knowledge that Spalding brought. This knowledge, Williamson-Cloud continued, "was technology, such as firearms and other things that had a tremendous impact on our lives at that time. …And so I think a lot of that was not so much that we were looking for religion or spirituality, because we already had that. But that we were looking for that type of knowledge and ways to access that."[19]

While the Nez Perce were interested in the technologies the missionaries brought, the missionaries themselves struggled to follow the guidelines established by the ABCFM to preach to the "Natives" first before undertaking other efforts such as teaching literacy or farming. David Greene, the ABCFM board's corresponding secretary, instructed Spalding and his fellow missionaries to preach the gospel, but to avoid establishing schools unless the Nez Perce were willing to pay for them.[20]

For the first few years of the missionaries' work, the Nez Perce came in large numbers for Sabbath services and provided much-needed food to the Spaldings. Henry Spalding wrote that on May 1, 1837, the Nez Perce brought fresh trout "weighing from 8 to 10 pounds." And in September he received forty salmon as gifts, which he salted, and also fresh game, including the "hames [sic] of 15 or 20 deer." A party of Nez Perce also travelled to Fort Colville and returned to Lapwai with pork, peas, corn, and some ninety pounds of flour.[21] As the Nez Perce people had kept the Lewis and Clark expedition alive by generously sharing their food, so too did the Spaldings survive due to the generosity of the Nez Perce.

As Spalding and his fellow missionaries shared their knowledge of agriculture, religion, and other topics with the Native inhabitants of the region, they demanded that the Plateau peoples to whom they ministered give up their traditions to be "reborn out of their old lives into utterly new ones."[22] According to Spalding, "while we point [the Nez Perce] with one hand to the Lamb of God which taketh away the sins of the world, we… point with the other to the hoe."[23] This process of conversion included more than religious belief and ritual. It also involved the Nez Perce abandoning their traditional lifeways and adopting Euro-American sedentary agriculture and dress. Many Nez Perce resisted this assault on their culture by simply staying away from Spalding.

In October 1839, Spalding confided in his diary of the low numbers of Nez Perce participating in the Sabbath. "Not quite as many as usual. Many have left for roots, game, fish &c. Nothing can be done for this people till they are settled. Oh hasten that day, Gracious God."[24] According to Spalding's biographer Clifford Drury, "Spalding never wavered in his conviction that the Indians had to be settled if they were to be saved."[25]

In addition to advocating for sedentary agriculture, Spalding and his fellow missionaries proscribed a vast array of Nez Perce customs. The missionaries attempted to regulate Plateau social customs by forbidding sex outside of monogamous marriage, gambling, and warfare. Spalding and his missionary colleagues sought to end traditional religious practices including ceremonies that involved drumming, singing, dancing, and wearing regalia.[26] For Spalding, religious conversion and assimilation to Euro-American culture combined in the "civilizing" process. As the historian Elliott West notes, this process of forced assimilation practiced by Spalding and his missionary peers was an aspect of a broader national effort of Indian removal forcing Native peoples west into Indian Territories where missionaries and government agents could have time to assimilate them while other settlers exploited the resources found on ceded Indian lands.[27] This forced assimilation was also part of a larger colonial project whereby colonizing nations exploited colonial peoples economically and culturally by removing Indigenous cultural artifacts and sending them far away as "curiosities" for display in museums to demonstrate the superiority of Euro-American culture. Collecting of Native American culture continued as government officials and others believed that Native cultures would disappear as they were assimilated into Euro-American society.

Museums in turn collected Native American material culture from the late nineteenth century onward without regard for the communities who created the items. Curator Chip Colwell cites three reasons: the first was the "salvage ethic," the idea that Native peoples were on the verge of extinction and thus their materials life should be preserved before it was too late; secondly, the political disempowerment and economic desperation of many Native American communities who suffered gravely at the close of the Indian Wars led communities to sometimes sell sacred materials to make ends meet or made them powerless to stop government authorities from taking cultural materials and ancestral remains; and finally, the idea of the museum as an instrument of the public good, animated by its sense of public duty. Colwell noted that "this new motivation allowed museum administrators to pursue their work at whatever the cost to (typically) distant Native Communities because it could be justified by the public service the museum was providing."[28]

As Nakia Williamson-Cloud observed, "a lot of the collections came to be at that point in time where there was the thought across the nation, especially in the institutions of higher learning, that we were no longer going to be here. That was the beginning of anthropology in the U.S.; let's document these people because they're not going to be here in another 100 years."[29]

Chapter 2

Collecting Native American Material Culture

Traditions of collecting Indigenous material culture began centuries before Henry Spalding established his mission to the Nez Perce. The European discovery of the Americas in the fifteenth century coincided with the advent of Renaissance collecting. The events would later influence the context in which Spalding operated. The earliest explorers, missionaries, and colonialists sought out objects of material culture from Indigenous peoples for their own personal collections or to trade or sell upon return to their home countries.[1] In this way, collecting represented one aspect or form of conquest. The arrangement of these collected artifacts served as material signs of victory over their former owners and places of origin.[2]

Early areas of collecting included Indigenous religious objects to show the need for Christian missionary work and objects of military technology, demonstrating what European explorers faced or ultimately what they conquered. Scholar and curator Christian Feest noted that "solders and missionaries probably destroyed more native works of craftsmanship than they preserved."[3] According to Feest, "only a small fraction, perhaps as little as one percent, of the objects collected in America ever entered the collections established by princes and scholars, and later by educational and religious institutions across western and central Europe."[4] Furthermore, according to curators Bob Chenoweth and Tabitha Erdey, the European collectors "seldom understood or recorded the cultural context in which Native Americans created these objects." Their assumption of European "cultural and religious superiority further obscured understanding of the cultures that had created the coveted objects."[5]

The earliest method of museum display consisted of cabinets of art and curiosity, or *kunst* and *wunderkammern*, established "upon the idea of the universal representation of the works of man and nature" with "rarity of execution or availability" as the "primary criteria of selection."[6] The earliest materials included in these cabinets came from the regions Europeans colonized including Mexico, Brazil, Greenland, Florida, and French Louisiana. The tradition of displaying "cabinets of curiosities" persisted into the twentieth century. Objects included in such displays had only minimal labels and scarcely any explanation as to their importance or to the culture or individual that had created them. Through the late nineteenth and into the twentieth century, curators and anthropologists "erroneously presented the items as relics of static or vanishing cultures."[7]

Although the impulse of Europeans and later, Americans, to collect "curiosities" of Indigenous peoples of the Americas dates back to first and sometimes violent contact, hundreds of years later museums remain reluctant to return these collections. European, Canadian, and American museums hold vast troves of material culture created by the Indigenous populations of the Americas. For example, one of the earliest artifacts of the contact between Europeans and Indigenous peoples of the Americas—a large headdress, made of more than 400 Quetzal feathers, gold, and precious stones, reputedly given by the Aztec emperor Moctezuma to Hernán Cortés in 1519—remains in the Austrian Weltmuseum (Museum of the World). Austria refuses to return it to Mexico despite two decades of formal requests from the government of Mexico. Austria's ambassador to Mexico, Eva Hager, argued that "it can't be transported without risks."[8] Yet it remains on display in Vienna, to the dismay and humiliation of the people of Mexico.

The earliest extant collection of Native American objects from the Pacific Northwest comes from George Vancouver's voyage to the Northwest coast in April 1792. In June 1792, Vancouver claimed ownership of the area that is now Washington state and named it "New Georgia." During a stop at the Strait of Juan de Fuca, Vancouver's surgeon and first mate, George Hewitt, collected objects and created a list describing them. Among the items Hewitt acquired were utilitarian objects from coastal peoples including bowls, spoons, combs, and two anthropomorphic objects: a carved grease dish and a standing figure wearing a hat.[9] During this voyage, Hewitt also participated in a survey trip with Lieutenant Broughton, Vancouver's second-in-command, that took them one hundred miles up the Columbia River. On that trip, likely in the area of The Dalles, Hewitt collected the earliest surviving and documented Plateau object: a woman's hat of vegetable fiber (perhaps hemp), bear grass, bark, and leather. This hat became part of the British Museum's collections in 1890 when A. W. Frank acquired the Hewitt Collection on behalf of the museum.[10]

In 1805, thirteen years after Hewitt's collecting, Meriwether Lewis, William Clark, and their expedition travelled down the Columbia, documenting the Native peoples of the West. In addition to their written accounts, Lewis and Clark collected specimens and Native American artifacts for President Thomas Jefferson. Jefferson later donated the Lewis and Clark Collection to Charles Wilson Peale's museum in Philadelphia. In 1850, the Peale Collection was sold to P. T. Barnum and the Boston Museum. A fire subsequently destroyed the collection acquired by Barnum, while the Peabody Museum at Harvard University acquired the Boston Museum materials.[11]

The artist George Catlin acquired three skirts and a whale bone bark shredder (used by a western Washington tribe) from William Clark in the late 1830s, when Clark served as governor of the Missouri Territory and superintendent of Indian Affairs. Clark displayed his personal collection (mostly acquired after his famous travels with Meriwether Lewis) in a brick museum he had attached to his home. Clark's museum also served as a council chamber where he met Native delegations. Upon Clark's death in 1838, his collection went to the Western Academy of Natural Sciences in St. Louis where it later burned in a fire in 1869.[12] Catlin took his collection to Europe where, after becoming financially destitute, he was forced to sell it to Joseph Harrison. In 1884, the Smithsonian acquired the Catlin Collection from Mrs. Sarah Harrison.[13]

Two more early Northwest collections came to Europe via Hudson's Bay Company trading posts in the Northwest. An early collection of Coast Salish art that included Salish canoes carved with figures and mountain goat horn bracelets went to the Perth Museum of Scotland when the museum acquired the Colin Robertson Collection. The second collection came to the British Museum from Captain Edward Belcher, who had visited the Hudson's Bay Company's fur-trading post at Fort Vancouver in 1839. During his journey along the Columbia River, Belcher acquired a mountain sheep horn bowl, a carved wooden ladle, a cedar bark skirt, several Chinook/Clatsop style baskets, and an oblong Klickitat basket.[14]

Prior to the arrival of Henry Spalding, maritime exploring and fur-trading expeditions dominated the collecting of Native American material culture from the Northwest Coast. With very few exceptions, the material culture came from Native groups who inhabited the lands along the banks and the mouth of the Columbia River. Since those doing the collecting were Europeans or were financed by European companies, the majority of the surviving artifacts went to European museums. The high tide of European collecting of ethnographic material from around the world came with the second wave of colonialism in the nineteenth century when European museums began grouping collections by peoples and cultures. An outcome of the vast expansion of collections was a tremendous overcrowding of exhibit displays. Nor did architects design these museums to accommodate the future growth of collections, with the result that they quickly became overwhelmed.[15] By the end of the nineteenth century, European museums began acquiring fewer Native American collections, while North American museums with substantial funds for acquisitions developed extensive collections.[16]

Chapter 3

The Spaldings and the Allens

Henry Spalding began the wave of collecting by Americans that would come to dominate the Columbia Plateau. However, collecting was a small part of the activities that Henry Spalding and his wife, Eliza, undertook. The two faced significant challenges as missionaries. They devoted much of their energy to basic survival. Goods in the Oregon Country were expensive, basic supplies had to be shipped great distances, and the ABCFM provided only $500 per year, per family. In their efforts to obtain the goods they needed for survival, missionaries such as Spalding relied on donations from eastern US supporters sent in barrels by ship.[1]

In June 1841, Spalding received one such barrel from his former college friend and ardent supporter, Dudley Allen. Not only did Spalding appreciate the goods packed inside he also made use of the barrel itself. Writing to Allen, Spalding mentioned "it now contains our beef. We need another for pork. We had nothing but small kegs and they usually leaked."[2] Spalding wrote in his diary regarding the arrival of another barrel that he found, "a large b[a]r[re]l from my friend Dr. Allen, Ohio, the former containing native cloth & a few articles & the latter $100 worth of clothing judiciously selected & not highly priced, not injured though put up some two years ago."[3] The two years the barrel spent in transit reflects the isolation from the eastern United States in which Spalding labored. The Pacific Islands and portions of Africa and Asia, though geographically farther away from the headquarters of the ABCFM in Boston than from the Oregon Country, were nevertheless more closely linked to the East Coast of the United States by sea travel.

In February 1842, Spalding started collecting Indian goods to send to Allen. He wrote to Allen alerting him to his progress and setting low expectations, "I am making out a box of Indian clothing and implements to send to you and hope to get it ready to send next fall....I do not know as I shall meet your expectations, do not put them high."[4] Spalding's initial estimate of the time required to assemble the collection proved overly optimistic. In a July 1843 letter to Allen, Spalding apologized, "I am ashamed to say that I have not yet made up a box of specimens for you." He explained the delay came "more from the indescribable press of business of all kind, translating, Printing, (not used to the business), Preaching, Building, farming, and the sick; this last takes most of my time."[5]

On August 20, 1847, the first two boxes of "Indian curiosities" that Spalding shipped to Allen in Kinsman, Ohio, arrived damaged. Allen wrote with advice for Spalding's future packing, "your boxes came to house in bad state. One containing the saddle had been broken to pieces. You should hoop with raw leather or iron or wood any boxes for the W. State." The contents of the boxes also suffered on the long journey, "the skin had bread moths & was spoiled & the moths had hurt the dresses &c, eat up the woolens ornaments &c & injured the skins some." But all was not lost, as Allen continued, "still they look handsome. I thank you for them.... I want more. They are all worth the having! I will try and pay for them all in due course of time. If you see proper you will oblige me by any different curiosities, that you can send me."[6] After providing Spalding with updates on local news, Allen cautioned his friend, "In writing to me for the Public Eye—keep separate our private affairs in way of Barter, not only on my account but on your own. But all of your news—your business, your wants everything of your person situation I want to show to our people." He continued, "Our ladies, all read the letters."[7] Allen's caution to Spalding indicates that their collecting was something that they should keep quiet, something not for public consumption, apart from the Spalding's missionary news aimed at the general public. Allen's desire to keep the "private affairs in way of Barter" indicated that something unsavory was going on in Spalding's acquisitions and shipment east of Native objects.

These private dealings between Allen and Spalding led Nez Perce tribal historian Allen P. Slickpoo Sr. to observe, "In all my years of studying our tribal history, I have never heard that the board of missions expected their spiritual workers to set up trading posts among their converts." He continued, "It does seem a bit odd that Dr. Allen was writing to Rev. Spalding telling him to keep their dealings quiet. What was he trying to hide?"[8]

As for the amount that Allen would pay in bartered goods for the collection, he relied on Spalding's evaluation of what the items were worth.

Spalding did so in a detailed letter dated April 27, 1846, describing the collection he mailed to Allen separately from the barrels containing the artifacts. Spalding wrote regarding his difficulties in obtaining items for Allen from the savvy bargaining Nez Perce: "it is no easy matter to obtain these things from the natives as they always want to extort a great price as soon as they find I want them." He continued, "some times [*sic*] for a small stone a shirt is demanded, which of course is not given, & perhaps for an important Geological specimen is taken away and sold to some other person who cares nothing about it, for a single flint."[9] It is important to consider the relationships between Spalding and the Nez Perce. Spalding's missionary work was at their pleasure, and it was the Nez Perce people who determined if they wanted to trade with Spalding or not.

Spalding then noted his estimation of the monetary worth of the items he shipped to Allen. The prices Spalding included in his letter to Allen were not the prices Spalding paid—for the Nez Perce and the other Plateau peoples did not operate in a money economy. Rather Spalding traded other manufactured items for the goods he collected. He also may have received some of the items as gifts from Nez Perce who wished to demonstrate to Spalding their desire to join his church. Spalding wrote, "I give the cost of the articles that you may judge whether you will send for more. The property in my possession belongs to the A. B. C. Fr. M. You can think best about paying for them." However, Spalding clearly did not want Allen to pay the missionary organization as he next made clear, "in my estimation you have already more than paid for them. But should you feel disposed to pay," Spalding wanted Allen to send, "clothing for myself & family, table furniture, such as plates, cups & saucers, bowls, etc, etc, calico, cheap for Indian shirts etc, will be better than money."[10] Spalding then requested specific items he needed: "will you have the goodness to send me in the next B[ar]r[e]l from the Ladies Soc[iety] a dung fork & 3 pitch forks, a hair sieve for meal rather fine."[11] Trade goods mattered more to Spalding than money. To spend money Spalding had to go down to Fort Vancouver. However, he could use the trade goods and tools sent by his benefactors at his Lapwai mission site in exchange for Nez Perce labor, food, and goods. Spalding also required specific tools unavailable in the region for his extensive missionary enterprise, such as the hair sieve for his grain mill.

In his description of the collection in the letter to Allen, Spalding provided information about the Nez Perce people that reflected his own

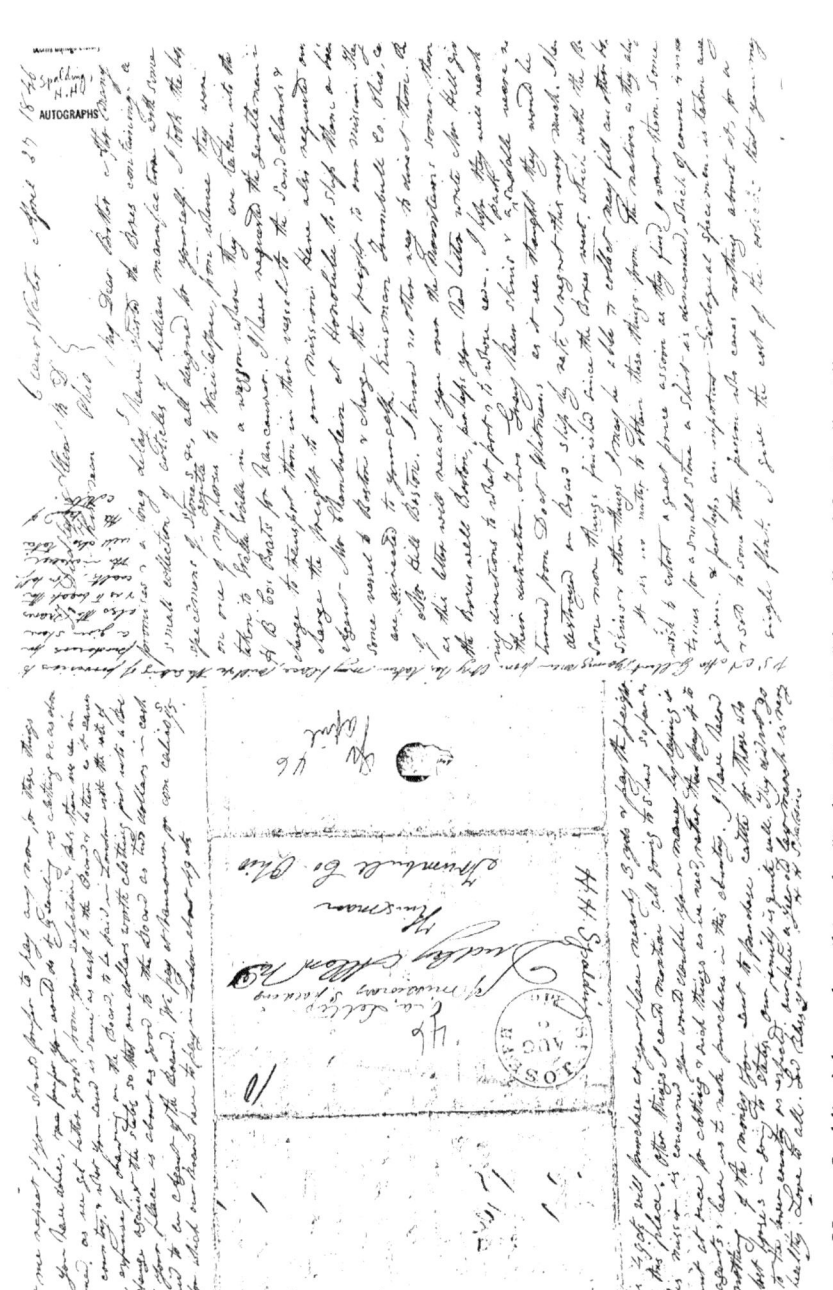

Henry Spalding's letter describing the "Indian Curiosities" he collected for Dudley Allen.

To the lower right of the image are the values Spalding assigned to items in the collection. Courtesy of the Oberlin College Archives.

prejudices and he emphasized the monetary value of the Nez Perce goods he collected for Allen. He also sought to demonstrate his expertise in Nez Perce material culture. Spalding noted that the two dresses he sent were "worn by the rich" and often valued for "3 horses." The dresses included precious dentalium shell decorations and rare elk teeth. According to Spalding, "the elk teeth upon one dress as also upon the cradle are obtained only from the Buck Elk, two from an animal." Spalding claimed that dresses such as he shipped to Allen "would sell... in the southern states for $50 or $60 a piece."[12] It is likely that this is a fanciful estimation on Spalding's part intended to emphasize the cost of the goods sent to Allen, if Allen sought to purchase similar dresses without Spalding's aid. Yet Spalding valued the two dresses at the bargain price of $27, emphasizing the deals that he could make on behalf of Allen.

Dresses such as those that Spalding shipped to Allen would have engaged the skills of an entire family. As Jacqueline Peterson and Laura Peers noted in their description of one of the dresses Spalding acquired, "female relatives designed, beaded, and sewed the dress. Male relatives hunted for deerskins and traded for the dentalium shells and black and white pony beads, which were expensive. It might have taken a year to trade for the ornaments on this dress."[13]

Spalding's prejudices and misunderstanding of Nez Perce culture are clear in his description of the cradleboard which he wrote was "made for the occasion." He continued, "This cradle with its vicitme [sic] is hung upon the horn of the saddle when camps moves [sic], hangs upon the mothers [sic] back when she goes for roots or wood, sits in the sun against a rock through the day when she digs her two or three bags of roots, going now & again to nurse it, or against the root of a tree while she cuts & binds up a bundle of wood weighing from 150-200 lb, to warm a gambling son or husband who may be at home a sleep [sic]."[14]

Cradleboards served an important function in Nez Perce culture: they kept a child close by and a woman's hands free. Jacqueline Peterson and Laura Peers wrote, "Indian women who still use cradleboards say that babies cry when they are removed. The snug wrappings made children feel secure, and the moss padding kept bottoms dry."[15] Nez Perce cultural specialist Josiah Pinkham objected to Spalding's description of the Nez Perce men, who according to Pinkham, "had to be as industrious as the women. It's just that it was a different nature," said Pinkham. "They would have been out checking on horses, they would have been out fishing, they would have been out hunting. I mean, that's hard work, too. Because I know that. It's a lot of fun to go out and hunt. But it's also a lot of work."[16]

In his letter, Spalding itemized the materials he packed for Allen with the heading, "price of things as nigh as I can recollect."

2 dresses Woman... $27.00
1 pr. Men's Leggings... $2.50
Red Bear Skin... $.50
Childs Cradle... $3.00
Woman's Leggins [sic]... $2.50
6 pr. Mocisons [sic]... $1.50
3 Woman's hats... $.60
2 Small Baskets... $.40
1 Whip... $.30
3 Hemp Bags... $4.00
2 Men's Shirts... $14.25
1 Woman's Saddle $4.37
2 Hair cords ... $.38[17]

Although this listing is the most detailed account of any Native American collection from the region, it nevertheless includes major silences. Spalding does not directly tell us how he acquired most of the goods or talk about the individuals who made them. Nor does he elaborate in the medium of exchange. "The thing, the frustrating thing," said Nez Perce National Historical Park curator Bob Chenoweth, "is that given all that Spalding wrote, he didn't write down where any of this stuff came from. Who gave it to him. And I don't believe that the Indian people themselves that gave up their things understood that they were going to be preserved."[18]

If Spalding had named the individuals from whom he acquired the items, the Nez Perce would have had an even stronger case through lineal descent to repatriate the collection from the Ohio Historical Society. We can only speculate on the circumstances of how he put the collection together. According to Allen P. Slickpoo Sr., ethnographer for the Nez Perce Cultural Resource Program, oral tradition recalls that "from the time Henry H. Spalding arrived in the Niimíipuu [Nez Perce] Country, in 1836, he began to tell our people that it was 'evil' to wear the buckskin clothing and the eagle feather. It was the work of the 'devil' to do so."[19]

Nevertheless, Spalding provided much more provenance for the collection he assembled for Allen than did other collectors of his era or the generations following. At least we know what he acquired, where and when these acquisitions took place, and that the collection included Nez Perce and Plateau items.

But how did Spalding acquire the collection? According to Chenoweth, Spalding almost certainly did not pay for these items, as he would have had no cash and the Nez Perce would have had no use for money. In June 1840, Spalding recorded in his diary how the Nez Perce traded with other tribes. "The Pondarays first brought into the circle their robes & laid in heaps their value for a horse. The N[ez] P[erce] then led up a horse to each bunch, & if the Pdys, thought the horse worth his robes &c, he put his rope on him & led him off & the N.P. took the robes, &c." Spalding continued, "Some 10 horses were traded in this way. Usually 3 robes and 1 Appishmore [blanket], or 2 robes & 1 gun or 2 robes, 2 App. & a shirt were given for a horse. This trade convinced me that the Nez P. are not the only sharp traders in the world."[20]

Likewise, Spalding traded goods for the artifacts he collected. As he noted in his diary on March 9, 1842, he "purchased one bag for Dr. Allen" by trading "2 knives & 10 loads, one cap, 1 knife…10 loads, 1 saddle pack, 20 loads."[21] Nakia Williamson-Cloud remarked that there exists:

> a lot of suspicion amongst people now, knowing some of that history from what we know from the written history, but also from our elders, that find it hard to believe that he [Spalding] was actually purchasing those items from Nez Perce people. Because we know the stories of how he would try to shame our people into thinking that those ways were backward, and those ways were somehow associated with the devil and things like that. And so he encouraged them to basically rid themselves of a lot of these type of items that came from our way of life. And so…a lot of Nez Perce people…feel…that's probably how he got them. Rather than actually paying hard dollars for them.[22]

Williamson-Cloud said, "It's pretty laughable to think he actually paid for them." Spalding strongly disapproved of Nez Perce material culture. Based on Nez Perce knowledge, he was burning traditional clothing at the time. "You can bet he was condemning those things to the original owners."[23]

Spalding had many opportunities to acquire Nez Perce items. In addition to direct trade, missionaries often received artifacts as presents or employed Native objects, such as baskets, rope, or tools, in their daily activities. Moreover, the process of conversion and baptism among Native Americans involved giving up traditions and material goods. As the scholar Sylvia Kaspryski noted, "converts were generally expected to surrender all their ritual paraphernalia before or after baptism," thus providing missionaries such as Spalding, "ample opportunities to get hold of such artifacts."[24]

Nez Perce Tribal Executive Committee member Bill Picard draws a distinction between the goods that the Nez Perce traded and the regalia made for their families. "And so these items that were taken [by Spalding] weren't made to be bought and sold." Picard explained that his community travelled along the Columbia River and bartered goods such as beadwork, buckskin, and elk hides. "These were the things that were materialistic, that were basically like money, to be bought or bartered with. But the items that they created for their regalia…it wasn't…to be bought and sold. It was material to be heirlooms, to be sacred, to be kept so that your children enjoyed these same things." Picard explained that this regalia was intended to be handed down. Say family members had "seen you dance and they were very impressed with the way you dance. They might give you an item to add to your regalia, so that when you dance it was something to honor you. So you don't sell something like that. There's a value that can't be put in dollars."[25]

Any monetary valuation of Nez Perce material culture is problematic. Bill Picard elaborated, "Well, my feelings on that is that you can't put a value on somebody's necklaces or eagle feathers or beaded dresses or ribbon shirts. You can't put a value on it, because…these items are handed down through generations." Furthermore, according to Picard, Nez Perce regalia provides connections between the Nez Perce and their ancestors. As Picard noted, "If I was wearing the regalia and I went to Pendleton, they would look and say, 'I remember his grandfather used to wear that.' Or, you know, 'His grandfather received that from this person or that person.'" To sell regalia was an abhorrent thought. According to Picard, such a sale would be like "selling [a] part of your body. Or part of like what Chief Joseph told his people was, 'Don't sell the land, because the land holds the body of your elders. It holds the memories of your people.'"[26]

The regalia in the Spalding-Allen Collection, Josiah Pinkham observed, has a value that is transgenerational in two senses of the term. Pinkham explained that the first aspect of transgenerational value came from passing the regalia through the family. The shirts, for example, would be made for a "leader of some sort and then be passed on to his next in line, his oldest son, his nephew, whomever that might be, and on down through the lineage." Pinkham continued, "A shirt like this also had, on the other side of the transgenerational interpretation, it had numerous women that were involved in the process. So his sister may have tanned the hide. His wife may have sat down with his mother and did the beadwork together while they were by the fireplace. And they would have been trading stories and talking and doing different things…I mean, that's where the real value is."[27]

Nakia Williamson-Cloud remarked that "when Spalding came, I think many of our people were receptive. And to compare it to what we already knew about our creator, it seemed like it was consistent with what they were saying." However, over time Spalding lost his standing among some of the Nez Perce since he operated as more of a trader than a spiritual leader. As his collecting and trading with Dudley Allen demonstrated, Spalding supplemented his missionary funds with acquiring items, such as regalia, that he told the Nez Perce they had to abandon to become converts. Williamson-Cloud continued, "He's just here, you know, buying and selling things.…Which was probably part of what he had to do to survive. But I think a lot of our people kind of did not take to that very well. And become somewhat disillusioned in his teachings and what he was espousing as a Presbyterian minister."[28]

Spalding held no qualms about collecting or bartering Nez Perce material culture. In his letter to Allen describing the collection, Spalding did not delve into the details of his acquisitions. He did, however, emphatically make the point again to Allen that he needed goods sent to him in return, not cash, "if you should prefer to pay any more for these things than you have done, we prefer you would do it by sending us clothing etc. as above named, as we get better goods from your selection & B[a]r[re]ls than we can in this country." Spalding argued for the benefits of this arrangement: "what you send is same as cash to the Board & better as it saves the expense of drawing on the Board, to be paid in London with the note of exchange against the States." Spalding remarked that one dollar in goods sent by Allen was worth more than two dollars of cash sent to the Missionary Board.[29]

On March 27, 1848 Allen wrote to Spalding, "in the Barrell forwarded to Boston last fall I sent you a few things, cannot tell now what, you will see in time I trust. If such articles are as profitable to you as money, why, I will continue to send them." Allen acknowledged that Spalding was operating in a region where bartered goods were more valuable than cash. Allen continued, "I rec[eive]d Your 2 Boxes at last. They were badly broken, especially the one containing the saddle & minerals; the last were nicely conglomerated. Moths hurt the dresses much. Still, I prize them more than the cost! At minerals and curiosities try your hand again if the opportunity offers. The clays were all safe. The dresses look tolerable." Allen continued with more packing advice for Spalding, "if you ever send anything animal [hides] insert it in Tobacco." Near the end of his letter Allen noted that Spalding would receive this letter and write again before Allen would ship another barrel so Spalding should "write again in full what you want. Our shippers say, dried fruit, honey, &c will spoil in sending. But write all books, or anything for the children, &c tools, &c. and we will send as convenient I trust."[30]

Dudley Allen also received Plateau material culture from Spalding's fellow missionary, Marcus Whitman. Whitman sent Allen a Nez Perce hat and three cedar root baskets. Allen's family later donated them to Case Western Reserve College in 1914. In 2003, Case Western Reserve University deaccessioned the items and sold them via Cowan's Auctions. Cowan's included the accession notes from Case Western Reserve University in their provenance information about the items. However, the provenance remained tentative because no other documentation survived describing the connection with Whitman. Bob Chenoweth, curator at the Nez Perce National Historical Park, purchased the items at very reasonable prices in 2003.[31]

In addition to collecting minerals and Indian "curiosities" for Allen, Spalding also sent plant samples back east, hoping for payment that would support his mission. In 1841, naturalists travelling with the Wilkes expedition visited Spalding's mission.[32] Afterward, Spalding requested books on rocks and plants from the secretary of the ABCFM. Two years later in 1843, the botanist Charles Geyer stayed with Spalding. Geyer wrote, "I owe [Spalding] the means of visiting another new field, the highlands of the Nez Percez [sic], where he accompanied me on my excursions… where previous botanists had but cursorily passed."[33]

In 1846, Spalding sent a box of plant samples to the Mission Board in Boston with the expectation that the sale of the samples would contribute funds toward his mission expenses.[34] His plant collecting was therefore part of his broader effort to fund his missionary work. Spalding noted in a letter to David Greene of the Missionary Board he had created

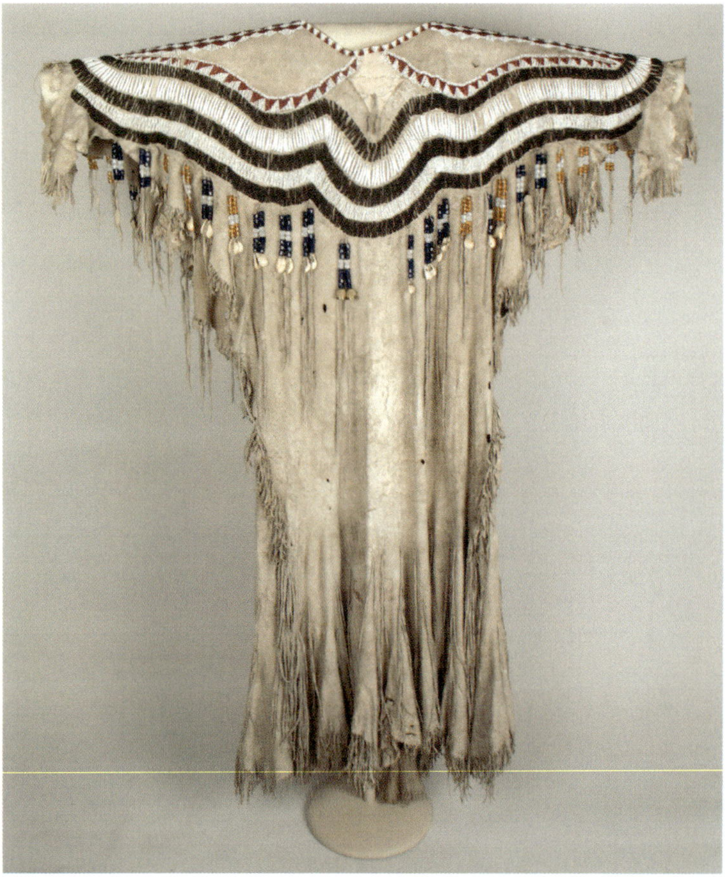

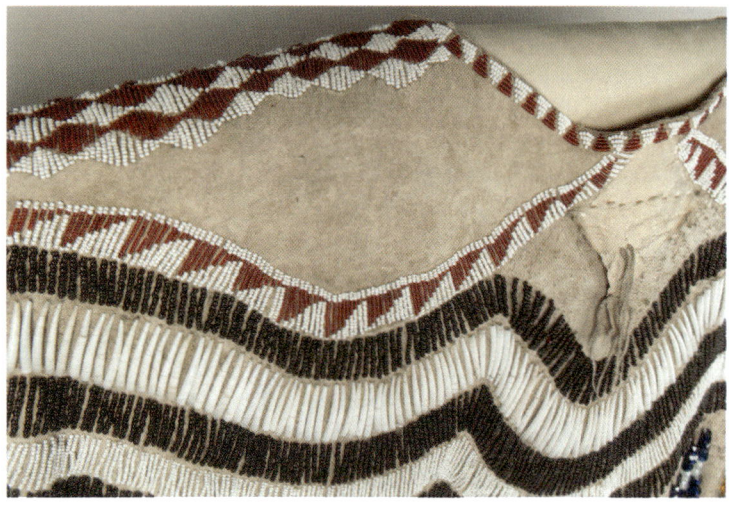

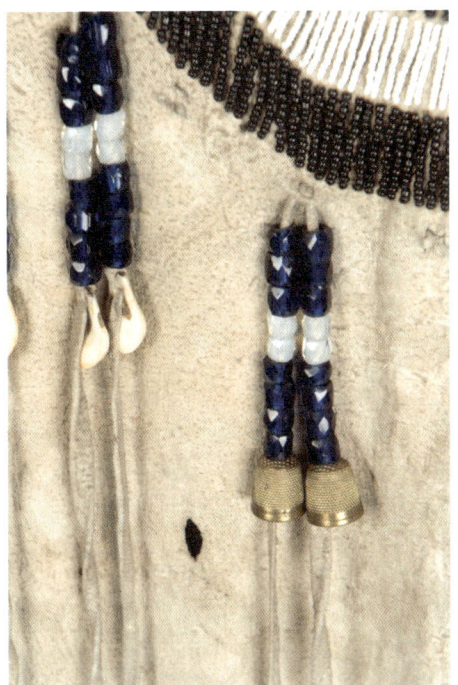
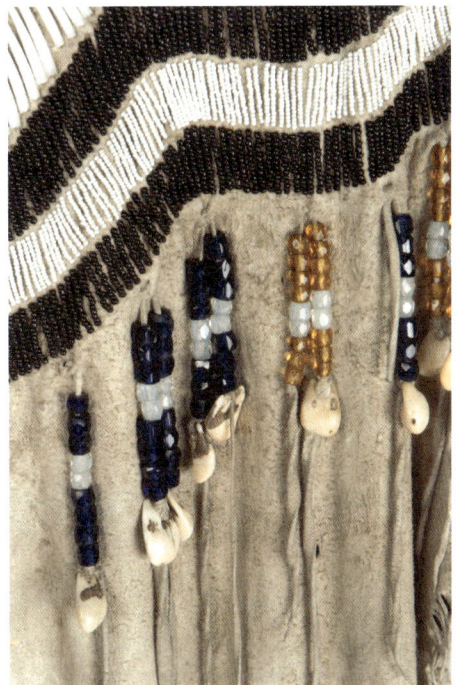

Nez Perce woman's dress collected by Spalding. The dress, manufactured between 1820 and 1840, consists of two deerskins and features dentalium shell, glass beads, elk teeth, two brass thimbles, and fringe. Photographs by Zach Mazur. Courtesy of the Nez Perce National Historical Park. NEPE 8758.

the collection with Eliza while "traversing the Plains, the vallies [*sic*] & hills looking after my cows, horses, &c, or as my duties called me to visit the different bands of this tribe at their root grounds, fisheries &c…Mrs. Spalding did most of the drying in papers." Spalding, commenting on the originality of his contributions to science, wrote, "no Botanist has ever spent a whole season in this vicinity or even in this country & therefore could not collect the flow[er]s which were not in existence at the time of his travels." Spalding continued, "I send them to you with the expectation that you will dispose of them as may be thought best. Should they arrive uninjured they will be worth $5.00 or $6.00 a hundred i.e. the Botanical Gardens in London offer that price for flowers from this country."[35]

The ABCFM turned Spalding's box over to Asa Gray at the Harvard Herbarium who later sent Spalding a detailed letter requesting that

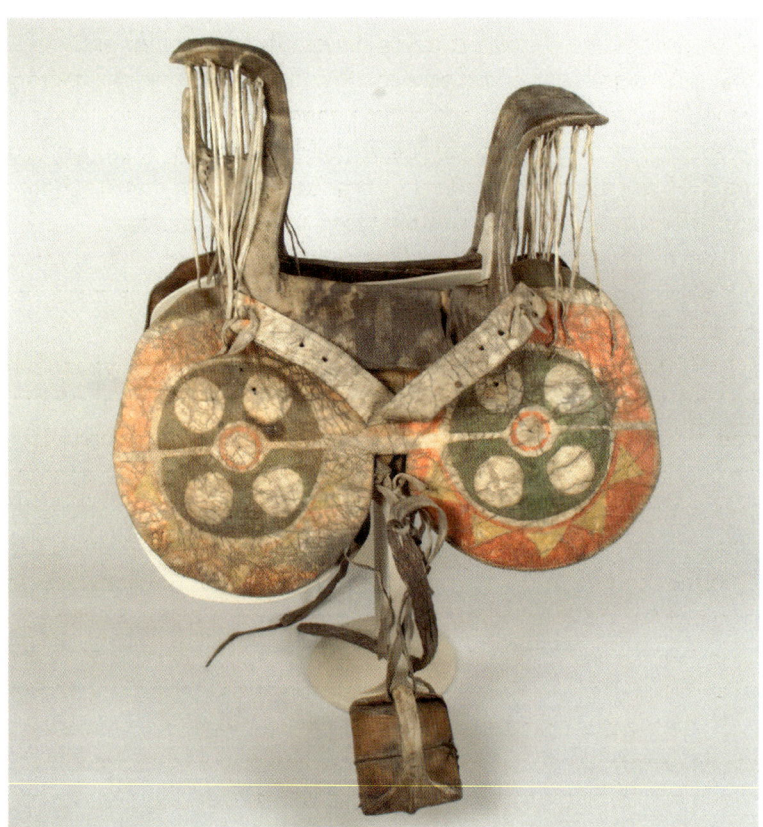

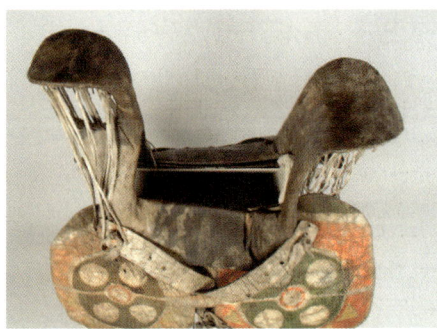
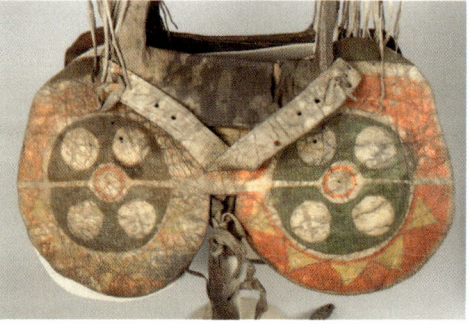

A decorated Nez Perce woman's saddle made circa 1830–1845 with cotton wood frame and painted geometric designs on the fenders from the Spalding-Allen Collection. Bison hide laces secure the rawhide inner pieces forming the pommel. Dr. Allen wrote to Spalding on March 27, 1848, that the box containing this saddle was badly damaged. Photographs by Zach Mazur. Courtesy of the Nez Perce National Historical Park. NEPE 8755.

Spalding collect samples of the foods gathered by the local Indians. Gray wrote that Spalding should thin the thick roots and bulbs "with a knife, when the specimen is pressed…it is very desirable to have." The ABCFM included these instructions in reams of pressing paper for shipment to Spalding. However, the box never left Boston, for the missions ended suddenly after the attack on the Whitman Mission.[36]

Spalding's collecting went beyond supporting his missionary work and enhancing his reputation. His activities were at the vanguard of a broader effort to claim the Oregon Country for the United States. As the historian Curtis Hinsley argued, the very act of "collection and removal to the core homeland of territorial resources—botanical, mineralogical, ethnographic—[serve] as the material metonymic proofs of conquest, proprietorship, and ultimately incorporation."[37] As Spalding packed the barrels of Nez Perce goods and shipped them to Allen and collected his botanical specimens, he was also aiding in the Oregon Country becoming part of the United States.

Spalding never sent the next shipment of artifacts he had collected for Allen. While Allen's boxes and letters were en route to Spalding's mission, Spalding and his family fled with the other ABCFM missionaries after the Cayuse killed Marcus and Narcissa Whitman and others at Waiilatpu on November 29, 1847. Spalding's mission at Lapwai was ransacked. When news of the attacks spread east, the ABCFM ended all of the Oregon Country missions.[38]

After the closing of the missions, the Spaldings moved to Brownsville, Oregon, where Spalding struggled to earn a living. He farmed, taught school, preached at the local Presbyterian church, served as school commissioner, postmaster, and Indian agent. Eliza Spalding died in Brownsville on January 7, 1851. Spalding remarried and returned to Nez Perce County in 1859 where he farmed until he received an appointment as Indian commissioner which lasted until 1866. During this period, he quarreled with other Indian agents and blamed the Catholics for the attack on the Whitman Mission. He died in Lapwai on August 3, 1874.

Spalding had mixed "success" as a missionary. In the early years of his missionary efforts, he and Eliza welcomed large groups of Nez Perce for Sabbath services and learning. He converted several key Nez Perce leaders: Timothy, Lawyer, and Joseph. This (old) Joseph was the father of Chief Joseph who became famous for his leadership during the 1877 Nez Perce War. But as Spalding's insistence on giving up traditional practices became understood, many Nez Perce stayed away from the mission.

Spalding maintained discipline at his mission by whipping or having other followers flog the Nez Perce who broke Spalding's rules. While there was a cultural precedence among the Nez Perce for whippers to discipline older children, publicly whipping young men was shameful.[39] As for Spalding's memory among the Nez Perce, according to NPS curator Bob Chenoweth, "I think people in this community [Nez Perce] are conscious of all the perspectives about him." Chenoweth continued, "I've never heard anybody stand up and say, oh, he was like the greatest thing since sliced bread. They say generally it's a good thing that he brought Christianity. But don't go too deep into who he was as a person."[40]

Slickpoo wrote that Spalding's mission and that of Whitman were initially successful "by both Indian and white standards," but that began to change. Slickpoo argued that "we preferred our mat houses to the log cabins that took so much time and work to build. Also we felt that a man's status depended upon his ability as a hunter and fisherman, and it was woman's work to gather berries and such." Slickpoo continued, "It seemed to us that the white men were asking us to become like women when they wanted us to garden." "Unfortunately," Slickpoo wrote, "the missionaries interpreted this reluctance to change our way of life as laziness, a notion that could hardly have been further from the truth."[41]

Spalding created lasting divisions among the Nez Perce between his select followers and traditionalists. According to Nez Perce oral tradition, one way that Spalding rewarded his supporters was through his distribution of potatoes. As Nez Perce cultural specialist Josiah Pinkham related the memory:

> My aunt Mary Waters was telling me about how one of the practices that he [Spalding] utilized to gain his fellowship was along the lines of when he would distribute potatoes that came in, when he received a shipment of potatoes, he would take some of those potatoes and he would cut the eyes out of them. And then he would keep those aside. And then there came a point where he would distribute potatoes to his fellowship. And to those individuals that were ardent followers of Christian faith, or that were performing above and beyond the call of duty of the time, he would give the potatoes that had eyes. And then those people that maybe needed a little bit of a nudge or weren't doing, weren't following as ardently as the rest of the small amount of Christian Nez Perce, that he would give the potatoes that didn't have eyes. And he'd say, "Go forth and plant." And they would do so.
>
> And then the Nez Perce that received the potatoes with eyes, they would come back and they'd say, you know, "Look at all our potatoes."

And he would proclaim, "Oh, God has blessed you. Your faith has been rewarded." And he would talk it up really big.

Those Nez Perce that received the potatoes without eyes wouldn't come forth with anything. And he'd say, "See? God's punishing you, because you're not as faithful as your brethren or your siblings over here."[42]

Spalding was clearly not above using deceit to get his way. Spalding's use of physical punishment among the Nez Perce lingers as a troubling aspect of his missionary work. Spalding's biographer Clifford Drury, a historian and Presbyterian minister, viewed Spalding's work in a very positive light, going so far as to excuse Spalding's use of the whip on the Nez Perce. According to Drury, "it is hard for us to pass judgment [on Spalding] when all of the factors are not known to us. We must remember that these few white people were living among uncivilized Indians, and perhaps times did arise when the only language the natives understood was that of force."[43] While it may be easy to dismiss Drury's analysis as pro-missionary and racist, he remains the only biographer of Spalding and a key secondary source for early Nez Perce history.

According to vice chairman of the Nez Perce Tribe, Bill Picard, "I've heard stories of Henry Spalding. But I've also read articles and books on the Nez Perce Tribe. And they refer to Henry Spalding and they say that Henry Spalding…would whip adult men and women for not attending church on time, or not doing something that they were supposed to." Picard continued "we discipline our children to raise them up the way they should be raised. But when they're an adult, they need to make their own decisions. And if their decision isn't to do this or that, for a man to hold another man down and spank him, I don't think…that's proper." Picard argued that Spalding "brought his way of thinking. Not the Christian belief, or not the word of God in the Bible. But that he brought out his own opinion of how things should be done. So he used the Bible to influence or dictate his way of thinking and force that on the Nez Perce."[44]

Spalding did not tolerate being an Indian *and* a Christian. As Picard explained, "Right now, I go to church. But I also go to pow wows.…I praise God but I also hunt and fish…So my culture is, I can be an Indian and still be Christian.…But with Henry Spalding, you had to be one or the other. You couldn't be both. And if you were an Indian, you were a heathen." Picard continued, "And if you weren't, then you were a good Indian. And that was his [Spalding's] belief. But that's not the way Jesus or the Bible teaches.…I've got a lot of stories from a lot of people that say that he was forcing his belief—not the Bible's belief, or not the Christian way of life—but that his belief is what he was forcing on the tribes."

To the Nez Perce people, religion served as the basis of secular success and when this secular success did not materialize, many Nez Perce came to resent Spalding. However, Spalding did introduce many innovations to the Nez Perce including new medical practices, a printing press, mills, and gardens. Spalding established a school at the mission and also introduced a new form of Nez Perce administration with a head chief and twelve sub-chiefs, each with five police assistants.[45]

Regardless of Spalding's later reputation or his achievements as a missionary, he collected an important cultural heritage and documented it. According to Nez Perce cultural specialist Josiah Pinkham, Spalding "put a lot of time into securing objects and centralizing them in a way that showed a broader spectrum of material culture than others are capable or have the desire to amass." Unlike Whitman, who collected only baskets, Spalding collected expansively: garments, a saddle, bags, baskets, rope, and other items of Niimíipuu life. Pinkham noted that what Spalding acquired "was visually…representational of the nicer stuff that the Nez Perce people had. And I think that says something about, it says something about Spalding's eye."[46]

The goods Spalding sent to Allen were, according to Drury, "undoubtedly, the best assortment of old Nez Perce articles in existence today."[47] Josiah Pinkham echoed Drury's assessment of its significance: "to the Nez Perce Tribe as a whole, I think, is that the collection embodies the earliest and greatest centralization of ethnographic objects for the Nez Perce people. You don't have a collection of this size, this age, anywhere else in the world."[48]

Allen kept the collection and Spalding's letter at his home in Ohio. The setting of Allen's mansion was a regal one for the collection and reflected Allen's wealth and privilege as well as his capacity to support Spalding's missionary efforts. The Allen residence included Greek revival details on the exterior, a temple-fronted façade with ionic pilasters and richly detailed interior window frames and ornaments in the Federal style. Architecture historian Richard Campen described the house as "the masterpiece of early architecture in Trumbull County."[49] This was the first home for the Spalding-Allen Collection after its journey from the Columbia Plateau.

Part 2

Away from Home

Chapter 4

The Ohio Years: From an Indian Cabinet of Curiosities to Oberlin College

These few items are among the oldest documented Nez Perce items known to us and do represent examples of our culture that cannot be found elsewhere. We are anxious to see these items return to their homeland where all can see and appreciate them.

—Richard Halfmoon

While the Spalding-Allen Collection remained in Kinsman, Ohio, momentous change came to the Nez Perce Tribe between 1848 and 1893. In 1855, nine years after Spalding shipped the Nez Perce materials to Ohio, Washington territorial governor Isaac Stevens negotiated a treaty with the Nez Perce and other Plateau tribes, including the Yakama, the Cayuse, and Umatilla, to establish reservations east of the Cascade Range.[1] In these negotiations, the Nez Perce maintained the largest portion of their ancestral lands while the Cayuse and the Umatilla saw their lands greatly diminished and were forced to share a reservation.

Nez Perce chiefs Looking Glass and (old) Joseph signed the 1855 treaty, as did Chief Lawyer, a follower of Henry Spalding. The 1855 Nez Perce reservation boundaries included seven million acres and represented roughly half of their traditional territory. The treaty contained a provision that the Native nations had one year before moving to their reservations. However, any others might "enter upon and occupy as settlers any lands not actually occupied and cultivated by said Indians at this time, and not included in the reservation." Thousands of gold seekers and settlers soon poured into the region after Elias Pierce discovered gold within Nez Perce territory in 1860.[2]

The gold rush unleashed a flood of white miners who soon illegally built the new supply town of Lewiston within reservation boundaries. A. J. Cain, Indian agent at Walla Walla, proposed a much smaller reservation in 1863 that took away the area around Lewiston, the gold fields, the Wallowa lands of northeastern Oregon, the Salmon River territory, and more, thereby reducing the Nez Perce Reservation by roughly 90 percent. Several prominent Christian Nez Perce leaders including Chief Lawyer supported the 1863 treaty and the diminished reservations. However, many non-Christian leaders including Looking Glass and (old) Joseph refused to sign the 1863 treaty, gaining them the moniker "non-treaty" Nez Perce.

The 1877 Nez Perce War started over disputed land and the incursion of settlers into ceded Nez Perce territory. After the killing of eighteen hostile settlers by young Nez Perce warriors, the United States mobilized more than five thousand troops to fight against five bands of non-Christian, non-treaty Nez Perce and Palouse. These included (old) Joseph's son, Chief Joseph of the Wallowa, the followers of Looking Glass, the White Birds, the Palouse, and the followers of Toohoolhoolzote.[3] The war consisted of a 1,170-mile tactical retreat by the Nez Perce through Idaho and Montana.

Following the last battle of the conflict at Bear Paw, Montana, two hundred Nez Perce including Chief White Bird escaped to Canada. Chief Joseph and four hundred other Nez Perce, including all of the children and the elderly, surrendered to Colonel Miles who promised they would be allowed to return almost immediately to Idaho. After years of imprisonment first at Fort Abraham Lincoln, Dakota Territory, then Fort Leavenworth, Kansas, and finally at the Quawpaw Reservation, Oklahoma, 150 Nez Perce, including Joseph, were sent to the Colville Reservation in May 1885, and only 115 came back to the Nez Perce Reservation in Idaho.[4]

Chief Joseph never returned home. After the 1877 conflict, Joseph was ordered to remain at the Colville Reservation. There he continually advocated for the return of Nez Perce lands as had been negotiated in the 1855 treaty ratified by the federal government. On September 21, 1904, Chief Joseph died on the Colville Reservation, far from his beloved Wallowa Valley. He was sixty-four. His doctor ruled that Joseph died of a broken heart.

Further reduction of Nez Perce lands was to come. In 1887, Congress passed the Dawes Severalty Act, or Allotment Act, and the Nez Perce became one of the first tribes to suffer allotment, the division of commonly held reservation lands into individual parcels.[5] The implementation of this law resulted in the appointment of Alice Fletcher who supervised the division of the rest of the already diminished Nez Perce Reservation. This process disrupted patterns of communal living that had sustained Native peoples for thousands of years.[6] Fletcher, although an exceedingly honest civil servant, nevertheless demonstrated her partisanship toward the Christian Nez Perce when she used the former house of Presbyterian missionary, Kate McBeth, as her headquarters for determining who received which allotments. Fletcher went so far as to have her allotment laborers rebuild McBeth's front porch and spent another six weeks repairing McBeth's church at Kamiah.[7] After Fletcher made allotments favoring Presbyterian Nez Perce, fully half a million acres remained. This land was put up for sale and was quickly purchased by settlers, resulting in a patchwork of Nez Perce land holdings.[8]

The Spalding-Allen Collection at Oberlin College

As the allotment process was underway on the Nez Perce Reservation, back in Ohio, Dr. Allen kept the Nez Perce "curiosities" that his friend Henry Spalding had sent him in a cabinet in his home. We can only imagine Dr. Allen displaying his magnificent home, wealth, and knowledge to guests when he gave tours of his cabinet. The Spalding-Allen Collection remained first at the Allen home and then later at his son Dudley Allen's residence in Oberlin, Ohio. Dudley Allen subsequently left the collection to Oberlin College and donated enough money to have the college name the art museum after him.

In May 1893, an employee in the Oberlin Museum recorded the collection that Dudley Allen donated as accession no. 401, "1 lot of Indian clothing, trinkets, etc."[9] The connection with Spalding was not explicitly stated, only implied. Spalding's letter describing the Nez Perce collection also came to Oberlin. However, when Oberlin staff described the Allen donation, Spalding's name as the collector of the Nez Perce artifacts was not indicated. Officials at Oberlin divided the collection: the objects went to the Oberlin Museum housed in the A. A. Wright Laboratory; the letter Spalding wrote to Allen documenting the collection went to the library. By splitting up the collection (a common practice then and now), and not

clearly connecting the objects with the letter or the Spalding-Allen relationship, Oberlin curators endangered the provenance of the collection.

As Oberlin staff accessioned the Spalding-Allen Collection, another
collector, George Gustave Heye, began assembling what would become
the largest, most important collection of Native American material culture
in the United States. Eventually Heye's collection would become part of
the Smithsonian Institution's National Museum of the American Indian
(NMAI). Heye initially treated his collecting as a hobby, but over time
he became obsessed with creating his own museum. After sixty years of
collecting from multiple sources, funding archaeological digs, and buying
entire collections, he amassed over eight hundred thousand objects.[10]

Heye began collecting in 1897 with the purchase of a Navaho man's
shirt. Heye's father was an early associate of John D. Rockefeller at Standard Oil, and he grew up in a family of wealth. He started his own investment bank and by 1915, inherited a trust of ten million dollars.[11] Heye,
like other collectors of his era, believed the demise of Indian peoples was
inevitable and that it was up to collectors like himself to acquire collections and put them in museums. He developed his Museum of the American Indian in New York City. Initially he stored his collection in his
apartment but soon outgrew the space and established a storage facility
in the Bronx. These collections eventually became the core of the Smithsonian's National Museum of the American Indian.

Back on the Oberlin campus, the association between the Allen gift
(the "lot of Indian clothing, trinkets, etc.") and the collector Henry Spalding was lost for nearly thirty years until Robert Fletcher, assistant professor of history at Oberlin College, realized the connection between
Spalding's letter held in the Oberlin archives and Allen's gift of Native
American artifacts. In August 1929, Fletcher gathered in one case the
"majority" of the "articles of Indian manufacture mentioned in this letter." It is telling that by 1929, only the "majority" of the collection could
be located—unfortunately not all of it, for some contents had been lost.
As Fletcher noted, "the name of the distinguished missionary has never
until now been associated with the articles in the museum." Fletcher
wrote an essay on the collection for the 1930 *Oberlin Alumni Magazine*
in which he invited his readers to see the Spalding-Allen Collection:

> Here now, if you come to Oberlin, you may see the women's dresses
> with their elaborate bead work and elk tooth pendants. The deer skin
> or elk skin, of which these dresses are made, is still as soft as chamois....

Here are the men's shirts with their brilliant porcupine embroidery…
all made by the Nez Perce over eighty years ago, are in excellent condition. When you look at these things, remember that they came down the
Columbia in the Hudson Bay Company boat, thence to the Sandwich
Islands, way round the Horn to Boston in one of the splendid Yankee
sailing ships.…Remember that they were gathered by Henry Spalding,
Presbyterian Missionary.…Remember that these relics started on their
long journey in 1846, the year of the final establishment of the American claim to Oregon and not much more than a year and a half before
the tragic termination of the historic missionary venture of the American
Board in Oregon.[12]

Fletcher made a significant contribution to the life history of the Spalding-Allen Collection. By publishing this article, he left a trail (one cited
by Clifford Drury in his biography of Spalding) that would lead others
back to the collection. Most importantly, Fletcher reestablished the provenance of the collection and emphatically connected it to settler colonialism, arguing that the "relics" of the Spalding-Allen Collection served as a
reminder of the American claim to Oregon.

In the life history of the Spalding-Allen Collection, this was a key
moment in its preservation. However, when items in a collection are separated, as was the case with the Spalding-Allen Collection where the artifacts and the documentation—in this case Spalding's letter to Allen—
were kept separate, the provenance was forgotten. If the provenance of a
collection is not maintained, if its documentation is lost, its research and
monetary value is diminished. However, a collection with a well-documented provenance, one that includes highly collectable items, may dramatically increase in value. In the 1980s and 1990s, the appraised value
of the Spalding-Allen Collection dramatically increased because of the
rarity and provenance of the collection.

We have no way of knowing how many people heeded Professor
Fletcher's call to see the collection in its display case. Evidence of at least
one visitor remains. In the summer of 1935, Clifford Drury, the biographer of Henry Spalding and a Presbyterian pastor, was hired by E.
O. Holland, president of Washington State College, to collect primary
sources related to the missionaries of the Oregon Territory. Drury wrote
a detailed letter to Holland describing his collecting activities, including
his visit to Oberlin, where he saw Robert S. Fletcher, who showed Drury
the "Spalding collection of Indian relics sent to Dr. Allen and then given
to Oberlin."[13]

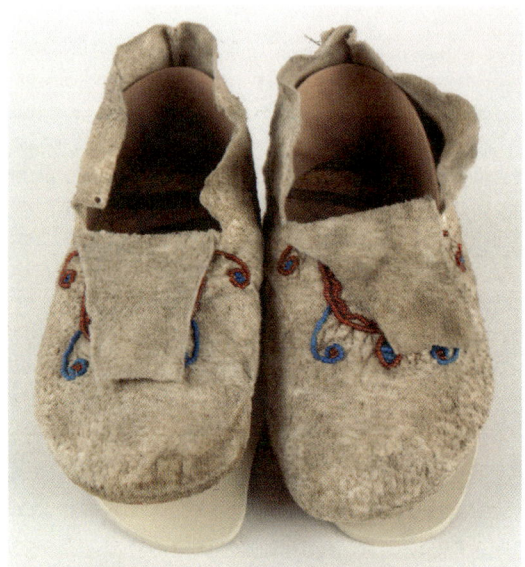

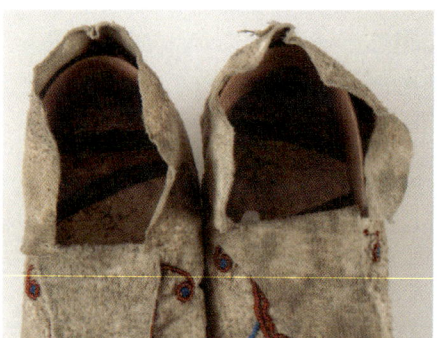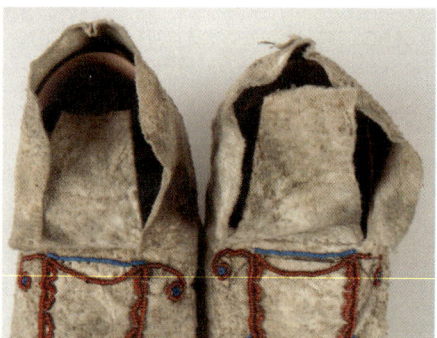

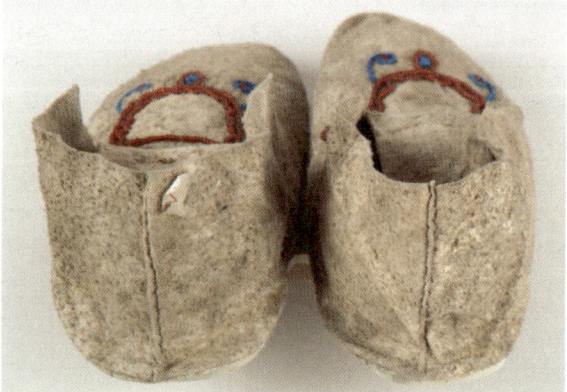

One of two surviving pairs of moccasins in the Spalding-Allen Collection. Spalding wrote to Allen that he sent six pairs. This pair, made circa 1840, includes a decorated/reused parfleche sole and beadwork. Photographs by Zach Mazur. Courtesy of the Nez Perce National Historical Park. NEPE 8738-39.

Chapter 5

A Return to Self-Governance

The United States government and state officials continued their destructive policies toward Native Americans, confining them to reservations and seizing their lands through reservation allotments and other measures in the years that the Spalding-Allen Collection was held at Oberlin College. From a Native American population once estimated between four and seven million in the region of the United States, the census of 1900 registered only two hundred thousand Native survivors. It took decades longer for American Indians to gain the right to vote. Congress granted citizenship of native-born Indians in 1924, but some states denied the rights of Native Americans to vote into the 1950s.[1]

Federal policy toward Indian tribes changed during the administration of Franklin Delano Roosevelt. Starting in 1934 and continuing until his resignation in 1945, John Collier, commissioner of Indian Affairs, advocated an "Indian New Deal" with increased federal support for social services, including healthcare and education. Collier's Indian Reorganization Act shifted federal policy away from forced assimilation to self-governance and self-determination.[2]

The Nez Perce Tribe, along with many other tribes, developed a written constitution during this period. The Niimíipuu adopted their constitution in 1948 and revised it in 1961. In their constitution, they defined membership in the Nez Perce Tribe as those names that appear on the membership roll of 1956, children who are of at least one-fourth Nez Perce ancestry and whose parents enrolled them before the age of 18, and persons adopted into the Tribe. All enrolled Nez Perce would meet twice a year as a Tribal General Council to vote on major issues and to elect a nine-member governing board, the Nez Perce Tribal Executive Committee (NPTEC). NPTEC's members and chair would serve three-year terms and would represent the Nez Perce Tribe in negotiations with federal, state, and local governments, and with private corporations. NPTEC also would administer programs to protect the health, education, and general welfare of the Tribe, and to disperse unrestricted Tribal funds.[3] This organization later played a key role in the struggle to keep the Spalding-Allen Collection.[4] Today, NPTEC and its chair speak on behalf of Niimíipuu interests and enter into negotiations with other governmental entities.

As the Nez Perce developed their constitution, Oberlin College officials transferred the Spalding-Allen Collection. In 1942, the storage conditions on campus led Oberlin officials to move the Spalding-Allen Collection to the Ohio Historical Society (OHS), presumably to ensure that it received better care. Oberlin dean Carl Wittke recommended that the Oberlin College Prudential Committee, "loan for an indefinite period the Spalding Nez Perce Indian Collection, now improperly housed in the Wright Zoological Laboratory, to the Ohio State Archaeological and Historical Society for exhibition purposes in the Ohio State Museum at Columbus."[5] The following day, Wittke wrote to a Mr. Shetrone at the Ohio State Historical Society requesting that he draw up a document stating that Oberlin College is loaning "this material" and that OHS "undertakes to care for it properly." Both parties would sign the agreement, at which time "the matter would be closed and your truck could stop by to take the material to Columbus at your early convenience."[6] The extent to which OHS cared for the collection "properly" would be debated later. It is important to note that Oberlin College loaned the Spalding-Allen Collection to the OHS where it could be properly stored. However, Oberlin did not cede its ownership of the collection.

Decades later, it would turn out to be unfortunate for the Nez Perce Tribe and the National Park Service that that Oberlin officials transferred the Spalding-Allen Collection to OHS. At the time of the collection's "rediscovery" in 1978, Oberlin professor Mark Papworth offered to return the Spalding-Allen Collection to the Nez Perce without charge. Ultimately, however, Papworth could not do so because he could not locate the collection.

Chapter 6

Asserting Their Rights

During the transfer between Oberlin and the Ohio Historical Society (OHS), the items in the Spalding-Allen Collection were mixed with other OHS collections. This may have resulted from the varied sizes of items in the Spalding-Allen Collection requiring their storage in multiple locations, such as the woman's saddle being placed apart from the smaller artifacts. The result was that the provenance of the collection was disturbed. Spalding's original letter to Allen, the key source of provenance for the collection, remained at Oberlin. But that was not all that stayed behind at the college. According to Nez Perce National Historical Park curator Susan Buchel, surviving clues indicate that more of the collection might have remained at Oberlin College.

A 1958 list of the materials transferred between the Oberlin Zoological Museum and the Dudley Allen Art Museum includes items that appear to match Spalding's 1846 letter to Allen but that are not part of the present collection. For example, there is mention of a pair of women's leggings, described as item "57.138 American Indian leggings, beadwork."[1] Spalding mentioned six pairs of moccasins, but only two pairs are present in the current collection. Spalding also listed three hemp bags, only one of which remained in the collection held by OHS. From the incomplete records and brief listings, there still exists the possibility that other Spalding-Allen materials may be at Oberlin College or at OHS.

As the Spalding-Allen Collection remained in storage at OHS in the 1950s, the Nez Perce asserted their sovereignty in a dispute with state and federal officials over the loss of fishing grounds at Celilo Falls. After intensive research and the deposition of elders, the Nez Perce appealed an initial decision denying their rights to fish at Celilo Falls by testifying before the US Senate Committee on Appropriations. Before this Senate committee, the Nez Perce persuasively argued that Celilo Falls was indeed part of their "accustomed fishing places." Though the Tribe asked for $6,400,000 (a settlement in line with other Native communities located closer to Celilo), the Nez Perce received a judgement of $2,800,000 which was distributed to the Tribe on a per capita basis.[2] This payment was the first of a series of cash settlements that would over time help fund Nez Perce government. Beyond the settlement payment, the Nez Perce Tribe asserted their sovereignty and ancient connection to the land.

In 1960, the Nez Perce Tribe recovered a judgement of $44,200,000 as compensation for the unfair price paid by the US government in the Treaty of 1863 and a further $3,000,000 for gold seized by settlers from Niimíipuu lands. These resources were divided, with 87 percent going to the Nez Perce Tribe of Idaho and 13 percent to Joseph's band of Nez Perce on the Colville Reservation. Some of these settlements went to individual members of the Nez Perce Tribe, but a large amount remained for tribal use as directed by the Nez Perce Tribal Executive Committee.[3]

Nez Perce people continued to assert their fishing rights through the 1960s. In 1967, a jury voted 11–1 to acquit Jesse Green, a Nez Perce charged with two counts of fishing with fixed gear in the Columbia River near John Day Dam. After the judgment, Green's attorney, Theodore Little, issued a statement that the verdict upheld treaty rights between the US government and Nez Perce Tribe for members of the Tribe to fish in the Columbia River.[4] The case against Green hinged on whether the portion of the Columbia River near the John Day Dam was part of the Nez Perce's "usual and accustomed" fishing sites. The testimony of Nez Perce elders, including Alex Pinkham and James Miles, led to a quick trial and acquittal for Jesse Green. The outcome of the trial beyond the resolution of Green's case helped to uphold and bolster the treaty rights of the Nez Perce Tribe.[5]

Searching for the Collection

As the Nez Perce Tribe asserted their sovereignty, the Spalding-Allen Collection languished at OHS for a generation. During this period, the staff paid little to no attention to the collection. Oberlin Dean Wittke's expectation that the collection be used for "exhibition purposes" was not realized. The benefit to the collection was that this extended "rest" helped preserve the original condition of the objects. Since they received little curatorial attention, the items in the collection, other than the cradleboard, remained in the OHS storage vault, protected from natural light. Bill Holm, director of the Burke Museum at the University of Washington, heard of the collection in 1976 while in England and arranged to stop in Columbus, Ohio, to see it on his way back home. As a museum director, Holm was interested in the collection for possible exhibits in the Northwest. He found OHS's care of the Spalding-Allen Collection less than ideal.

According to Holm, "They brought out most of the things [but] some of it was scattered at that time. Some of it was at Piqua, Ohio [a historical site associated with the Ohio Historical Society] and some was at a reproduction old town that they had next to the OHS museum [in Columbus]."[6] In scattering the collection, its documentary and historical value was greatly diminished. Holm saw most of the pieces on the list in Spalding's letter; however, "it's typical of those old time collections that there wasn't any real documentation and the pieces had been assembled according to the list." That is to say, the individual artifacts were never labeled as part of the Spalding-Allen Collection, but rather OHS curators checked the early transfer lists (and perhaps a copy of Spalding's letter to Allen) to retrieve the collection for Holm. Holm remarked that OHS museum curators had "tried to sort them out and attach associations to them," but Holm was sure they were not all accurate. Before concluding his visit, Holm conveyed to OHS staff that the collection was "terribly important and very valuable."[7]

Chapter 7

Raising Their Voices: A Portrait of Two Institutions

Prior to Holm's rediscovery of the Spalding-Allen Collection in the 1970s, Congress passed a 1965 bill establishing a National Historical Park to tell the story of the Niimíipuu people. On the site next to Spalding's mission at Lapwai, the National Park Service built the headquarters for the Nez Perce National Historical Park (NEPE) and developed other interpretive sites associated with the 1877 conflict in Idaho, Montana, Oregon, and Washington. The new NEPE headquarters included a museum exhibit space and storage for collections. NPS officials working with the Nez Perce Tribe sought materials to exhibit in the space. They envisioned the Spalding-Allen Collection as the key collection for this exhibit area.

In 1969, Nez Perce National Historical Park superintendent Jack Williams contacted Oberlin College in search of the Spalding-Allen Collection. He likely saw references to it in Drury's biography of Spalding or read the 1930 *Oberlin Alumni Magazine*.[1] Mark Papworth, an Oberlin College faculty member from the Department of Sociology and Anthropology, replied to Williams's query, stating that he had "assumed responsibility for the various collections and single specimens forwarded to Oberlin by its graduates over the past years." Papworth indicated that the collections were "scattered in storage across campus" making it "quite a job to reassemble and assess the condition, value, and proper identification of all items." At that point in time, he had not found "any designated or recognizably distinct Nez Perce artifacts or reference to such." Clearly memory of the "indefinite" loan to OHS was long forgotten, and documentation of the transfer buried in the Oberlin Prudential Committee minutes.

Papworth concluded his letter to Williams with the magnanimous offer that "this may mean that they are long gone or, more hopefully, that they are still at large in the basement storage of the Art Museum or etc. If and/or when I do find them you are welcome to the collection. I will keep looking as I sort this considerable supply of ethnographic debris."[2] Papworth likely concluded that the collection belonged with the people who created the objects, in its historical and geographic context, not lost in storage in Ohio. It was the ethical thing to do, and he made no mention of seeking a financial payment for the return for the materials.

While Williams prepared new exhibits for the Nez Perce National Historical Park, Native Americans began publicly protesting for greater rights. Some Native activists, taking a cue from the Black Panthers, formed the American Indian Movement (AIM) to protect Native Americans from false arrests and police harassment. AIM lunched several major protests that garnered national attention. A group of eighty-nine Native Americans occupied Alcatraz for nineteen months between November 20, 1969, and June 11, 1971, arguing that under the terms of the Fort Laramie Treaty (1868) between the United States government and the Lakota Nation, any abandoned federal land was to be returned to the Lakota.

The occupation made national news. Doris Purdy, who worked at the Bureau of Indian Affairs in Berkeley, made a film of the occupation.[3] Grace Thorpe, the daughter of Jim Thorpe, Native American Olympic gold medalist and football player, was one of the occupiers. She reached out to celebrities, including Jane Fonda, Anthony Quinn, and Marlon Brando, to visit the island and show their support. Grace Thorpe not only brought attention to the occupation, she also donated supplies, including a generator and water barge, and even established an ambulance service to the island. The band Creedence Clearwater Revival donated $15,000, used to purchase a boat to ferry supplies to the group.

The Alcatraz Occupation lasted for nineteen months and was forcibly ended after federal officials cut off power and later took back the island. While this demonstration did not yield the results asked for by the AIM activists, which was to return Alcatraz to Native ownership and the development of a new cultural center, it did bring national attention to the plight of native communities suffering from poverty.[4] Media reporters produced stories on the plight of Native American communities and the lack of resources available to them.

The protest inspired American Indians across the country. George Horse Capture, working in the Bay area as a civil servant for the State of California, quit his job and joined the protest. After the protest ended, Horse Capture attended UC Berkeley where he took any course that "touched even remotely on Indian affairs." According to Horse Capture, "Alcatraz was a beacon that awakened us and set us on a new course. It taught us that we were Indians."[5] Horse Capture would go on to help found the Smithsonian's National Museum of the American Indian.

For many Americans, the status of Native American communities was largely ignored until large and well-publicized protests demanded attention. The Alcatraz Occupation also inspired more than two hundred instances of civil disobedience among Native Americans. Although the American public, and even many Native leaders, did not agree with the AIM protests, Native American activists could not be ignored.

This activism spread to museums, where Native American curators and their supporters advocated for exhibits that included Native voices and perspectives. Native communities responded to the issue of who curates Native culture by founding their own museums and cultural centers in the 1960s and 1970s. In addition to the formation of the Nez Perce National Historical Park in 1965, other tribes on the Columbia Plateau opened museums including Tamástslikt Cultural Institute, the Yakama Nation Museum and Cultural Center, and the Colville Tribal Museum.[6]

In this context, while officials at the National Park Service searched for the Spalding-Allen Collection, Brad Baker, collections technician in the Department of Archaeology at OHS, became interested in the Spalding-Allen Collection. On September 23, 1978, Baker wrote to Roderick Sprague, an archaeologist and expert on Plateau culture at the University of Idaho. Baker planned to apply to the National Science Foundation for funding to "properly" conserve, store, and document the collection. According to Baker, "currently, the material is in fairly stable condition considering the neglect it has received for many years. Through the grant I hope to remedy this neglect and to insure the future care of this largely unknown collection." Baker hoped that Sprague might help to determine the rarity of the collection. "I know of certain extant Nez Perce collections, but I have very little information on documented collections from the 1840s and earlier. Do you know of any such collections?"[7] Baker never received funding for his proposal; however, the correspondence with Sprague likely alerted park officials and the Nez Perce, with whom Sprague worked closely.

In December 1978, two months after this exchange, Steve Shawley, curator at the Nez Perce National Historical Park and a graduate student of Sprague, visited OHS to view the Spalding-Allen Collection.[8] When Shawley returned from his visit, he informed NPS officials that the OHS would loan the collection to NEPE "providing that ownership in the collection may be established with the Ohio Historical Center."[9] It appeared that OHS was not prepared to loan the materials because the institution did not own the Spalding-Allen Collection but only held it on "permanent loan" from Oberlin College.

The ownership of the collection by the Ohio Historical Society was far from clear. Richard Spear, director and professor of art at Oberlin College, wrote to Raymond Baby, curator of archaeology at OHS on October 20, 1978, regarding plans by Oberlin to publish a catalog of the college's holdings of American Indian art, "the source of much of the material is documented in the College Archives." Spear continued, "with the growing interest in this field, such a catalogue could be highly useful to scholarship in the field... at some future date we would like to come to Columbus to examine the collection with a view to removing it to Oberlin for examination, cataloguing and eventual exhibition."[10] However, the return of the Spalding-Allen Collection and other Indian artifacts owned by Oberlin College never occurred.

Curators at the OHS moved to establish their ownership of the Spalding-Allen Collection, perhaps as a result of Steve Shawley's loan request and Professor Spear's desire to have the collection returned to Oberlin College. On May 10, 1979, Martha Potter Otto, head of the Department of Archaeology at OHS, wrote to the president of Oberlin College, Emil Daneberg, enclosing three copies of a Deed of Gift and closing her letter with the statement "we are extremely grateful for this donation and will see that the collection is maintained and utilized according to the best professional standards."[11] Apparently President Daneberg signed the collection over to OHS without consulting with Professor Spear or anyone associated with Oberlin's Allen Museum. This decision to relinquish Oberlin's ownership of the Spalding-Allen Collection would have far-reaching consequences. When the Nez Perce Tribe and the National Park Service later sought to bring the Spalding-Allen Collection home permanently to Nez Perce Country, Oberlin College officials—unlike OHS—were amenable to the return without charge.

On May 26, 1979, President Daneberg wrote to Leslie H. Fishel, a member of the OHS Board of Trustees, "it seems appropriate after all these years to turn the [Spalding-Allen] collection over to the Historical Society and this letter can serve as official notice of that unless you would prefer some different form."[12] However, Daneberg turned over much more than the Spalding-Allen artifacts.

Curiously, the OHS deed which "conveys and transfers to the OHIO HISTORICAL SOCIETY the following described property irrevocably and subject to no conditions or restrictions whatsoever" included numerous Native American collections not part of the Spalding-Allen Collection. The OHS Board of Trustees meeting on August 3, 1979, officially recorded the receipt by Daneberg, president of Oberlin College, of a "Nez Perce Collection per the attached list" as accession no. 1994. The first four items listed were described as Plains Indian objects, including a fire bag, leather knife sheath, and another "parfleche" bag. Likewise, items six to eleven had no relation to the Nez Perce and included a harpoon from Norton's Sound, bows and arrows attributed to Plains Indians, and moccasins. In all, some twenty-two items appeared to be from the Spalding-Allen Collection while eighteen did not. In general, the items were briefly listed, many with question marks next to their descriptions reflecting the jumbled state of the Spalding-Allen Collection. Its provenance was disturbed, and it was far from its source of creation and far removed from the expertise of the descents who originally fashioned the objects and curators knowledgeable about Plateau material culture. From this list, OHS loaned nineteen items to the National Park Service.

Understanding the immense significance of the Spalding-Allen Collection to the Nez Perce Tribe and the exhibit program of the Nez Perce National Historical Park, Russell Dickenson, regional director of the National Park Service, lobbied OHS to donate the collection rather than loan it. On July 18, 1979, Dickenson wrote to Dr. Thomas Smith, director of OHS, in preparation for a meeting of the OHS Board. Dickenson noted "the acquisition of the 22 items of the Spalding-Nez Perce Collection belonging to the Ohio Historical Society would be of immense interpretive value to the Nez Perce National Historical Park. We would appreciate your consideration of our request to have the collection become a permanent part of the Nez Perce National Historical Park Collection [as it] is a cornerstone of Nez Perce tribal pride and culture." Dickenson noted that the request was based on the National Park Service's role as charged by Congress to preserve and interpret the nation's cultural and natural resources. According to Dickenson, "the interpretive use of the Spalding-Nez Perce Collection on the site of its cultural origin and collection would be of great public interest and support. We feel that should it be possible to make the collection a part of Nez Perce National Historical Park, we would thereby ensure the future care and interpretation of this unique collection."

After describing their plan for new museum facilities at the Nez Perce National Historical Park, Dickenson continued, "We have found the one-year loan policy established by the Ohio Historical Society Board of Trustees in 1977 to be too restrictive for us to justify the costly expense of conservation treatment and exhibit design, preparation, and installation for any short term. We feel that our request for a permanent assignment for the collection by gift or permanent loan, if a gift is not feasible, is in the best interest of the collection."[13]

The Nez Perce Tribe also lobbied OHS for the "permanent assignment, gift or loan of the items collected among our people in the 1840s by Reverend Henry H. Spalding." On November 13, 1979, Richard Halfmoon, vice chairman of the Nez Perce Tribal Executive Committee, wrote to curator Amos Loveday at OHS, "These items are part of the Nez Perce Nation's national heritage, a matter of pride and cultural interest of the Nez Perces today." Halfmoon emphasized the significance of the collection. "These few items are among the oldest documented Nez Perce items known to us and do represent examples of our culture that cannot be found elsewhere. We are anxious to see these items return to their homeland where all can see and appreciate them."[14] Halfmoon's arguments to OHS did not result in any concessions. However, considering the efforts of the NPS and the Nez Perce Tribe, the message that the Spalding-Allen Collection was incredibly important must have been clear to OHS. However, OHS was not willing to agree to NPS requests or those of the Nez Perce Tribe, to return valuable cultural patrimony back to the community that created it.

In the late 1970s, OHS was a powerful well-funded organization. It had a new museum and a large network of historical sites. From its founding in 1885 until the 1960s, OHS had been a fairly small, private organization with informal ties to Ohio state government. Its emphasis was on publishing essays on Ohio history and caring for historical sites and collections. This all changed in 1965 when Ohio governor James Rhodes wanted OHS to play a major part in the state's growth. OHS's director, Erwin Zepp, met Governor Rhodes regularly for lunch and as a result of these meetings the two men planned an expansive role for OHS. The result was a new law, Ohio Revised Code 149.30, which stipulated a massive contract for services by OHS to benefit the state.[15]

The contract specifies a vast range of services, charging OHS with the following responsibilities, among others: operate a public system of state memorials; protect and repair monuments in its care; maintain a state archives; operate a state historical museum; identify historical and archaeological sites; publish research on Ohio history, archaeology, and natural science; collect, catalog, and provide access to collections related to Ohio history; inventory archaeological sites; coordinate history tours at the state capital; provide an annual report to the governor; and commission a portrait of each departing governor.[16] OHS remained a private organization while at the same time supporting the state with this broad range of services. The arrangement worked well for OHS in the 1960s and early 1970s as state budgets grew. However, when state revenues declined, OHS struggled to fulfill its varied obligations.

The Nez Perce National Historical Park was a very different organization from OHS. Established by Congress on May 15, 1965, as Public

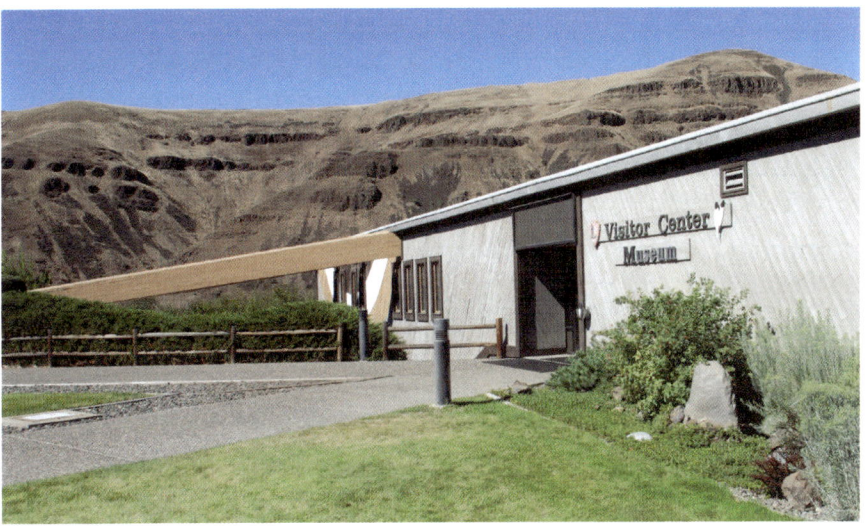

The Nez Perce National Historical Park Visitor Center and Museum entrance located next to the site of Henry and Eliza Spalding's mission. Courtesy of the Nez Perce National Historical Park.

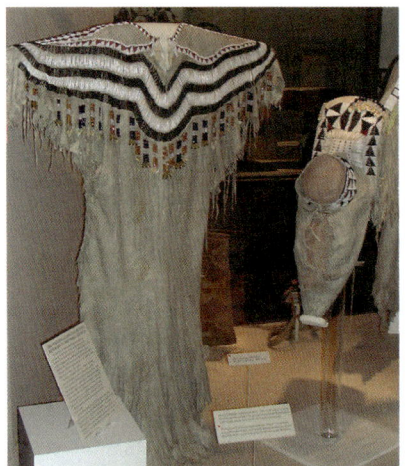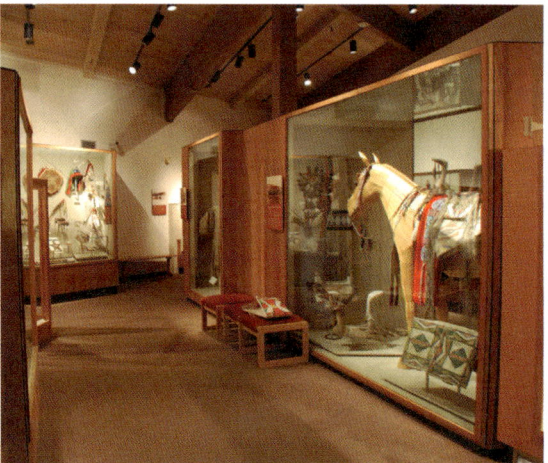

Nez Perce National Historical Park displays. Left: Woman's dress and cradleboard from the Spalding-Allen Collection. Right: Display featuring items from the Spalding-Allen Collection. (Note that the Spalding-Allen Collection was taken down as part of an exhibit update in 2020.) Both images courtesy of the Nez Perce National Historical Park.

Law 89-19, the park was created through a partnership between the Nez Perce, officials in the Department of the Interior, and Idaho's congressional delegation and included twenty-four sites.[17] Managed by the National Park Service, the Nez Perce National Historical Park grew to include sites in Washington, Oregon, and Montana, with a visitor center located beside Henry and Eliza Spalding's mission site in Spalding, Idaho. These sites included many locations that were managed but not owned by the National Park Service. By 1995, the park had fifty cooperative agreements with twenty separate communities and had a very close working relationship with Nez Perce leaders.[18] The very structure of the Nez Perce National Historical Park compelled NPS officials to work collaboratively with the Nez Perce and many other constituencies.

In January 1980, OHS came to an agreement with the NPS and the Nez Perce for one-year renewable loans and, later that year, OHS loaned most of the collection. Unfortunately, OHS refused to loan the cradleboard—the primary artifact sought by NEPE curators for an exhibit interpreting Nez Perce children. OHS informed NPS that the cradleboard was exhibited at an OHS branch museum. The cradleboard remained in Ohio for another sixteen years. Eventually, the Nez Perce were able to purchase it for $25,000.[19]

The terms of the OHS loan to the National Park Service included one-year loans with an indefinite number of renewals, insurance carried by the NPS, an appraisal of the collection every five years, and identification of the Ohio Historical Society as the owner of the collection. OHS had the Spalding-Allen Collection appraised in Ohio prior to the loan. In December 1980, the objects (not including the cradleboard) were valued at $52,700 and were insured at $52,900.

Prior to exhibiting the artifacts, the NPS sent the Spalding-Allen Collection to the Harper's Ferry Center for conservation treatment. There NPS conservators stabilized the artifacts for exhibition, incurring a $12,000 conservation fee for the NPS Northwest Division.[20] This expense was the first and only significant investment made to conserve and stabilize the collections. The NPS also purchased climate-controlled exhibit cases and custom mounts for displaying the objects.

According to the terms of the loan, the National Park Service paid for a reappraisal of the collection every five years. In 1985, an appraiser from the Northwest, recognizing the cultural significance and its unusually fine provenance, valued the Spalding-Allen Collection at $104,850, roughly double the appraised amount from 1980. In the five years between appraisals, the value of the two dresses declined, but that of the men's hide shirts increased more than fourfold. This dramatic increase in the appraised price of the shirts reflected the changing nature of the market for Native American material culture and the demand from collectors for large, fine examples with excellent provenance. In Spalding's day, colorful beadwork impressed collectors; however, over time, buyers had shown an increasing appreciation for quillwork. According to NPS curator Bob Chenoweth, beads were easier to work with and more colorful. With quills, there were more design limitations because dying the quills and attaching them to a garment required a lot more work.[21]

The appraiser also confirmed that three baskets included in the loan were of African origin and were not made by the Niimíipuu or part of Spalding's collecting activities. The National Park Service returned the African baskets to the OHS in 1986. The misattribution of three African baskets as part of the Spalding-Allen Collection indicates that OHS had not kept the provenance of the collection and had allowed other collections to become mixed in with the Spalding-Allen Collection. While Oberlin College left the Spalding-Allen Collection with OHS for "proper care," OHS curators jumbled the Plateau artifacts with other random collections. The fact that the OHS identified and sent these African baskets as Nez Perce artifacts demonstrated that the OHS curators did not have an even basic knowledge of Nez Perce material culture.[22]

Challenges at the Nez Perce National Historical Park

In 1980, the Nez Perce National Historical Park had a number of curatorial challenges. It was no paradise for collections. Prior to the completion of the visitor center in 1981, park officials kept collections in a former auto service garage without insulation.[23] The park's first museum curator, Stephen Shawley, started his position in 1977. Shawley, the son of missionaries, had grown up with Nez Perce and knew firsthand about their traditions and material culture. Yet, with a bachelor's degree in anthropology, Shawley had no professional training as a museum curator. Park superintendent Whitaker was concerned about Shawley's performance when it became clear that Shawley had neglected his work cataloging collections, had failed to identify whether objects were gifts or purchases, and had even mixed some collections, thus confusing their provenance. Worse still, Shawley treated the park's collections as his own by trading and not documenting the items.

Susan Buchel, who worked as a curator three years after Shawley, recounted that for him, the "line between being a curator, being a material culture expert and being a possessor of collections on his own, that line was hazy."[24] After years of investigations, Shawley resigned in 1985 under threat of indictment for the theft of collections.[25] After his departure, the park hired trained museum curators. Fortunately, the Spalding-Allen Collection, on exhibit in the visitor's center, remained safe from Shawley's grasp.

When Nez Perce National Historical Park curator Susan Buchel started at the park in the spring of 1988, she found the terms of the Spalding-Allen Collection surprising, particularly the annual renewal provision for objects in a permanent exhibit. As a collection manager, she remembered asking, "what's this all about?" Buchel recounted an anecdotal conversation with OHS registrar and loan contact Melinda Knapp. When Buchel asked Knapp about the one-year terms, Knapp replied, "Well, didn't you hear the story?"[26]

The story, according to Knapp, was that during Steve Shawley's visit to OHS in 1978, the "Ohio Historical Society got a good preaching to about how this material shouldn't be in Ohio." Buchel noted that Shawley did not know when "to let off and let go and what tone to take. And according to Melinda [Knapp], that annual loan renewal was mostly for spite.…It was done kind of as a resistance to being told what to do kind of thing." This encounter also resulted in the cradleboard not being part of the loan. As Buchel recounted, the end result was "there you are, and now you've got an annual loan."[27]

As the NPS and the OHS settled on the terms of their loan agreement, other Native American communities, following the example set by the Nez Perce Tribe, began achieving successes in legal cases against the United States. In 1980, the Cow Creek Band of Umpqua (southwestern Oregon) received a settlement of $1.5 million for lost lands. The Sioux (Dakota, Lakota, and Nakota) won some partial legal victories in their efforts to retrieve the sixty million acres of the Black Hills guaranteed by the 1851 Fort Laramie Treaty. The discovery of gold and the forced shrinking of that land base resulted in an 1877 treaty signed by only 10 percent of the adult male Sioux. The Indian Claims Commission sided (in part) with the Sioux to compensate the tribes with the value of the land in 1877 plus interest. Some Sioux groups including the Standing Rock Reservation voted to accept the award, but most refused it, holding out for a return of their land. The awarded compensation remains in an interest-bearing account and in 2005 was worth some $700 million. An estimate of the value of resources extracted from the same land in the Black Hills is $4 billion.[28] These cases represent an increasingly vigorous and public campaign by Native communities to articulate their rights and demand redress for their stolen lands and resources.

Another major development during the 1980s was the creation of a new National Museum of the American Indian (NMAI). The founding of the museum, how it operated, and how it cared for its collections became part of the national dialog on the best care and exhibition for Native American collections. Conversations around the founding began in the 1970s as land on the National Mall was reserved for a future Smithsonian museum. The director of the National Portrait Gallery, Marvin Sadik, suggested to Smithsonian secretary S. Dillon Ripley that the Smithsonian create a museum dedicated to Native American heritage following the Museo Anthropologia in Mexico City. Sadik wrote to Ripley that it was "high time that the American Indian was seen primarily on his own terms, rather than solely through the eyes of ethnologists, sociologists, historians, art historians, etc."[29]

During the 1980s, the trustees of the Museum of the American Indian, Heye Foundation, New York City, which had been founded by Heye and featured his massive collection, initiated talks with the Smithsonian about affiliating with the Smithsonian. In 1987, the negotiations were nearly finalized. In 1989, the legislation that created the NMAI Public Law 101-185 passed Congress. The law indicated that the Smithsonian would initially operate a museum in the Alexander Hamilton US Custom House in New York City (opened in 1994); then collections would be relocated to a new Cultural Resource Center in Suitland, Maryland (completed 1998); and finally, a new museum would be built on the last available site on the National Mall (opened in 2004).[30]

The planning for the new collections center and Smithsonian Museum would be different from previous Smithsonian endeavors. As the Smithsonian's deputy director Douglas Evelyn put it, "the act launched a rather new type of cultural museum, to be developed with the direct involvement of Native peoples. It was not a museum produced by others for American Indians, but rather one created by American Indians themselves." Evelyn stated that it would be a place for "Native people to celebrate and share their achievements and aspirations as Americans and citizens of the world."[31]

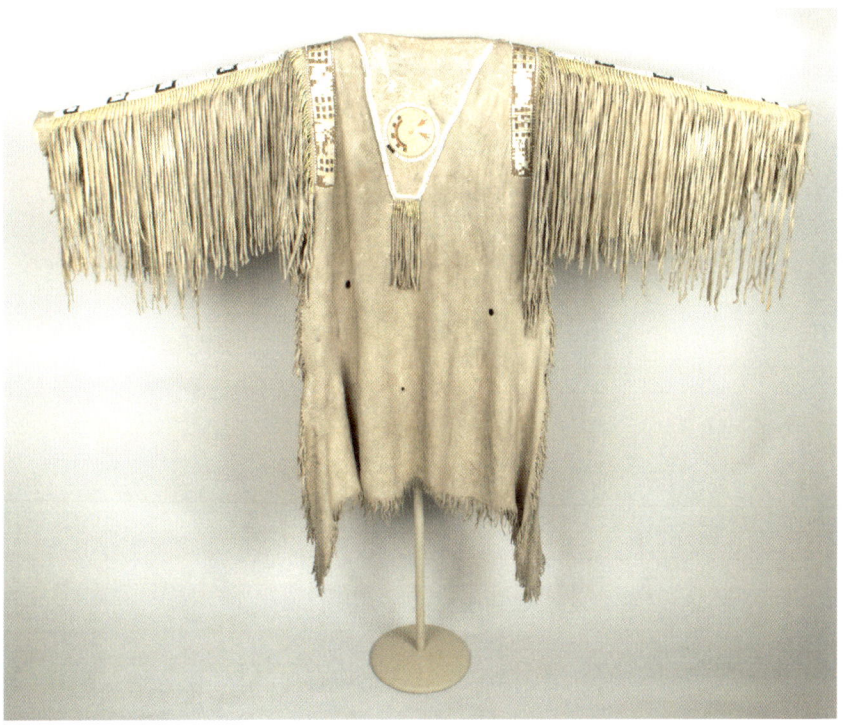

Nez Perce man's tanned hide shirt decorated with porcupine quillwork and black and white Venetian glass beads. This is one of two shirts in the Spalding-Allen Collection and one of the most valuable pieces in the collection. Photographs by Zach Mazur. Courtesy of the Nez Perce National Historical Park. NEPE 8760.

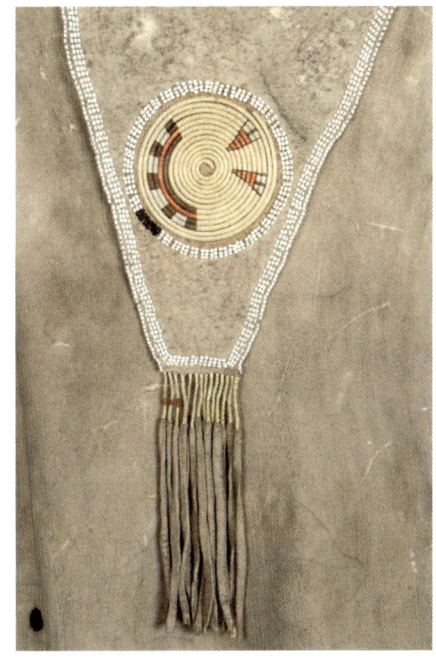

Part 3

The Campaign

Chapter 8

From Loan to Recall

OHS really didn't understand that concept of live native peoples who cared about their history and culture as compared to scholars studying an historic culture. I really don't think that understanding was ever truly reached, although they did finally realize the importance of the collection to the Nez Perce and that it should be in Nez Perce country.

—Frank Walker, Nez Perce National Historical Park superintendent[1]

While the Spalding-Allen Collection remained on display at the Nez Perce National Historical Park, other Native American communities worked to halt sales of their cultural heritage. In May 1991, the Hopi and the Navajo sought to stop a Sotheby's auction of sacred katsinam—masklike decorated objects representing kachina spirits that the Hopi (and other Pueblo people) consider spiritual beings. One of the katsinam, a painted design of cloth on panel intended to be worn by Chief Kachina, a dancer representing an ancestral spirit, had a pre-auction value estimated at between twelve thousand and eighteen thousand dollars. Although it received two letters from the Hopi and Navajo arguing for cancelling the auction, Sotheby's declined to halt the sale.

According to Native American Graves Protection and Repatriation Act (NAGPRA), the Native communities did not have a legal case to stop the sale. If put up for sale by a museum or any organization that received federal funds, the katsinam would have been covered under NAGPRA's provision to repatriate sacred objects and thus returned to the Hopi and Navajo.[2] However, as this sale came from an individual collector, the NAGPRA regulation did not apply, and Hopi were unsuccessful in their legal case. Instead, they made an ethical argument for the return of the katsinam.

Leigh Jenkins, director of the Hopi Cultural Preservation Office, noted that "we object very strongly to the marketing of these items. They are not pieces of art in the way the public sees them." Daniel Deschinny Sr., secretary of the Dineh Spiritual and Cultural Society, wrote that the Navajo object could be used in contemporary religious ceremonies; it was not, he added, "an obsolete relic of lost ceremonies." At the time, the head of Native American art sales at Sotheby's, Bernard de Grunne, could recall only one instance in the previous four years when a Native American community objected to the sale of an item. In that case, the Zuni Nation objected to a 1988 sale of a Zuni war god figure in the Andy Warhol collection. In that case, the Warhol Foundation withdrew the carved figure from the sale and returned it to the Zuni.[3]

While the Hopi and Navajo Nations fought unsuccessfully to regain their material culture from the marketplace, the new National Museum of the American Indian (NMAI) got underway at the Smithsonian. Officials from NMAI began two years of extensive consultations with Native communities. As W. Richard West Jr., a member of the Cheyenne and Arapaho Tribes of Oklahoma and the first director of the NMAI recounted, after two dozen consultations with Native communities in the United States and Canada, three main concerns emerged. According to West, "first, while acknowledging our deep past, Native peoples want to be seen as communities and cultures that are very much alive today." He continued, "second, we want the opportunity to speak directly to museum visitors through our exhibitions and public programs, and to describe in our own voices and through our own eyes the meaning of the objects in the museum's collections and their importance in Native art, culture, and history." And finally, "we want the museum to act in direct support of contemporary Native communities."[4]

While Richard West and his colleagues planned the NMAI and forged a new type of relationship between museums and Native Americans, the Spalding-Allen Collection was soon at the center of a major struggle between the Ohio Historical Society and the National Park Service and the Nez Perce Tribe.

OHS Recalls the Spalding-Allen Collection

In the spring of 1992 after twelve years of renewable loans, OHS requested a recall of the Spalding-Allen Collection to Ohio for evaluation. The recall letter came as a shock to park officials, especially as OHS requested that the collection be returned within three weeks. Park officials requested more time to pack the collection and plan a replacement exhibit for the visitor's center. Frank Walker, superintendent of the Nez Perce National Historical Park, described what the recall would mean to the community. "It will be a great loss to the Nez Perce people and to all people who live

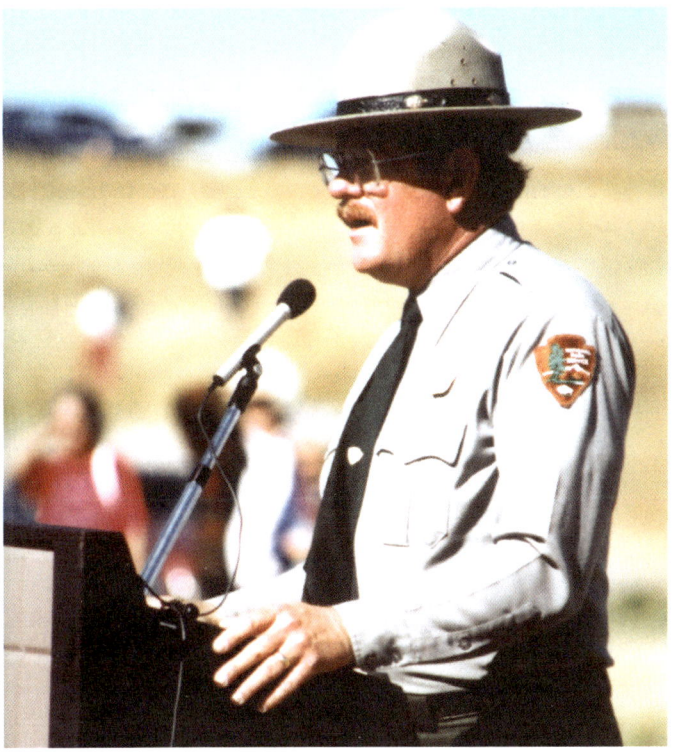

Nez Perce National Historical Park superintendent Frank Walker, Bear Paw Commemoration, 1993. Courtesy of the Nez Perce National Historical Park.

in the Northwest. They are a piece of the Northwest that if it goes away will never come back." Walker continued, "it will be a loss of inspiration for Nez Perce artists and Nez Perce people that will never come back. They are like great pieces of art, or great literary works."[5] OHS took this delay on the part of Walker and the NPS as a refusal to cooperate.[6]

Nez Perce National Historical Park curator Susan Buchel recounted that OHS officials asked the NPS if the collection was so important to the Nez Perce Park, then why was the park willing to loan the dress to the Burke Museum for a year? According to Buchel, the NPS's response was that, by loaning it to the Burke Museum for the centennial of Washington state, new audiences would see it in "context with other materials and other tribes in a facility" that was "quite capable of doing it in a really stellar, stellar way, which they did."[7] This question from OHS reflected their apparent lack of understanding of the importance of curating the Spalding-Allen Collection in context.

Why Recall the Loan Now?

Several factors led to the recall decision. Amos Loveday, curator for OHS, attributed it to new scrutiny over all loans after a court case in 1977 that was decided initially in the favor of the OHS but was then overturned on appeal in 1980.[8] The case centered on a loan to OHS by Mary Houser of items she inherited from her ancestor, General Israel Putnam. Upon receipt of the items in 1934, OHS provided Ms. Houser with a loan receipt for a term of "one year, or more, when they may be withdrawn upon presentation of this receipt." Ms. Houser died in 1952, and in 1975, her estate administrator, Helen Houser, discovered the receipts from OHS and requested the return of the items. OHS refused the request. Helen Houser took OHS to court over the loaned goods in 1977 and lost her case. However, she appealed the ruling, and in 1980, the courts compelled OHS to honor the initial receipt.[9] The result of the case caused OHS to better document ownership of its collections, including the Spalding-Allen Collection on loan from Oberlin College. However, it is hard to see this lawsuit as the reason for the recall of Spalding-Allen Collection from the National Park Service, since the case was litigated between 1977 and 1980, and the recall occurred in 1992. It seems apparent that the primary reason OHS recalled the Spalding-Allen Collection was their growing realization of the importance of the collection and its value.

Loan Requests Highlight Value of Collection

Two major loan requests alerted OHS officials to the significance of the Spalding-Allen Collection. To celebrate the centennial of Washington state in 1989, the Burke Museum in Seattle planned a major exhibit titled "A Time of Gathering: Native Heritage in Washington State." When the curator of the Burke exhibit, Robin Wright, contacted Buchel regarding the possibility of an eight-month loan, Buchel indicated she had no objection and suggested that Wright contact OHS.

On July 25, 1988, Wright wrote to the president of OHS, Gary Ness, to request the loan of the Nez Perce woman's dress with dentalia decorations, currently on display at the Nez Perce National Historical Park, and the Nez Perce cradleboard held at OHS. She enclosed in her letter slides of the dress and cradleboard that Bill Holm had taken of the objects during his visit to OHS in 1976.[10] Wright also requested high-quality color transparencies of both objects for an exhibit catalog. According to Wright, "the dress and cradle from your collection are among the earliest, finest and best documented Nez Perce pieces I have seen in the more than 30 museums I have visited in preparation for this exhibit."[11] OHS granted the loan request.

To deliver the requested items, Buchel drove with the dress to Seattle, agreeing to arrive at the Burke Museum on the day that OHS collection manager Bradley Baker arrived with the cradleboard. Buchel was eager to see the cradleboard, since only black-and-white photographs of it had been available to her. According to Buchel, Baker was eager to check on the condition of the dress. As Buchel described that meeting:

> We have the two boxes sitting on a table. And there's a number of people from the Burke around us. And Baker is on one side and I'm on the other side. We're both opening our packages. And as we're opening our packages, I all of a sudden had to step away. There was like a whoosh of air come up out of both packages. And it made me jerk backwards. And this whoosh thing, I don't know what it is, rose up above the box and was kind of swirling around, up above of both boxes. And was kind of swirling around. And I felt this immediate sense of joy, reuniting, just happiness. And I can't even explain it.
>
> And I looked at Baker to see, and he says, "What's the matter?"
> And I said, "Didn't you feel that?"
> And he goes, "No. What?"
> And I looked at everybody else. And they thought I was crazy. They thought I'd tripped or something. And I definitely felt that. It took me a second before I actually looked into Baker's box. And the second I looked at that cradle board in real life, and not in black and white, it was like oh my god. That cradle board is made by the same woman who made this dress. They belong together. We have kept them apart for, I don't know, whatever, 135 [years]…through our own management of these things, or mismanagement of these things. And they belong together.
> And of course, Baker could see that, too, looking at them.[12]

As Buchel recalled, the high-profile loan to the Burke Museum and all the interest in the dress and cradle board from Burke Museum curators made the Spalding-Allen Collection "something real to the OHS again. Maybe when Steve [Shawley] had been there in the '70s, it became real again." Buchel continued, "But for this generation [at the Ohio Historical Society], it had a new value that they hadn't recognized before. So I think that the Burke Museum's request for this thing was the beginning of this whole real acknowledgement on the part of Ohio that they had something significant."[13]

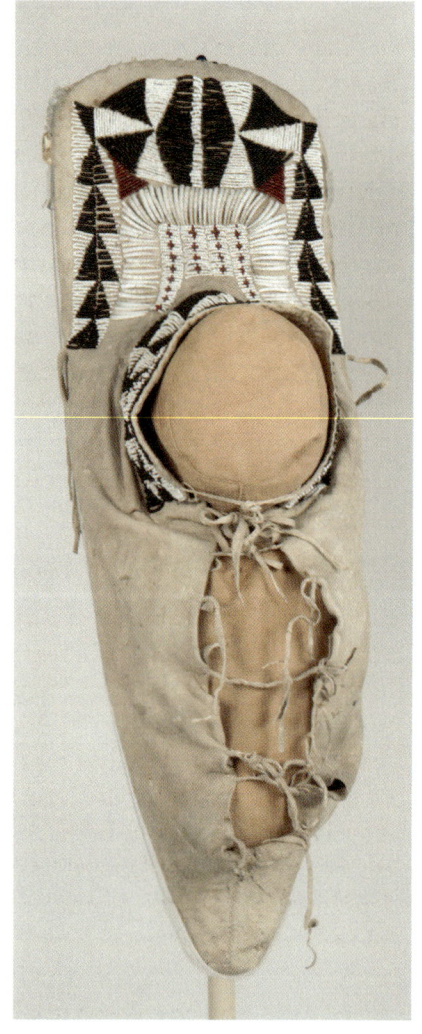

On the heels of the loan to the Burke Museum, the OHS received another major loan request for the Spalding-Allen Collection. This request for a travelling exhibit with significant support from the National Endowment for the Humanities focused on missionaries and Plateau Indians titled "Sacred Encounters: Jesuit Missionaries and the Indians of the Rocky Mountain West."[14] One major component of the exhibit centered on the work of Jesuit missionary Pierre Jean De Smet. On April 6, 1990, the director of the exhibit, Washington State University professor Jacqueline Peterson, wrote to Melinda Knapp, the registrar of OHS, indicating that, after visiting the Nez Perce National Historical Park, Peterson had identified several items from the Spalding-Allen Collection that she wished to borrow from OHS for the exhibit and a travelling tour.[15]

On May 17, 1992, Knapp replied to Peterson that the OHS Board "tentatively agreed to the loan request, subject to several conditions. The primary condition is the recall of the five artifacts currently at the Nez Perce National Historical Park to the OHS headquarters in Columbus." Knapp wrote, "As part of a general review of Society holdings, the entire collection has been scheduled for recall at the end of the current loan period in early July. The five artifacts are being recalled early to enable the Society to assess their condition before the next Board meeting in mid-April." Knapp continued, "The board will require this assessment before

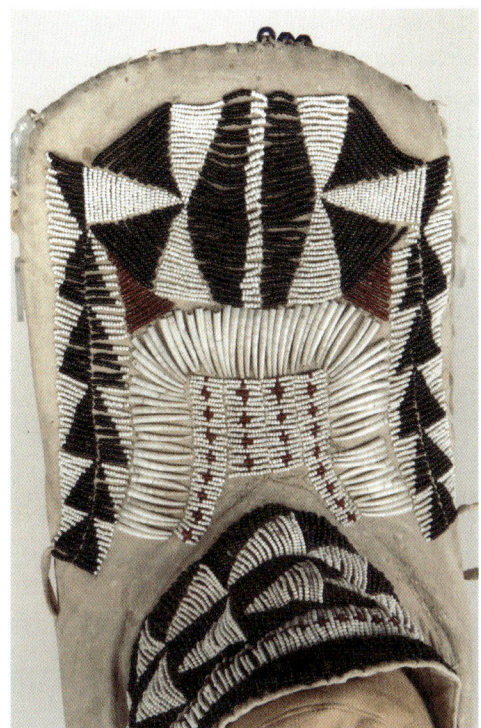 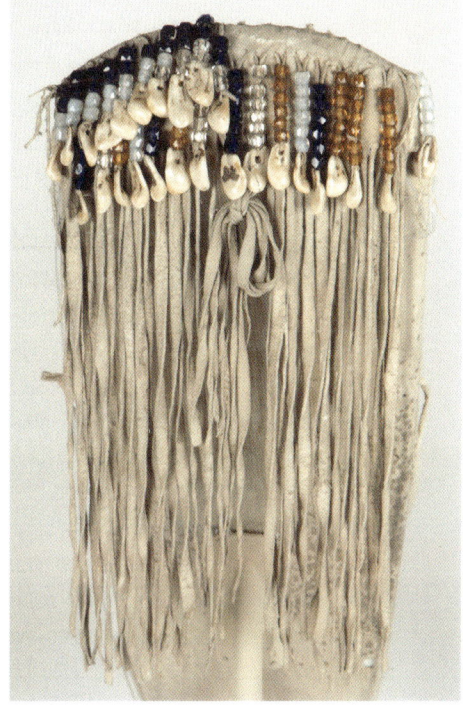

Nez Perce cradleboard circa 1846. The teardrop-shaped wooden board is covered with buckskin and decorated with black, white, and red glass beads, dentalium shells with elk teeth attached to top fringe, and was made by the woman who also fashioned one of the dresses in the collection (NEPE 8758). OHS withheld this piece from the original loan of the Spalding-Allen Collection to NPS. Photographs by Zach Mazur. Courtesy of the Nez Perce National Historical Park. NEPE 33887.

giving final approval....The Society is very interested in participating in Sacred Encounters."[16]

Though OHS was "very interested" in the exhibit, officials at the Nez Perce National Historical Park were less enthusiastic. As Buchel recounted, "When the De Smet project came...I recommended to Frank that we not be as on board with that as with the Burke [exhibit]. And that was going to be a traveling exhibit. It was going to go on for quite some long while. And we basically left that to Ohio to talk to the De Smet people about [it]."[17]

On May 12, 1992, Pavelka, exhibition coordinator for the Sacred Encounters exhibit sent Jacqueline Peterson a fax reporting that the OHS loans "may be in jeopardy." After he placed a call with Knapp, Pavelka wrote that although Knapp in no way indicated the following to him, his "interpretation of the situation is that OHS (on the board level) promised these things to Nez Perce [National Historical Park] on a permanent loan status and the Nez Perce (on the board level) is angry that OHS is authorizing/approving the loan of them for Sacred Encounters and disrupting its installation for a lengthy period of time."[18]

On July 1, 1992, Knapp sent a fax to Pavelka with an update. The OHS Board did not receive a recommendation from OHS staff regarding the Sacred Encounters request because the Nez Perce Park had not yet returned the collection. Weeks earlier, OHS's chief curator, Amos Loveday, had placed a call to the National Park Service regarding the recall of the Spalding-Allen Collection.

The Call Demanding the End of the Loan

On June 9, 1992, Frank Walker, Nez Perce National Historical Park superintendent, received the call from Amos Loveday regarding the Spalding-Allen Collection loan. A detailed four-paragraph, single-space, typed record of that conversation, made by Walker, survives in the National Park Service records. According to Walker, Loveday "demanded" a formal request to extend the loan further. Walker characterized Loveday as "rude" and "demanding." Loveday reported to Walker that "this [the loan agreement] was only between the National Park Service and the Ohio Historical Society and did not concern the Nez Perce Tribe." Walker reiterated the point that a recall would greatly "concern" the Nez Perce and that "returning them would be a great loss." Loveday's response was that this "was not with the Nez Perce people and was just between the National Park Service and the Ohio Historical Society." Walker let his temper show at the end of the conversation when he asked Loveday "if he worked for Dr. Ness or was it the other way around." Loveday responded that "he worked for Dr. Ness, but we [NPS] had better get our request in immediately." Walker concluded that "this was a verbal request for an extension" and that he "requested a written response concerning this call from Dr. Ness."[19]

Walker ended the call visibly shaking. Decades later, he remembered this telephone call as a point of momentous significance for his career. Walker said that Loveday "wanted the loaned collection sent back immediately. There did not seem to be any concern about the impacts the return might have on the park or the Nez Perce people. I got the feeling at that time that the OHS didn't care about the impacts on the Nez Perce." OHS's position was, according to Walker, "we own them and want them back."[20]

Walker sent a letter to Ness the following day, copying NEPE curator Buchel, and Samuel Penney, chairman of the Nez Perce Tribal Executive Committee (NPTEC). He communicated to Ness that he had "indicated a willingness to have a representative from OHS come to the park to assess the pieces' condition." If an OHS conservator could not make the trip, Walker offered to arrange a conservation assessment by an independent party.

Walker wrote that instead of a return call from Ness, he received a "heated almost belligerent, pompous, and demeaning phone call from your Curator, accusing my staff and I of being 'unprofessional.'" Walker noted that when he asked about the site visit by OHS, he instead was "cut short." Walker continued, "this leads me to believe that the call back of this loan really has nothing to do with the condition of the objects." Walker pressed Ness, "Does Mr. Lovejoy's [sic] phone call accurately reflect the position of the Ohio Historical Society, or does your most recent correspondence? I thought you and I, as directors of our facilities, were engaged in an open discussion, but instead I find the communication changed dramatically." Walker concluded with a formal request to extend the loan and asked for notification if the loan would not be approved so his staff might "properly plan for the major exhibit rehab the loss that material would necessitate." Walker conveyed that he was "shocked, not only by Mr. Lovejoy's [sic] demeanor, but by his statement that the Nez Perce have 'nothing to do with' this loan or these materials.

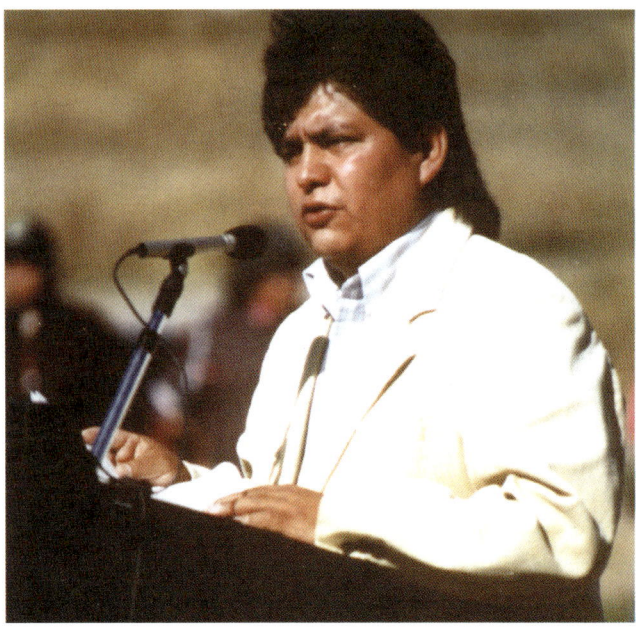

NPTEC chairman Samuel Penney at the Bear Paw Commemoration, 1993.
Courtesy of the Nez Perce National Historical Park.

Such a statement, coming from a curator of Native American cultural
material, shows a dismaying lack of sensitivity for the most basic significance of the very material for which he is the caretaker."[21]

Walker's letter resulted in a phone call two days later with Ness.
Again, Walker took detailed notes of their conversation. Ness relayed that
the OHS Board wanted the OHS curators to "recommit" to the Sacred
Encounters travelling exhibit and that the Spalding-Allen Collection
needed to be returned to Ohio. Walker countered that rather than sending the collection across the country, NPS could deliver the requested
items to the Sacred Encounters exhibit less than one hundred miles away.
Ness related that an onsite visit by OHS officials was not possible, in part
because he did not want a board member or a conservator to be put in a
"political situation" with tribal leaders.[22]

After further negotiations, Gary Ness, Amos Loveday, and George
Carroll, a professor at Urbana College and a member of OHS's collections committee, agreed to visit NEPE on October 25, 1992. Walker and
his staff at NEPE closely coordinated the visit with Samuel Penney, the

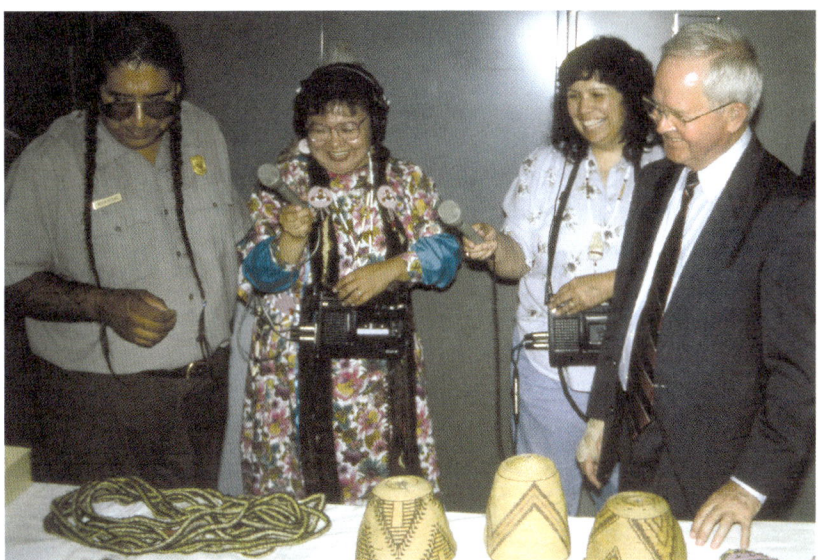

Kevin Peters, Mary Sando-Emhoolah, Tirsea McNeil, and Gary Ness during an OHS visit to Nez Perce National Historical Park on October 25, 1992. Courtesy of the Nez Perce National Historical Park.

chairman of NPTEC. Walker and Penney wanted to convey to OHS the proper care that they had taken of the Spalding-Allen Collection. Walker issued a memorandum to all NEPE employees on the significance of the Spalding-Allen materials. He also arranged for Herman Reuben to tell Nez Perce stories followed by a dancing performance by Sam Slickpoo and his father. Walker reminded his staff that "the building will be clean, the lobby will look professional and this group [the OHS delegation] will see how vital the Spalding collection is to our operation."[23]

When the delegation arrived, Carroll and Loveday noted that the National Park Service did not properly display OHS ownership of the Spalding-Allen Collection as was specified by their loan agreement. This lack of attribution led Dr. Carroll to surmise that the NPS "more or less concluded that it was their material."[24] OHS curator Loveday later recalled that his "suspicion" after that first visit "was that NPS never had any intent to honor the loan agreement."[25] According to park superintendent Walker, the Niimíipuu people "showed up in force and explained the significance [of the Spalding-Allen Collection] to their history." Eventually this message began to resonate with OHS. Walker recounted that OHS simply "didn't get it" when working with Native American communities. OHS was accustomed to working with Native American collections in a museum setting. As Walker noted, "OHS really didn't understand that concept of live native peoples who cared about their history and culture as compared to scholars studying an historic culture. I really don't think that understanding was ever truly reached, although they did finally realize the importance of the collection to the Nez Perce and that it should be in Nez Perce country."[26] Nakia Williamson-Cloud echoed this sentiment. Scientists and officials at other institutions, like museums, often draw lines between the people of the past and the people of today, he said, "All of this is wrapped up together; that's our experience as a people."[27]

Buchel recalled the visit of OHS to the Nez Perce country. "It still gives me goosebumps, thinking about it, when those trustees came. And I don't know what they expected. But…people who have never experienced the warmth, sincerity and depth of a culture, and then have it thrust on them in a way that they can't not see it, it changes you." The visit, Buchel reflected, "helped in a way that no amount of talking or letters or other meetings between officials could ever have done…it changed the minds and hearts of at least a few people in that group. That was an amazing thing that we put together."[28]

The following spring, OHS extended the loan of the collection for another year while the National Park Service and the Nez Perce developed a proposal to "permanently return the objects to the Nez Perce Country." Walker proposed consulting with the Nez Perce to plan an acceptable range of options, to send an NPS/Nez Perce/academic delegation to Ohio to see the other Spalding items still held there, and to get an independent appraisal of the collection.[29] In an email to Walker on March 15, 1993, Buchel listed the options under consideration: a congressional appropriation to cover the purchase, private fund raising, or exchange of the Spalding-Allen Collection for other NPS collections. In her message, Buchel wrote "if using this option [private fundraising], I personally think we need to strongly consider transfer of ownership to the Tribe rather than NPS."[30]

Walker immediately contacted Nez Perce leadership to gauge their interest in the collection and their level of involvement in keeping the collection at the Nez Perce National Historical Park. Buchel recalled that she and Walker were like-minded on the question over ownership of the collection. According to Buchel, "It doesn't matter who owns it. In our mind...it didn't have to be the park service. What mattered was that it was whole and it was where it belonged. And ownership was the least of our interests." Buchel continued, "The value of the collection was not in Ohio. The value of the collection was out here where it belonged with the people."[31]

The topic of retaining the Spalding-Allen Collection caused a heated debate at the Nez Perce Tribal General Council Meeting, held twice a year and open to all tribal members. Park superintendent Frank Walker told the gathering that the collection might be worth between $500,000 and $1 million, and that they could either negotiate a sale of the collection with OHS or an exchange. Walker asked for the Nez Perce Tribe to work with him and the National Park Service but given the monetary value of the artifacts, he cautioned, "It's not something most of us can reach into our back pockets for."[32]

The discussion over the possible purchase of the Spalding-Allen Collection led to some sharp remarks from the audience. Tribal member Beatrice Miles said that after the arrival of Christianity with Spalding, Nez Perce were forbidden to wear their own regalia, and it is possible that Spalding just took some of it with him. She accused Spalding of stealing land from the Nez Perce. According to Miles, Spalding "was nothing but a crook to me....Maybe he stole those articles, and here we are having trouble now." She elaborated, "He was mean to the people," though she added that Spalding's wife was a much nicer person and was well-liked. Another participant suggested that since Spalding was Presbyterian, they should ask the Presbyterian church to pay for the collection, a sentiment echoed by Beatrice Moffett. Richard Ellenwood spoke of the history of the white man (*soyapo*) exploiting Indians. "We have to buy our land back. Now we have to buy our regalia back," he said. "This belongs to us, and it belongs to the future of our grandchildren." Ellenwood suggested that each tribal member contribute five dollars, perhaps by missing a meal. By doing so according to Ellenwood, "We can buy some of our culture, some of our history." Bill Picard, a member of the Nez Perce Tribe Executive Committee (NPTEC), observed that the tribe needed time to negotiate and suggested asking the OHS for period of three years' time to come up with the money, and then asking the US Congress to pay for it. NPTEC member Barry Moffett eventually made a motion to form a committee with members from NPTEC, a representative from the Tribe's cultural program, a representative from the National Park Service, and four representatives from the general council. This motion passed with a charge for the committee to develop a plan to finance the purchase and to report to the council in May the following year.[33]

To formalize their shared efforts, the National Park Service and NPTEC signed a memorandum of understanding to work together to "bring about the acquisition of the Spalding-Allen Collection of the Plateau materials by the Nez Perce Tribe and ensure their long-term care." As part of the agreement, the Nez Perce pledged to provide resources and staff time, to allow the materials to remain on loan to the NPS for exhibit for a period of no less than five years, and to administer all proceeds of any fundraising. NPS agreed to devote staff time and "provide routine and specialized preservation cares, including the costs associated with such care."[34] This government-to-government document laid out their shared interests in the collection and formalized what would become an epic struggle to keep the Spalding-Allen materials.

In May 1994, a delegation from the NPS and the Nez Perce Tribe travelled to Columbus, Ohio, to meet with OHS officials and discuss the future of the Spalding-Allen Collection.[35] The participants did not come to an agreement, however, and the following winter OHS recalled the Spalding-Allen Collection effective December 31, 1995.[36] However, on March 3, 1995, Ness wrote to Bill Walters, NPS acting director for the Pacific Northwest region, to notify him that the board of the OHS would be "willing to entertain an appropriate offer to purchase" but that OHS would "secure an independent appraisal of our Spalding-Allen collection so as to establish a current value" after which "any negotiations leading to the purchase could proceed from that point."[37]

Chapter 9

Appraisals and Greed

On May 10, 1993, Paul Raczka of Sun Valley, Idaho, completed a new appraisal for OHS based on his examination of the Spalding-Allen Collection and a comparison of sales of similar objects through private galleries and current auction records. Raczka noted in his appraisal that "the most significant factor in the valuation of this collection is the provenance which is exceptional for Native American material." Raczka explained, "All of the items were collected…from a specific, identified, location, and by an identified collector." The most valuable items in the collection, according to Raczka, were the two men's shirts both made by Nez Perce between 1830 and 1845. Although the condition of one shirt was only "good" with "some damage to quillwork" and the other "fair" with "heavy quill damages" and a replaced "bib," the valuations of the shirts were $250,000 and $225,000. Raczka commented on the more damaged shirt, "Despite the condition, valuation is affected by the provenance and rarity."[1] For insurance purposes, the total replacement value of the items on loan to the National Park Service (NPS) was $583,100, according to Raczka.

When Spalding sent the collection to Allen, he indicated a $27 value for the dresses while listing shirts as worth $14.25. Raczka explained the difference between Spalding's estimate and a modern appraisal. "At the time Spalding was sending these pieces back the dresses were larger and flashy compared to the shirts. This was a visual response rather than an artistic evaluation. Meaning at that time there was little concern or interest in the methods of decoration." Raczka continued, "The quill wrapped horse hair shirt strips are much more difficult to accomplish and we recognize that today. That skill and artistic genius is acknowledged today, while it was not even considered back then."[2] Nez Perce artist and NPS ranger/cultural interpreter Kevin Peters explained the skill

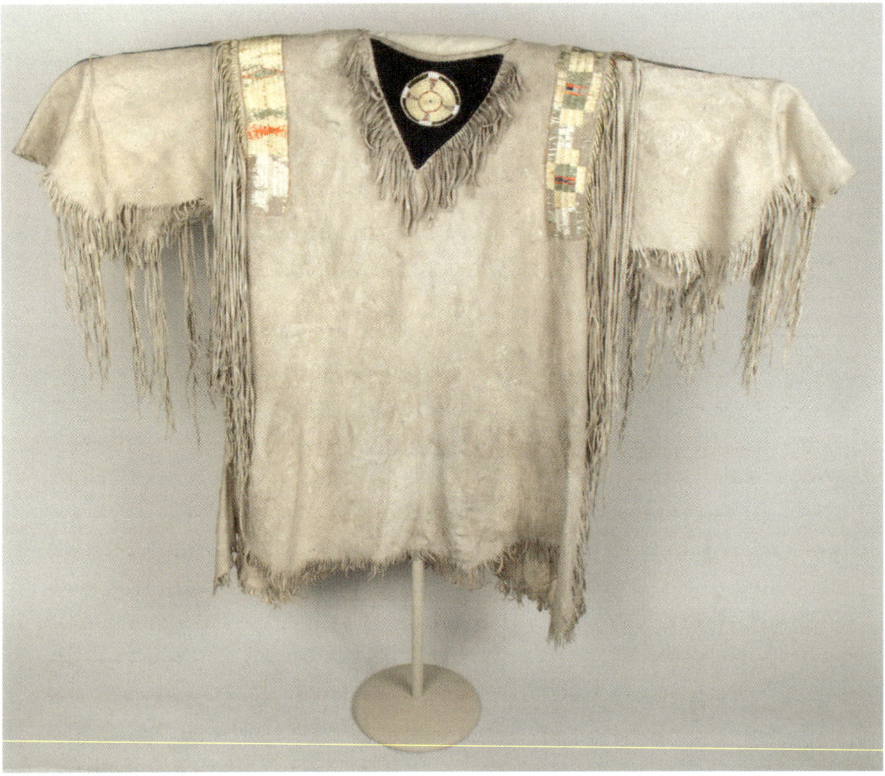

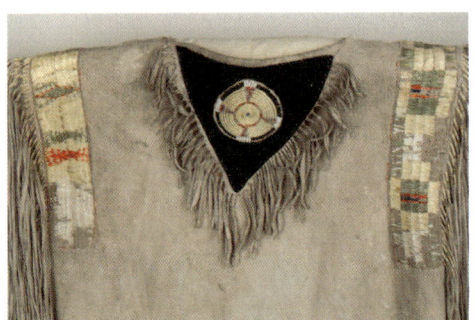
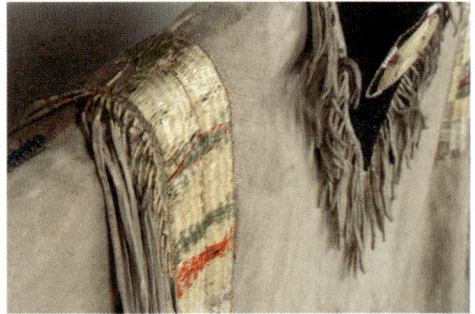

Nez Perce man's hide shirt from the Spalding-Allen Collection decorated with dyed porcupine quillwork and Venetian glass beads. The two men's shirts in the Spalding-Allen Collection remain the most expensive appraised items.

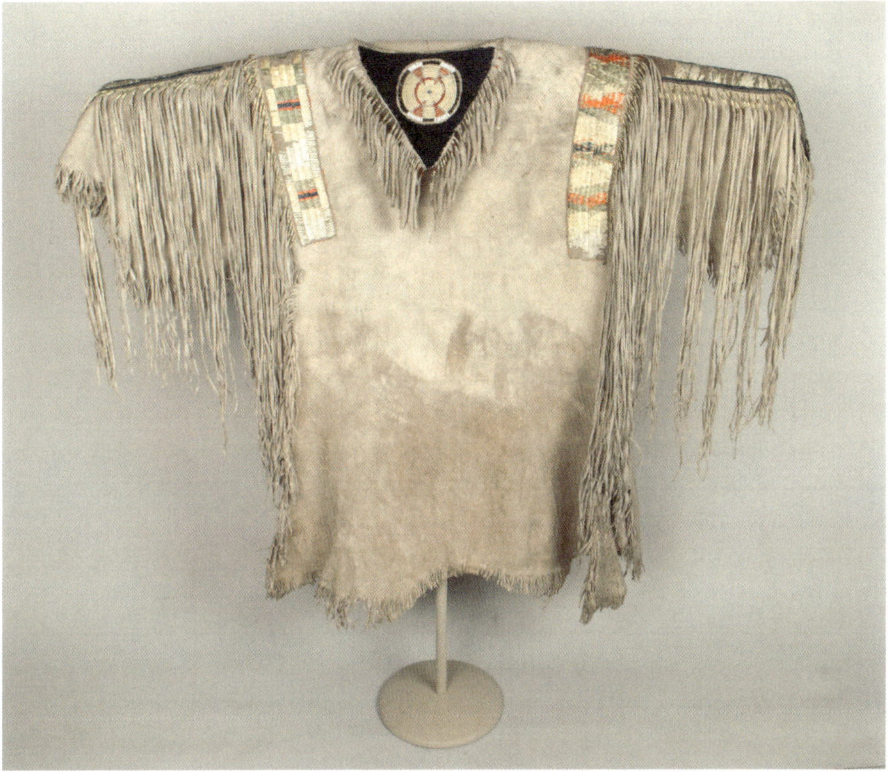

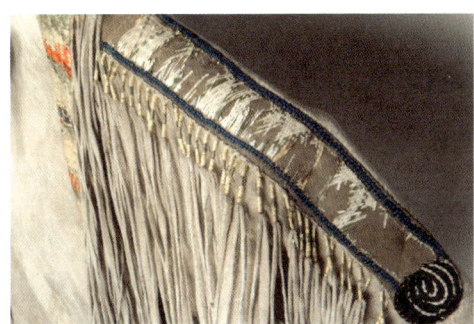
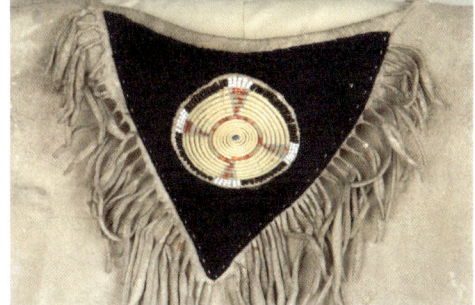

They represent some of the finest examples of American Indian shirts from the mid-nineteenth century in existence. Photographs by Zach Mazur. Courtesy of the Nez Perce National Historical Park. NEPE 8759.

involved in this technique: "Now I have a hard time tying my shoes, and this person is putting together horsehair, wrapping quill, punching holes and sewing it down all at the same time. I'm just amazed by the intricacy of the item and how you can manipulate your fingers doing that. It's…totally amazing."[3] The Nez Perce cultural specialist Josiah Pinkham agreed that wrapped horsehair is the most difficult decorative element to master. According to Pinkham, "Because just the manipulation of the materials is more intricate and detailed, thus more difficult than to do beadwork or plaited quillwork."[4]

The Nez Perce and NPS officials worried that, with the dramatic increase in value of the materials, if they returned the Spalding-Allen Collection to the Ohio Historical Society, OHS would then sell the collection on the open market. Such a sale would certainly break up the unity of the collection. As Nez Perce cultural resource specialist Josiah Pinkham observed, "being parceled out to different bidders…the collection would never again be put together in one place. And so that was a big challenge for the Nez Perce Tribe." Pinkham continued: this "collection embodies the earliest and greatest centralization of ethnographic objects for the Nez Perce people. You don't have a collection of this size, this age, anywhere else in the world. And that was huge for the Nez Perce to be faced with the potential loss of that collection, that meaning, that connection with our ancestors."[5]

To keep the Spalding-Allen Collection, the Nez Perce sought support from other stakeholders. In June 1995, participants at the Mid-Year Conference of the National Congress of American Indians, held in Spokane, Washington, passed Resolution SPK-95-070 Support of the Nez Perce Tribe to Recover the Spaulding-Allen [sic] Collection. "Whereas, the Nez Perce Nation is in a situation of losing an irreplaceable tribal historical collection…which were collected in the 1840s by the Reverend Henry H. Spaulding [sic], in his quest to civilize the Nez Perce people by prohibiting ceremonial customs and practices and confiscation of tribal regalia, and were shipped to his family in Ohio." This last statement that tribal regalia were shipped to Spalding's "family in Ohio" is not accurate. Spalding shipped the items to his supporter and friend Allen, not family, but the interpretation of Spalding's acquisition of the items is revealing of Native American perspectives on the collecting of missionaries and how the suppression of traditional customs and regalia is tied up with the acquisition of material culture.

The resolution continued, noting that although the collection had been displayed for the last fifteen years as part of an OHS loan program to the National Park Service, it must be returned to the OHS by "December 1995, unless the Nez Perce Tribe can purchase these collection items at the appraised value of $600,000." The NCAI "supports the Nez Perce Tribe's request in their efforts to retain the Spaulding-Allen [*sic*] Collection to be permanently displayed where they rightfully and culturally belong, in the homeland of the Nez Perce Nation."[6]

While Ness and his OHS colleagues communicated with National Park Service officials, they ignored letters and requests from the Nez Perce Tribe. On June 1, 1995, NPTEC chairman Samuel Penney wrote to Ness regarding his conversation with superintendent Walker about "the publicity generated by a recent interview with tribal elder Richard M. Ellenwood concerning the important cultural value of the Spalding-Allen collection to the Nez Perce People and our desire that these objects remain in our homeland." Penney explained that the Nez Perce general council had elected Richard Ellenwood to chair the Spalding-Allen Collection Committee on September 24, 1993, and charged the group with pursuing acquisition options. To do so, the committee needed a copy of the most recent appraisal completed for the Spalding-Allen Collection. Former NPTEC chairman Hayes had written to Ness two times (September 28, 1994, and March 3, 1995) to obtain the monetary appraisal, but OHS had yet to send this information. Penney concluded that "the Nez Perce Tribe is…again reaffirming our desire to negotiate in good faith."[7] Niimíipuu officials could not negotiate for the collection without knowing its monetary value; yet OHS avoided engaging with the Nez Perce Tribe.

OHS director Ness finally replied to Penney on June 23, 1995, with a three-page, fourteen-point letter outlining the OHS perspective on the status of the Spalding-Allen Collection. Ness argued that "the quality, fragility, and significance of the Spalding-Allen collection requires curatorial attention which is commensurate with the collection's value." I find this an ironic statement given that such curatorial attention was never provided by OHS. Indeed, OHS's own collections technician Brad Baker spoke about his organization's "neglect" of the collection. It was the National Park Service and not OHS that paid for the professional conservation of the Spalding-Allen Collection.

Money was a major theme of the letter. Ness noted the significant cultural and monetary value of the collection and of the "fiduciary" responsibility of OHS. Given the monetary value of the collection, he noted that "no transfer of ownership should occur with appropriate 'consideration' being offered in exchange." Ness wrote that the appraised "financial value" of the collection was a variable factor. Therefore, he continued, OHS "will consider that the insured value is an appropriate approximation of monetary worth" so that the price can be "validated" by appraisal "if and when a timetable for purchase is negotiated between OHS and the buying party." It is telling that Ness did not specify the Nez Perce as the assumed purchaser, implying that OHS might put the collection on the open market.[8] Superintendent Frank Walker recalled, "We kept hearing that OHS had other buyers in Germany and Japan who were offering over a million dollars for the collection. These [rumors] were unsubstantiated, but fed the process."[9]

Ness also indicated that once the Spalding-Allen Collection was received, "examined, and treated (as necessary), OHS expected to utilize the collection in exhibitions, including the possibility of loaning to appropriate organizations and facilities." In the statement, Ness appeared to confirm concerns that once the collection was sent to Ohio it might never return to the Nez Perce National Historical Park.[10]

Nez Perce chairman Penney countered Ness's letter with an offer for Nez Perce tribal representatives to travel to Ohio and meet with OHS board members to negotiate the deal and to pay for an OHS curator to travel to Idaho so the Spalding-Allen Collection would not have to be removed from their "exhibit cases and subjected to the hazards of handling and shipping." Penney added, "Since we are requesting the Ohio Historical Society to do an appraisal of the collection, it would appear to be more convenient to perform the appraisal in conjunction with the inspection of the condition of these materials in their present location" at the Nez Perce National Historical Park. Given the impending expiration of the OHS and National Park Service loan agreement on December 31, 1995, Penney reminded Ness that it was "imperative" that they negotiate an acquisition agreement "well in advance of that date."[11]

While Penney and Ness exchanged letters, Richard Ellenwood, chair of the Nez Perce Spalding-Allen Collection Committee, spoke with local reporters. Ellenwood said that the Nez Perce would offer the appraised price of the Spalding-Allen Collection, or $583,100, even though many

Niimíipuu people could not "understand why the tribe should pay for artifacts of their own culture." According to reporter Joan Abrams, OHS demanded the return of the collection by December 31. The Nez Perce prepared a brochure on the collection in which Nez Perce artist (and later director of the Nez Perce Tribe Cultural Resource Program) Nakia Williamson-Cloud stated, "We want these things to be here, they reflect another way of living, another way of life. These objects are important for our generation and future generations." Ellenwood added, "If my grand-children have to go see these things in Ohio, the journey will be long and our hearts would be heavy on the return."[12]

After an emergency meeting of the Nez Perce Spalding-Allen Collection Committee, Chairman Ellenwood appealed to the Presbyterian church to keep the items on the Nez Perce Reservation. They asked "for reparation for past policies of wrong-doing against Native Americans," said Ellenwood. He explained, "The Rev. Spalding was Presbyterian and during the time he lived in Lapwai area, he prohibited tribal members from practicing their native spiritual customs or wearing ceremonial clothing." Indians discovered "dancing or drumming were punished, often by a public whipping, and their ceremonial clothing was taken away."[13] The Presbyterian church did not respond.

Ellenwood took his case to other reporters, and he was quoted by the Associated Press in a story that newspapers around the country published arguing that the collection "rightfully belongs here [in Idaho] because of the significance to this area. They have no significance to Ohio at all. There are no Nez Perce at all in Ohio." According to Ellenwood, many Nez Perce people were outraged that the collection had to be purchased in the first place. At the semiannual Nez Perce General Council meeting in Kamiah, Idaho, Ellenwood reported, "Our people expressed to the General Council that it's ours and should be returned to us without paying." He remarked that the Nez Perce generally are calm people, "but when you start taking things away—our land, our fishing and now, literally, the shirts off our backs…now wait a minute, you've already taken so much when is it going to stop?"[14] The publicity generated by Ellenwood drew a response from OHS which, up to this point, had largely ignored the tribe. According to Ellenwood, "It really stirred the whole pot. It really got it boiling again."[15]

OHS president Ness responded in the Associated Press story by saying that the collection needed inspection and preservation treatment and should be returned to Ohio because it was "unusual for items to remain on loan for so long."[16] Ness was accurate in stating that fifteen years of renewable loans was unusual; however, it was the National Park Service who paid for the curatorial costs associated with exhibiting the collection and its preservation treatment. The conservation work done on the collection and its valuation by experts in Plateau material culture were the major factors in its increased monetary value. NPS had also invested in custom cases and mounts to display the collection, while OHS never paid for the collection or devoted curatorial time to conserving, researching, or exhibiting it. The one-year loans required by OHS also put a burden on NPS curators.

The Associated Press reporter made a significant error in the penultimate paragraph of story. In describing the provenance of the collection, the reporter accurately stated that "Allen was an alumnus and trustee of Oberlin College and its first major art benefactor." However, the next sentence, "the historical society bought the items more than 100 years ago from Oberlin" was completely false. OHS took the Spalding-Allen Collection on permanent loan in 1942 and obtained title to it only in 1979 on the eve of the loan to the National Park Service.

Ann Frazier, a spokesperson for OHS, responded to the negative stories regarding OHS's conduct, arguing that OHS had already been more than generous. According to Frazier, the fifteen year-length of the loan was unusual, adding that OHS loans "items out quite often but always with the understanding that…they could be called back." Countering calls for OHS to give the collection back to the Nez Perce, Frazier indicated there was "no way the society would consider giving the collection to the tribe outright or selling it for less than market value." Why not, readers might ask? "For us to do that would to be remiss in our responsibility to the people in Ohio who support us financially," Frazier explained.[17]

On October 12, 1995, Chairman Penney wrote to the governors of Idaho and Ohio. In identical letters to Governors Philip "Phil" Batt (Idaho) and George Voinovich (Ohio), Penney requested assistance in his negotiations with OHS. Penney noted that since the 1992 recall by OHS of the Spalding-Allen Collection, the OHS board had agreed to delay the recall while the Nez Perce developed a proposal to acquire the collection. Penney wrote that on June 10, 1994, the Nez Perce had sent OHS three proposals: donation of the collection to the Nez Perce; sale of the collection to the tribe at a "substantially reduced price"; or use of in-kind services by the tribe and/or National Park Service "that could off-set the full market value of the collection."

Rather than directly replying to these proposals, OHS, according to Penney, responded to the National Park Service (not to the Nez Perce) that they rejected all three proposals and recalled the loan on December 31, 1995. Meanwhile the Nez Perce asked OHS for additional time to raise funds to purchase the collection. They also proposed a meeting between the Nez Perce and the OHS board in June of 1996. But, according to Penney, "There has been no response from Ohio." Penney continued, "The Nez Perce people are extremely concerned about these objects leaving our homeland and fear that they may be sold on the open market and never be returned to the tribe if they leave the state of Idaho." Penney implored the governors for their assistance in extending the OHS loan for another year so that the Nez Perce Tribe could raise the money to purchase the collection for "generations of our people to share with visitors to the Nez Perce National Historical Park."[18]

While these negotiations were underway, the Nez Perce explored their legal options. On November 1, 1995, Julie Kane, deputy counsel for the Nez Perce, prepared a detailed analysis for possible repatriation of the collection under the Native American Graves Protection and Repatriation Art (NAGPRA) for Samuel Penney. NAGPRA, which became law in 1990, provides Native Hawaiians and Native Americans legal protection and repatriation for funerary items, sacred objects, and artifacts of cultural patrimony. NAGPRA requires that any institution, state, or local government agency receiving federal funds prepare an inventory of Native American collections, including funerary objects, sacred objects, and items of cultural patrimony and provide notification to the affiliated tribes.

According to Kane's memorandum, for the Nez Perce Tribe to repatriate the Spalding-Allen Collection under NAGPRA they needed to: 1) establish the affiliation between the collection and the Nez Perce; 2) identify the artifacts as funerary, sacred, or cultural patrimony; and 3) establish that the OHS did not have a right of possession of the objects. In Kane's analysis OHS had "clear documentation that this collection derived from Reverend Spalding, who apparently lawfully obtained them and, in turn, lawfully sold them to Dr. Allen." Under NAGPRA the original collection of the artifacts needed to include "the voluntary consent of an individual." As Kane noted, when questioned if the items were acquired with "voluntary consent," some Nez Perce elders, such as

Beatrice Miles, stated that "Spalding took the items from individuals as punishment for not converting to Christianity." However, Kane concluded that the "documentation from the correspondence between Dr. Dudley Allen and Reverend Spalding [indicated] that Reverend Spalding, in fact, purchased the items."

After examining the subsequent transfers of the Spalding-Allen Collection to Oberlin and then to OHS, Kane concluded "all transactions seem to be well documented. Therefore, it is fairly well settled that OHS is the legal owner of the property" under the guidelines of NAGPRA. However, Kane noted, "It may be possible to establish that some of the objects are culturally or religiously significant." Yet even if items in the Spalding-Allen Collection qualified for protection under the act as sacred, ceremonial, or cultural patrimony, the OHS could "refuse to return them" based on their documentation of ownership. If Spalding had included the names of the individuals from whom he acquired objects, their "lineal descendants would have the right to reclaim them (if the requirements of the Act are met)." Unfortunately, Spalding never listed the individuals from whom he acquired the objects, so no paper trail survives.[19]

In addition to advice from their legal counsel, the Nez Perce Tribe sought an additional opinion. Tribal member Allen Pinkham, who served on the board of the Smithsonian's National Museum of the American Indian, spoke to the museum's director W. Richard West Jr. regarding a NAGPRA claim to return the Spalding-Allen Collection to the Nez Perce Tribe. In a letter dated June 2, 1995, West wrote that curator George Horse Capture reviewed the material Pinkham sent regarding the collection and reported "that none of the items in the collection are human remains or associated grave goods, and none appear to be sacred materials." West continued, "However, if items such as the dresses, moccasins, or particularly the shirts can be identified as having a Nez Perce Indian as the owner, a case of cultural patrimony could be established." This process, West cautioned, "would require extensive research in books, photographs, Spalding's letter and diaries, etc."[20] Repatriating the collection, or portions of it, under NAGPRA hinged on the provenance of the collection. Could ownership of objects in the Spalding-Allen Collection be traced back to individual Nez Perce?

For a collector of his era, Spalding provided more information on what he acquired than most. However, the label of "Indian curiosities" or assemblages of "Cabinets of Curiosities" reflect a more general pattern, especially the nineteenth-century practice of dehumanizing Native American culture. As Nakia Williamson-Cloud reflected, "It's like what you see in a lot of early nineteenth century material about Indian people. I mean, it wasn't even really enough to say Nez Perce. As long as it was Indian, that was good enough. Much less, this came from this family or it came from this individual....It was kind of that dehumanizing of our culture and devaluing our culture by just kind of putting these broad sort of general depictions of what our culture is about."[21]

Although Spalding did not record the individual names of the family members from whom he acquired the collection, Nez Perce Tribal Executive Committee (NPTEC) member Bill Picard eloquently made the argument that the Spalding-Allen Collection was closely associated to a broader conception of kinship among the Nez Perce. "We all feel that we're one big family and that we're related, whether it's through marriage or bloodlines. But we're all Nez Perce. And that we, if one of [us] hurts, we all hurt." Picard continued, "so even, even if it isn't specific families, basically what we felt was those items belonged to us as a family. They belonged to my sister. They belonged to my aunt. They belonged to my grandma." Picard drew a modern analogy to make his point, "Me and my wife, we raised probably twenty kids in this community in the time that we've been married. And most of them aren't related to us. But they call us aunt and uncle. And now they're grownups. And they still call us aunt and uncle." As Picard noted "that's how we consider family. And so when people say, 'well, how is this boy your brother?' to my daughter, she says, 'we were raised together.' And so even if there's not a bloodline, there's a connection. And so when you look at these items, you feel like these items were taken from my family, the Nez Perce Tribe."[22]

On August 16, 1995, Nez Perce National Historical Park (NEPE) curator Bob Chenoweth spoke with Paul Raczka who suggested that he not appraise the Spalding-Allen Collection again. Raczka told Chenoweth that OHS should find someone to do it, but "not too many people [are] willing or able to do it." Raczka said he would conduct another appraisal "if need be but feels it isn't necessary for the tribe to do another one." Also, if Raczka did an appraisal, he told Chenoweth, it would absolutely be "HIGHER" [emphasis in original] since the market is "going wild."[23]

With negotiations underway, but no resolution in sight, the National Park Service issued a press release on November 20, 1995, titled "Spalding-Allen Collection Returns to Ohio." The document quoted NEPE

Superintendent Frank Walker: "OHS has not been receptive to offers by the Nez Perce tribe to acquire the collection, so the National Park Service must now honor its obligation and return the loaned items. This is a sad day for Nez Perce Country." NPS officials invited the public to see the collection until November 26, when they would be removed and packed for shipment to Ohio.[24]

As the NPS prepared to return the collection, the Nez Perce fought back. Richard Ellenwood spoke to Joan Abrams, a reporter at the *Lewiston Morning Tribune,* arguing that the Spalding-Allen Collection's spiritual and cultural value to the Nez Perce is priceless. According to Ellenwood, "It's not right to put greed in front of something that sacred and put a price on it." The possibility of losing the collection forever had caused "broken hearts" among the tribe, particularly the elders. Ellenwood explained. "It's a feeling of losing a dear friend…someone we won't be able to see every day. It's like a loss of part of ourselves."[25] Bill Picard amplified Ellenwood's remarks: "There's a value that can't be put in dollars. You know, like if your grandpa was passing away and on his dying death bed he gave you something and said…'This was mine. My grandfather gave it to me. I want you to have it because that's how much you mean to me.' You wouldn't take that item and sell it," said Picard. "You'd keep it. You know, it's got that relationship between you and your grandfather. And the importance of it."[26] With the Spalding-Allen Collection, "you can't really think of it in terms of the way modern people think of clothing or heirlooms. It has a much deeper meaning to us," said Nakia Williamson-Cloud. "These are living pieces amongst our community. They have a life in the community."[27]

Ellenwood and the Spalding-Allen Collection Committee organized "a day of shame" on November 27, 1995. The text of the event flier reads, "The Ohio Historical Society insists it owns the items, despite the fact that Reverend Henry Spalding claimed to have paid next to nothing for these traditional garments and adornments. OHS now claims the collection is worth more than $500,000, but to our people the spiritual and cultural value has no price." The flier continued, "By surrendering these items to the Ohio Historical Society, the Park Service begins a process that will ultimately result in their being lost forever. To protest this callous act of greed and indifference, and to renew our pledge to continue the fight for the return of this collection to the Nez Perce people, please join us."[28]

Coinciding with Ellenwood's efforts, Allen P. Slickpoo Sr., ethnographer for the Nez Perce Cultural Resource Program, prepared a two-page document titled, "Insensitivity to the Native Religious, and Cultural Values." Slickpoo began his essay with a passionate critique of the historical context in which Spalding collected the Nez Perce items. According to Slickpoo, "The government began to exercise a policy of genocide, the insensitivity to the Native American religious beliefs and the traditional cultural values were suppressed by the movement to 'civilize' the indigenous people." Slickpoo wrote "from the time Henry H. Spalding arrived in the Niimíipuu Country, in 1836, he began to tell our people that it was 'evil' to wear the buckskin clothing and the eagle feather. It was the work of the 'devil' to do so."[29]

Slickpoo reprimanded the greed of OHS: "the dollar value of these items does not reflect their cultural sensitivity and sacredness for the Nez Perce people." However, Slickpoo concluded on a persuasive and conciliatory note, "I strongly hope that the question of retaining these artifacts will be resolved in an amicable manner, realizing that our children and their children must learn to appreciate the valuable history, to realize the interpretation and value of their native culture and lifestyles of their ancestors." Looking to the future, Slickpoo continued, "It helps restore the self-image and the pride in being a Nez Perce. Therefore, it is logical to conclude that those items belong here, in their homeland, in the place of origin."[30]

Slickpoo argued from perspectives of Nez Perce people, and confirmed by Niimíipuu elders, that twelve of the items in the Spalding-Allen Collection were "identified and categorized, as being sacred objects and cultural patrimony." Three of the sacred items included the men's quilled buckskin leggings and two shirts. "These kinds of decorated items were specially made for a man who may be an outstanding person of the village…a leader, a good family provider, a warrior or a spiritual leader." Garments such as these, decorated with quill, beadwork, and "trimmed with feathers or parts of animal pieces" had "a significant spiritual meaning" and "were definitely made for sacred ceremonial dance, religious, or 'medicine dance' rituals and other special family, or village ceremonies."[31] Similarly, the two dresses "decorated with beadwork, elk teeth, or sea shell ornaments, small animal parts and fringes" signified family symbols, or trademarks that held "special meaning" to the makers. According to Slickpoo, these were not everyday garments, but were "sacred to them. These kinds of dresses were made exclusively for special occasions."[32]

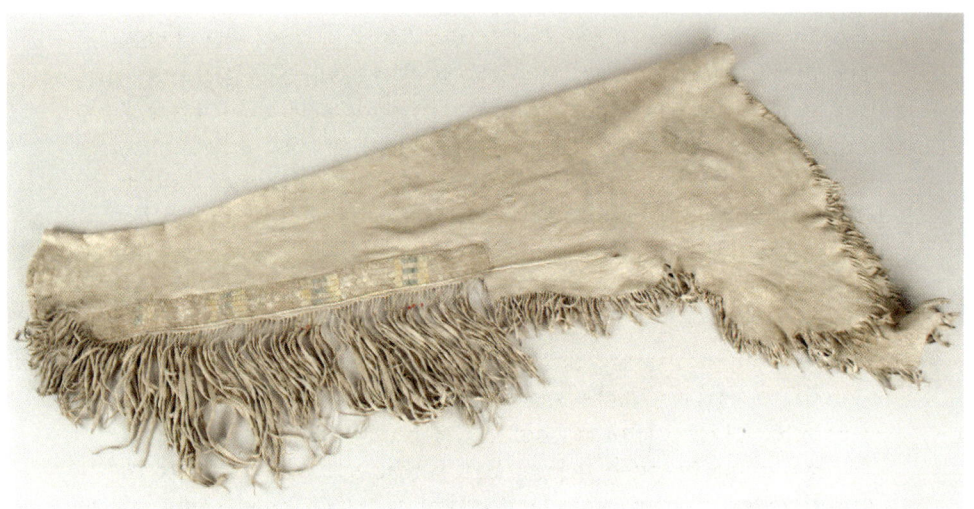

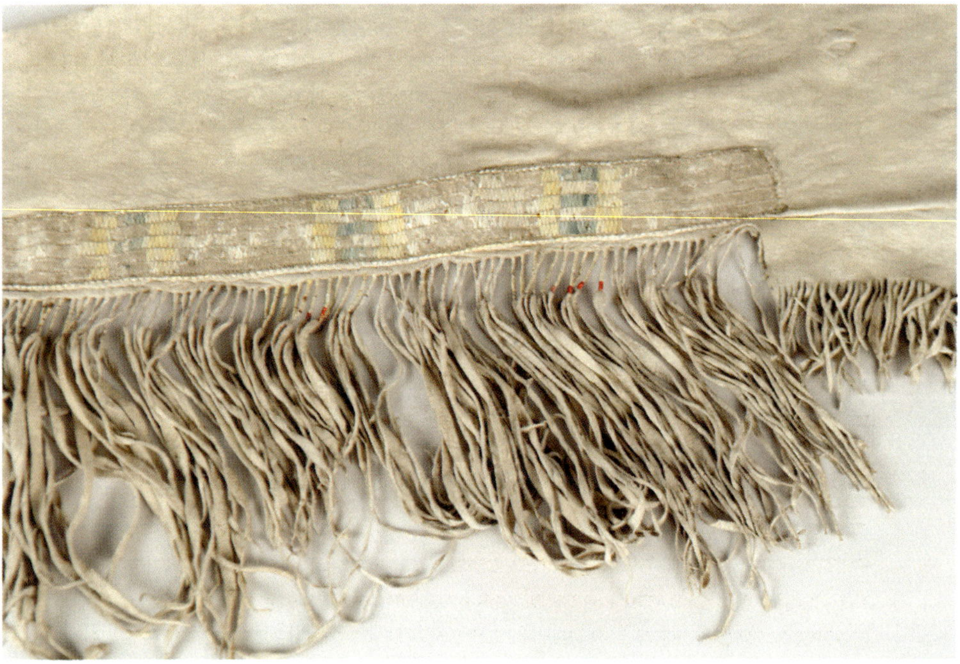

Men's leggings from the Spalding-Allen Collection made of deerskin and sinew with porcupine quill decorative panels. Photographs by Zach Mazur. Courtesy of the Nez Perce National Historical Park. NEPE 8751.

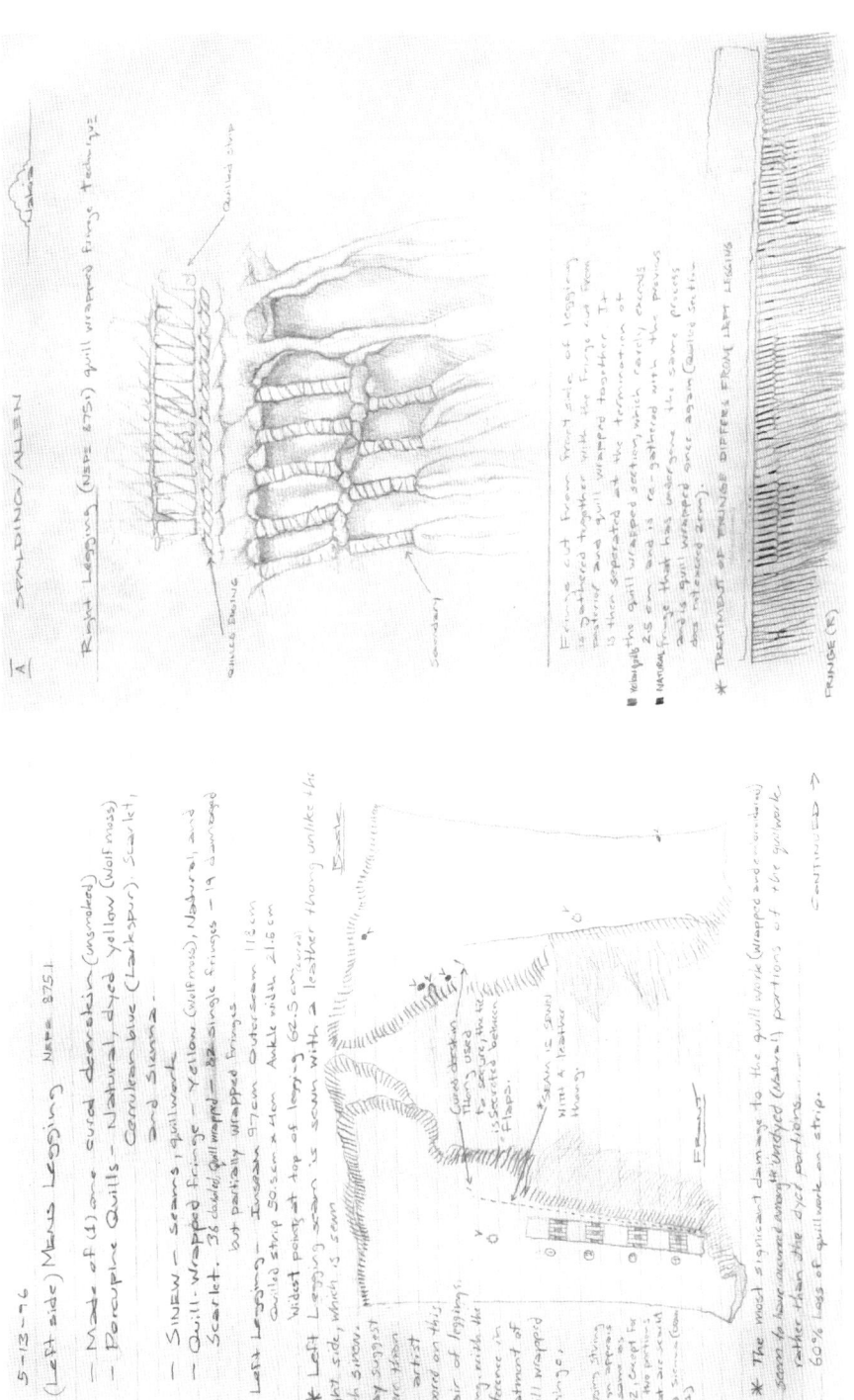

Technical drawings of men's leggings. Illustrations by Nakia Williamson-Cloud. Courtesy of the Nez Perce National Historical Park.

Another six items included examples of Nez Perce weaving: three hats and three bags. The hats, or *neets-kow* (also spelled *ni`caw*), were woven with hemp or cornhusk and featured designs made with natural dyes from plants or roots. Women wore these hats for special occasions, Slickpoo continued, including the "first feast of some kind of food, weddings, or burial purposes and other sacred ceremonial events." Similar to the hats, the decoration of the bags reflected particular family designs. The Nez Perce employed the bags for storing edible roots or bulbs "during harvest time and for winter storage." The bags would also be used for "ceremonial events, such as wedding trade, burials, or feast gatherings and 'giveaways' during memorials of a deceased member of the family village, or Tribe."

The final item highlighted by Slickpoo was the quirt. According to Slickpoo, "the Nez Perce people made special designed quirts (whip[s]) out of animal parts, such as antlers, or [the] carved wood of trees or brush. They became part of his or her horse." He continued, "Each quirt, with the design, had a significant meaning to the owner and his horse. It was a special tool that he/she carried during the long family travels" and for the hunter or warrior "who, at times, depended on the speed of his horse. The importance of a quirt was treated in the same manner as a weapon."

These twelve items in the Spalding-Allen Collection, concluded Slickpoo, "were part of their daily lifestyles. They were a part of their religion and sacred ceremonies. They were used in special ceremonial dances honoring the living and the deceased members of the family, the village and the Tribe." Traditionally items such as these would have been buried with their owner upon his or her death. The deceased "would wear the special made dress, shirt, or leggings, the hat and the tools they used and was so dear to them." Or depending on the wishes of the "departed, these items would be handed down to the eldest child," who in turn would distribute them to "the other children." Slickpoo continued, "From that time on, they became family heirlooms, to be handed down from generation-to-generation. They were sacred objects to be placed into continual use. They were items of cultural patrimony. They became part of the family history and culture of the Niimíipuu."[33] Despite these powerful arguments, OHS did not change their position on the collection.

OHS curator Loveday recalled that NPS worked so closely with Nez Perce that he thought NPS "was turning over the museum to the Tribe and [NPS] became increasingly difficult to deal with. It seemed to me at the time that NPS was in effect acting as an agent for the Tribe rather

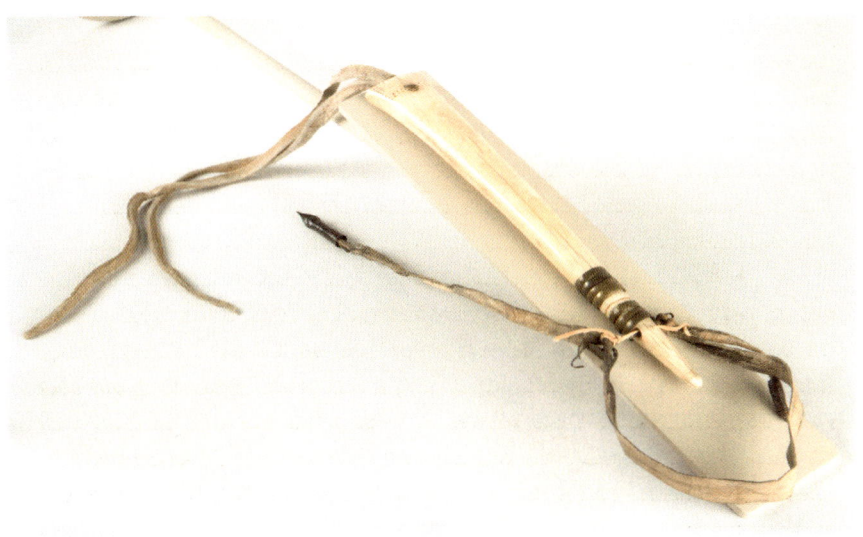

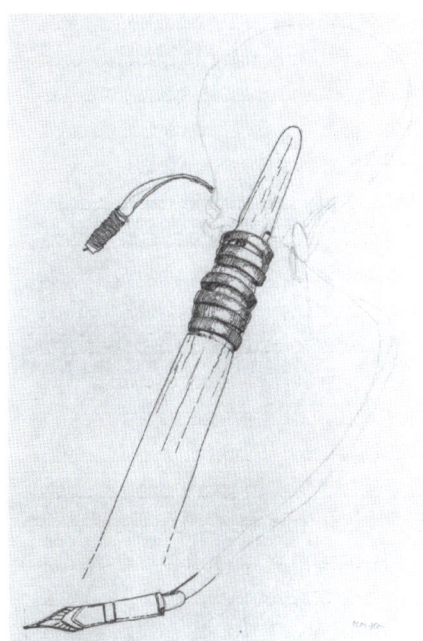

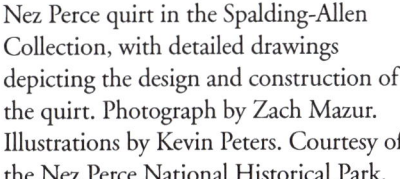

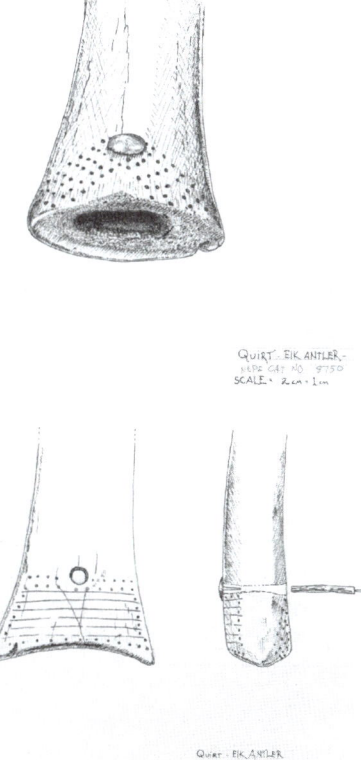

QUIRT - ELK ANTLER -
NEPE CAT NO 9750
SCALE - 2 cm = 1 cm

QUIRT - ELK ANTLER
SCALE - 2 cm = 1 cm

Nez Perce quirt in the Spalding-Allen
Collection, with detailed drawings
depicting the design and construction of
the quirt. Photograph by Zach Mazur.
Illustrations by Kevin Peters. Courtesy of
the Nez Perce National Historical Park.

than living up to the agreement it signed with OHS." He continued, "It was pretty clear that if OHS did not retake possession the items would be appropriated. So OHS dug in taking the position that items be returned so claims could be reestablished."[34]

The Spalding-Allen Collection belongs in Nez Perce country according to Josiah Pinkham because of the tremendous education opportunities. "If you…take that collection of phenomenal Nez Perce material culture and you plant it in the middle of the culture that manufactured them, the learning potential there is compounded," said Pinkham. And for the Nez Perce people, Pinkham explained, when they "look at these things, they study these things, and they can make them in the way that their ancestors made them. And that connection is…restored." This connection perpetuates a relationship, says Pinkham, "Not just with their ancestors, but with their landscape." In Nez Perce the term "is *anaqoonma* and…what that means is those that came before me. That means not just the ancestors like the people, my family, my parents, my grandparents, and all those behind me. But that also includes animal people. Because we regard them as the same way. They took care of our ancestors the same way that they're taking care of us now. They're the ones that came before us and they're our elder kinfolk. So we look to that connection to basically pass on the relationship to our children. So all of that has to basically keep going. So that's why this [the collection] is more powerful here in Nez Perce country than really anywhere else in the world. I mean, it perpetuates a pretty powerful connection."[35]

Fighting to Keep the Collection

With negotiations at an impasse, Superintendent Frank Walker sent an email to NPS regional director Bill Waters, apprising him of the situation. As of November 21, 1995, Walker reported that OHS was "firm on having the collection returned by December 31," unsure if the society was willing to sell it to them, and uncertain about the price. More distressing was the following, "So far the tribal Chairman Sam Penney and Gary Ness [OHS President] have NOT talked." After meeting with Nez Perce elders, NPTEC members, and Tribal counsel, Walker reported that their legal options, such as an injunction or NAGPRA claim, would not stop the removal of the collection to OHS. They discussed the need to take the story to the national press and to fully document the collection. This research would support a potential NAGPRA claim but had to be completed before the artifacts left the Nez Perce country. Chairman Penney proposed taking out a ten-year bank loan and offering a check for the appraised value of $583,100 to see if OHS was serious about selling. Walker also reported a proposal that reflected the desperation of the situation—one NPTEC member suggested going to the park and confiscating the collection. Both Walker and legal counsel reminded him of "existing federal and Indian laws prohibiting that action."[36]

The Nez Perce Tribe held a farewell ceremony to say goodbye to the Spalding-Allen Collection on November 27, 1995. Allen Slickpoo Sr. told the gathering, "It's ironic a person [Spalding] who preaches against (the clothing) as the work of devil would turn around and sell it to another person." He included one joke in his remarks, stating that he was not sure if he was good at it, but he put a hex on the Ohio State football team, and since the team lost to Michigan, "things are looking bright." Members of the Lapwai Veterans of Foreign Wars made up the color guard, and the Nez Perce Nation provided drumming and a song as did the young drummer's group, Wap'tes Juniors. Some participants wore regalia and danced, mourning the loss of their heritage.[37]

On Wednesday, November 29, 1995, the *Lewiston Morning Tribune* published an editorial in support of Nez Perce keeping the collection. The author chastised OHS by questioning how they with "no connection to the tribe and its traditions and little reason to display its artifacts can continue to list them as assets…Surely any society that cares more about history than pride would recognize that whatever the question of ownership of these pieces, the location where they should be displayed is here."[38]

On the same day, the Nez Perce Tribal Executive Committee issued an impassioned national press release. "Time is slipping away from the Nez Perce Indian tribe, as they strive to retain sacred and historical artifacts on loan from the Ohio Historical Society." The release outlined the efforts of the Nez Perce to negotiate the acquisition of the collection and their "inability to receive concise details on the proposed purchase from OHS." According to Richard Ellenwood, "It seems Ohio is blind to our smoke signals. We have heard nothing from them since July." Chairman Penney argued that OHS was unwilling to sell at the appraised prices because "they can get a much higher amount on the open market." Superintendent Frank Walker challenged the OHS position that the recall was an effort to preserve the collection. He noted that an independent conservator from Denver visited the park in 1992 and reported to OHS that the "collection was being well cared for and in good condition." Walker recounted that OHS curator Loveday commented during his last visit to the Nez Perce National Historical Park, "These items most appropriately belong here."

The press release concluded with elder Allen Slickpoo Sr. recounting oral history that Spalding "urged our people to give up their native lifestyles. He insisted the men cut their hair and families discard their native clothing. Our people became separated, identified as either 'progressives' or 'heathens.'" According to a park brochure, the growing demand in America and Europe for "Indian curiosities" provided a means for missionaries such as Spalding, as part of a larger colonial enterprise, to ship Indian culture to collectors in return for goods to finance the operations of their missions. The release then drew a parallel between Nez Perce history, when the Niimíipuu evaded US troops for 1,300 miles through the northern Rocky Mountains under the leadership of Chief Joseph, and the current struggle with OHS. According to a "defiant" Slickpoo, "I feel strongly that the Nez Perce Tribe should *not* surrender its rights. Chief Joseph did not give up easily. This is the precedent we should follow, regarding the Spalding-Allen collection."[39]

These events likely spurred OHS to finalize negotiations over the collection. The Nez Perce received the appraisal and on November 29, 1995, NPTEC chairman Penney wrote to Ness regarding the "retention of the Spalding-Allen collection in the Nez Perce National Historical Park on the Nez Perce reservation where, in our view, it rightfully belongs for a number of reasons." Penney made an "irrevocable offer" to buy the collection for $583,100, paid on or before June 1, 1996, "on the condition that the collection remains at the Nez Perce National Historical Park Museum during that time."[40]

On December 1, 1995, OHS chief curator Loveday sent a memorandum regarding the proposed sale to OHS president Ness with his recommendation and those of his fellow curators, Melinda Knapp and Martha Otto. The curators agreed that OHS should accept Penney's offer although "all recognized that the appraised price is dated and almost certainly below what might be had at auction." Loveday then shared three matters of concern. First, the offer did not include the Nez Perce cradleboard that could be added for another $25,000. Second, the OHS should "re-evaluate our insurance on the collection making sure that value is protected." As Loveday reasoned "once the asking price is published nationally, as it will have to be, the collection becomes more vulnerable to theft.

Since we have no control over the security arrangement, we must be satisfied that the value is protected." And finally, the curators requested that money from the sale be placed in the collection fund for the acquisition and conservation of OHS collections.

Loveday noted that he viewed the sale as a "good outcome; the materials will find a permanent home with the tribe in a publicly accessible museum, the OHS receives fair value for the materials, and years of negotiations are brought to a conclusion." Loveday's final assessment: "it's good for business health, good for our cultural psyche, and it improves our capability to acquire Ohio materials." The windfall of cash to OHS in exchange for a collection they gained ownership over only on the eve of loaning it, certainly was good for their "business health."[41]

While negotiations between OHS and the Nez Perce were underway, Nez Perce people continued to make their case to the media. On December 4, 1995, the *Oregonian* reported that "the artifacts in the Spalding-Allen collection are caught in a cross-country tug of war between the 12,000-member Ohio Historical Society and the struggling 3,000-member Northern Idaho Indian tribe." While OHS wanted the collection returned for evaluation after a fifteen-year loan to the National Park Service, "the tribe insists the collection belongs home, on the Nez Perce Reservation." Nez Perce schoolchildren wrote letters to OHS, including Raleigh Ellenwood, age twelve, who argued, "There are no Nez Perces in Ohio. It was ours in the first place." More to the point, Niimíipuu elder Roy White Sr. observed, "I don't see why we should have to buy our own things back." According to oral tradition, Henry Spalding "was a bad devil," White explained. "That's what my grandmother said. She said he was stealing from us."[42]

Local residents wrote to OHS executive director Gary Ness pleading with him to act justly. From Moscow, Idaho, Louise Barber wrote that OHS "has been most generous in loaning the nineteen items to the Nez Perce National Historical Park for many years. But I would like to implore you and members of your board or whomever has the power to decide the outcome of this entanglement to, very simply, do another right thing." Barber explained, "It is rare in the history of Indian-white relations that we in this nation any longer have straightforward situations that allow us to easily act either rightly or wrongly. The Nez Perce artifacts of the Spalding-Allen collection present just such a moment." She continued, "Ours is a history of cheating Native Americans at every turn...To leave these items where they are is the right thing to do. On behalf of those of us who would like to see trust begin to take hold in our relations, please act to ensure that this collection remains in the hands of the Tribe."[43]

The letters, pleas, and calls to act morally did not change OHS's position. Nor were OHS officials persuaded by tribal ethnographer Allen P. Slickpoo Sr.'s characterization of twelve of the items in the Spalding-Allen Collection as qualifying as sacred or funerary objects under NAGPRA. Maggie Sanese, communications manager for the OHS, countered, "It's pretty clear to us the [NAGPRA] act does not apply to this collection." At the heart of the dispute were two divergent ways of viewing the collection. OHS argued that Spalding had purchased the items from willing Nez Perce sellers, while members of the Tribe countered that Spalding more likely coerced sales or made the Niimíipuu give up traditional clothing and items when they converted to Christianity. The most distinguished non-native author of Nez Perce history, Alvin Josephy, supported the Nez Perce Tribe's position. According to Josephy, Spalding was a "parsimonious man. He would have used various means to make them give things up."[44]

Members of the Nez Perce Tribe continued to make their case to the media. Richard Ellenwood obtained a copy of Oberlin professor Mark Papworth's letter to Jack Williams sent in 1970 in which Papworth magnanimously offered to return the Spalding-Allen Collection to the National Park Service or the Nez Perce Tribe, if he could find it on campus. Ellenwood told the *Lewiston Morning Tribune* that Oberlin's promise to return the collection demonstrated that the "effort by the Ohio Historical Society to secure ownership of the property from Oberlin College was a clear effort to undermine that process." Ellenwood charged that efforts by the Nez Perce Tribe to negotiate with OHS were being ignored. Several Nez Perce officials and members of the Spalding-Allen Collection Committee sought a place on the agenda of the OHS's December 1995 board meeting to discuss the situation with the collection. According to Ellenwood, "the Tribe should be making movements and be prepared for legal action if such a meeting does not come about." Allen Slickpoo Sr. added that they would keep up their efforts to retain the Spalding-Allen Collection to prevent the collection from "being unlawfully removed a second time." Another member of the Spalding-Allen Collection Committee, Roy White, challenged OHS to produce evidence in tribal court that it had legal ownership of the collection. According to White, "if they

[OHS] think that Rev. Henry Spalding 'stole them fair and square' they should make that argument here."[45]

On December 10, 1995, Tom Kenworthy, a reporter at the *Washington Post*, wrote a story titled, "Fragile Links to the Past: Nez Perce Tribe Battles for Artifacts Taken in 1840s." Kenworthy argued that the Spalding-Allen Collection was taken, not purchased or acquired. After recounting the war of 1877, when the Nez Perce conducted "one of history's epic retreats," Kenworthy compared those events to the contemporary struggle with the OHS, "But more than a century and a quarter later, the Nez Perce are fighting again to preserve a part of their culture, this time in a quieter battle with the OHS over 19th century artifacts that the tribe believes should remain in Idaho but that the society intends to move to Ohio." According to the story, "Officials of the society, who believe their careful stewardship of the fragile artifacts has helped preserve them, worry the artifacts may be irreparably harmed if they are continuously exhibited." The reporter paraphrased OHS president Ness, "Although the society recognizes its position could be viewed as insensitive, he [Ness] added, it has a fiduciary responsibility to its trustees and Ohio citizens to hold onto the valuable collection." However, Kenworthy concluded "the loss of this link to their [Nez Perce] past is another sorry chapter in a long history of mistreatment by white society."[46]

The preservation argument has served museums and cultural institutions—including OHS—as a key justification for collecting all manner of cultural heritage. As the anthropologist Douglas Cole observed, "Preservation is, of course, partly just that, a justification. Collectors had their own agenda, be it self-aggrandizement (personal or institutional), playing to peers, building a career, profiting from a transaction. Nevertheless, behind all acquisition, all 'appropriation,' lies this justification, essentially a moral one." Spalding's agenda included collecting for self-aggrandizement to obtain necessary goods for his missionary work. Now OHS was set to profit greatly from the sale of the Spalding-Allen Collection.[47]

The Niimíipuu people soon found many supporters. To emphasize the seriousness of their position, the Nez Perce Tribe indicated that they would seek a restraining order to keep the Spalding-Allen Collection in Idaho. Richard Ellenwood said that OHS had refused to negotiate a purchase price and to communicate with the Tribe. According to Ellenwood, the collection's "spiritual and cultural value" was priceless.[48] This argument was about the preservation of religious and cultural heritage, not cashing out to the highest bidder.

Throughout the month of December, as the National Park Service took the Spalding-Allen Collection off display and packed it for shipment, Nez Perce people spoke out regarding the injustice of OHS's actions. "The articles belong here, on a bluff above the Clearwater River. There is nothing in Ohio to relate to the Nez Perce," said Herman Reuben, an elder and president of the Nez Perce Tribal Foundation. Former Idaho governor Cecil Andrus protested about the pending return of the collection stating that it would be "a shame and a crime to see these items removed." Andrus elaborated, "They are part of history, not only that of the Nez Perce but of this part of the world. Once again the white man in a distant place is making a decision that adversely affects Native Americans in the Northwest."[49]

Maggie Sanese, communications manager for OHS, countered the arguments of Herman Reuben and Cecil Andrus, stating "The missionary [Henry Spalding] who bought these objects was from Ohio, and he purchased them for a friend who was an Ohioan," she said. "These missionaries were Ohio residents who had an important role in the West. We look at our collections as a way not only to learn about Ohio's history, but the larger scheme of how Ohio fit into the history of the United States." OHS also remained noncommittal about finalizing the sale and hinted that they might decide to sell the collection to the highest bidder. According to Sanese, the society would "entertain discussions of sale" to the Nez Perce but would not commit to a price. When asked by a reporter, she replied, "Well, that depends....We had a preliminary appraisal in 1992, but of course these things change over time. I can't say what the price will be." OHS did not rule out sale to another buyer, even a private collector. "If someone made us an offer, the board would consider it," Sanese said. Current prices in the auction market indicated that the Spalding-Allen Collection might reach a million dollars.[50]

All of the discussion over price clouded the real value of the collection to the Nez Perce people. Herman Reuben explained, "When we teach our children, it is usually oral history. The children see the dress of our ancestors, the tools that they used, the bags and clothes and baskets used 150 years ago." He continued, "to me, it establishes an identity of what a Nez Perce was, how we came about and how we survived."[51]

On December 12, 1995, a Nez Perce delegation including NPTEC chairman Samuel Penney, General Council chairman Richard Broncheau, tribal legal counsel Douglas Nash, and Spalding-Allen Collection Committee member Allen Slickpoo Sr. flew to Ohio and met with OHS officials. They negotiated a verbal agreement for the Nez Perce to purchase the Spalding-Allen Collection. After the meeting, Slickpoo called Richard Ellenwood and reported that the meeting was friendly and there was little debate about the fate of the collection and, with a six-month extension of the loan until the purchase, the National Park Service would halt plans to ship the collection to OHS. Ellenwood told reporters, "We're very elated, very happy." He continued, "I'm glad we don't have to go into a legal battle.…We ended up in a situation where no conflict will come of it to the relief of both sides." The purchase price agreed upon would be $583,100, the most recent appraisal valuation and the amount previously offered by the Tribe. "I wish they had just given it back to us," Ellenwood admitted, "but I'm happy it's going to stay here. Now we have to roll up our sleeves and start raising money." When news of the agreement reached NPTEC, applause broke out, according to Vice Chairwoman Julia Dais, who confirmed, "we're all definitely happy about the news."[52]

As news of the verbal agreement spread across the Nez Perce Reservation, so did the feeling of relief of not shipping the Spalding-Allen Collection back to Ohio where many feared the most expensive items would be sold to private collectors. Superintendent Frank Walker said, "We're delighted. The efforts of the Nez Perce tribe to go back and meet with the people in Ohio was an excellent thing to do." Tom Keefe, a former Seattle-based US Senate aide and resident of the Nez Perce Reservation, spoke of the mood in the community. "There was a feeling of impending doom and grief around here when they were taken off exhibit and prepared for shipment," he said. "But the unity and cooperation of the eldest members of the tribe and the youngest members was a source of great joy." The joy in the news was not unmitigated. "Personally, I guess we all feel sorry that we have to pay for it," reflected Ellenwood. "It's like paying for our own Christmas presents. But we are relieved the collection is going to remain here."[53]

On January 3, 1996, OHS and the National Park Service and Nez Perce Tribe finalized the agreement for the Nez Perce to purchase the collection for $583,100, and the cradleboard for an additional $25,000, for a total of $608,100. This was $555,400 more than the $52,700 appraisal the OHS received at part of the initial loan in 1980. OHS agreed to extend the loan to the NPS until June 30, 1996, giving the Nez Perce only six months to raise the money.[54] The Tribe also agreed to house the Spalding-Allen Collection at a museum where it would be available for public viewing and preservation.

Not everyone thought that the terms of the agreement were just. NPTEC member Bill Picard recalled the deal, "No. I don't believe that the amount was fair. And I also feel that the timeframe that they put us under was not fair, either." Picard made the point that, in 1993, the price of more than $600,000 was a lot of money. "And so trying to collect that kind of money in that short of a timeframe. We didn't know if we could do it, but we put forth the effort."[55] Superintendent Frank Walker reflected to a *Washington Post* reporter, "It is very difficult to watch the Nez Perce, which is a small tribe of about 3,000 people, try to raise almost $600,000 to buy part of their culture back."[56] Managing attorney for the Nez Perce Tribe, Julie Kane, recalled that it was "A lot of money to raise in that short amount of time. It was a daunting challenge."[57]

Chairman Penney and his NPTEC colleagues devoted significant time in their efforts to keep the Spalding-Allen Collection in the Nez Perce country. Retaining this collection was one of a number of serious issues they were addressing at the time. Others included a 75 percent unemployment rate and a series of winter floods that had damaged homes on the reservation in Lapwai.[58] With such pressing problems confronting the Niimíipuu people, it demonstrates the importance of the Spalding-Allen Collection to the Tribe.

What Picard felt especially troubled by was that OHS "received these items without paying for them or without negotiating for them…without the tribal members whose items these belonged to, the families. There was no compensation given to the [Nez Perce] families." Picard continued, "not that the families would have sold the items anyway. But there was no negotiation, no compensation for these items. And then they want to sell them back. After they didn't pay anything for them."[59]

The Nez Perce Tribe faced a significant challenge. They needed to raise a lot of money very quickly to buy the Spalding-Allen Collection. Richard Ellenwood, in his role as chair of the Spalding-Allen Collection Committee, knew that it would be a tough job, but he said, "We'll certainly give it our best effort. If everyone in Idaho gave $1, we'd have enough." However, if they were unsuccessful, many believed that OHS would sell the collection to the highest bidder. If that should happen, the earliest, finest example of their material culture, when sold at auction, would certainly be dispersed among private collectors and most likely would remain forever inaccessible to the Nez Perce.[60]

Chapter 10

Securing the Collection

Regarding the agreement to sell the Spalding-Allen Collection, the Ohio Historical Society essentially said, "Put up or shut up."
—Bob Chenoweth, curator of the Nez Perce National Historical Park

The people of the United States have demonstrated that they value our Native American Heritage. We are deeply grateful to all those who have joined us in the spirited and successful effort.
—Samuel Penney, chairman of the Nez Perce Tribal Executive Committee

By bringing this collection home, we're helping Nez Perce people to survive.
—Josiah Pinkham

Although an agreement was in place between the Nez Perce Tribe and Ohio Historical Society (OHS) for the sale of the Spalding-Allen Collection, supporters of the Nez Perce Tribe argued that the $608,100 price was too high. The high selling price of the collection prompted the *Seattle Times* to run an editorial noting that "others were grumbling that the price was too high, maybe unnecessarily so."[1] The editorial supported a proposal made by Gerald Elfendahl, curator of the Bainbridge Historical Society, who in a letter to OHS suggested that "Ohio could generate much good will by *not* charging the tribe." Rather, according to Efendahl, "perhaps museums across the country can send you other Ohio historical items whose values can be deducted from your request to the Nez Perce." To that end, Efendahl had a "made-in-Ohio railway crane used in the construction of the Panama Canal" to offer up.[2]

Governor Batt of Idaho also weighed in. In a letter to Ohio governor Voinovich, Batt proposed a sale price of $100,000. Batt argued, "The tribe is being asked to pay an enormous sum for articles that are part of their heritage. I appeal to the citizens of your great state to help remedy this unreasonable situation." Batt pointed out the obvious, "The terms of the arrangement are inequitably stacked against the tribe" and that the need to raise more than $600,000 "in six short months is unfair and unrealistic. This would be a formidable task for any organization to undertake." According to Batt, the collection is important to the Nez Perce but "of much less value to anyone else."[3] Batt's proposal was not accepted by OHS.

Individual citizens also lobbied OHS to reduce their asking price. Tom Savage of Grangeville, Idaho, wrote the following to Gary Ness: "Now, the Nez Perce are confronted by the daunting task of ransoming certain artifacts, the Spalding-Allen Collection from the museum to which these artifacts were transported a hundred years ago, by a well-intentioned missionary.... The Nez Perce bend themselves to the task of overcoming yet another obstacle." Savage pleaded, "You, and the Board of Directors of OHS, and benefactors of the museum, have within your grasp a rare opportunity. You have the power to dignify a nation and, in doing so, to give the soul of these United States a boost toward heaven. Please forgive the six-hundred-thousand dollars and give back to the Nez Perce People their national treasures."[4]

In the face of this public opposition, I wondered why OHS decided to sell the collection rather than give it back or exchange it for another NPS collection. According to Dr. George Carroll, an OHS board member, the Spalding-Allen Collection was on loan for "too many years running." Although the "Native peoples did not make a fuss," indefinitely loaning the collection was a "bad idea." OHS came to an "amicable transfer" with the National Park Service (NPS) and the Nez Perce.[5] According to Carroll, OHS had a "tenuous connection" with the Spalding-Allen materials. Carroll noted that OHS could not claim an "ethnic association." And Carroll, with his background as a collector, noted that the OHS "could have done better with the selling price. I was upset that they did not get enough." However, since this was an agreement between museums, and considering the location of the Nez Perce National Historical Park and its strong cultural connection with the Spalding-Allen Collection, the OHS board determined the sale price was reasonable.[6] In this way OHS compromised to a certain extent. Carroll was likely correct that OHS could have received an even higher sale price than the appraisal indicated.

As the appraiser Paul Raczka observed, given the Native American art market at the time, OHS may have received a higher price if they had sold the collection as individual lots. According to Raczka, "more than likely dealers and individual collectors" would pay more for "individual pieces and not the whole collection. If the collection was put to auction it is also possible those higher prices would not materialize, auctions being auctions." The "selective buying by a small number of bidders would leave a number of items in the collection without a sale and scattering the collection to the winds."[7]

The purchase price of $608,100 was a significant sum, especially given the resources of the Nez Perce Tribe.[8] There was a stark contrast between the views of OHS and the Nez Perce about the collection. As Bill Picard noted, OHS saw the collection as something "that they [OHS] could make money off of them. And they did make money off of them....And the Nez Perce Tribe looked at them as we need to bring our items home to our families." According to Picard, for OHS, their claim on the collection was all about money. They considered Niimíipuu material culture as a "commodity, to be bought and sold. They turned them into like a car or a painting or something along that—but in our culture, these items aren't materials to be bought and sold. They're a way of life." Picard continued, "and when you get through using these things, then you hand them down to your children. And they, in turn, hand them down to their children. And so these items were handed down through generations and generations." The collection represented more than money to Picard. It's like "taking a picture of your grandson and instead of handing it down to him when he gets older, you sell it, and then have him buy it back five years later. You know, that's kind of how we were feeling."[9]

Picard explained that the material culture of the Nez Perce people represents who "we are. It was the way we dressed, the way we live. The way that we bead. The way that we design things. It was our story, our history, our culture that was taken, and then being sold back to us." For example, "even now, when a tribal member does beadwork and somebody comes up and goes, 'Oh, that's beautiful art.' But to us it's not really art. There's a reason for it, and it's part of someone's regalia. It's part of something." Picard continued with a personal example, "When I graduated high school, I was given a beaded belt buckle. And the lady that beaded it, she didn't give it to me as a piece of art or for me to sell it in ten years for money. She gave it to me from her heart to my heart. And so these items [in the Spalding-Allen Collection] that were taken weren't made to be bought and sold."[10] These objects made by Nez Perce hands transcend the specific purposes for which they were originally made. Native American artifacts, the scholar Sylvia Kasprycki observed, "may be regarded as statements about how people conceive of the universe around them, how they define their place and that of others within this universe, and how they interact with their natural environment, their fellow beings, and the supernatural world."[11]

As for OHS's negotiating position, Bill Holm, curator emeritus of the Burke Museum, said what many felt. "Deep down I believe Ohio should return the items....That would be the ideal thing."[12] When I asked the Nez Perce Tribe's managing attorney Julie Kane if it was fair to sell the collection back to the community that created it, she replied, "That was the question. Why did they [OHS] charge the tribe in the first place? I suppose they had to satisfy their group too. Everybody felt like that they should have just handed them over, but as the appraiser said, they were valuable artifacts."[13]

OHS viewed the collection in a radically different light than did Bill Picard or Bill Holm. OHS owned a valuable collection outside of their institution's collecting focus. If OHS was going to part with the Spalding-Allen Collection, they wanted the market value for it, regardless of the ethics of the sale. According to NPS curator Bob Chenoweth, the debate over the collection raised numerous issues about the ownership of cultural artifacts. An object, argued Chenoweth, "becomes a commodity when you take it out of a cultural context." He continued, "We [the non-native population] see religion as an institution. For the Nez Perce, there wasn't any separation. You lived and breathed your religion everyday.... [These items were] made that way because they were someone's personal medicine."[14]

OHS adopted a firm, unyielding bargaining position for selling the collection they termed their "fiduciary responsibility." Chenoweth recalled OHS essentially said, "Put up or shut up. You know, come up with the money. If you can't do it in six months, you probably can't do it. So we don't want this thing to drag on....I think it was beginning to be a public relations concern for them." Chenoweth continued, "Because as the story started getting out, even before the fundraising occurred, I mean people, the newspapers and TV and stuff all came."[15]

As the story caught the attention of the national press, the Nez Perce Tribe hired Tom Hudson, a community development consultant with a bachelor's degree in archaeology from the University of Idaho to raise the money for the collection. As part of his detailed proposal, Hudson affirmed that he was "personally committed to this undertaking [and]… while you would be contracting for my professional time, my spiritual and emotional commitment are given freely."[16] In an interview with the *Lewiston Morning Tribune*, Hudson described the negotiating position of OHS more starkly than Chenoweth: "my view is the tribe had a gun pressed to its head. The Ohio Historical Society said it was willing to sell to other parties.…[I]f the collection was returned to Ohio, we would never see it again and it would go to a private collector." Hudson noted that OHS viewed the collection not as historical artifacts but as financial assets.[17]

This position by OHS was hypocritical. Their 1996 website overview stated that "in 1885, a group of Ohioans gathered together, united in the alarm over the removal from the state of valuable objects by Ohio's prehistoric Indians." The text continued, "They established the Ohio Archaeological and Historical Society, proclaiming in its charter the goal of preserving such important prehistorical relics."[18] That the "valuable objects" came from an Indian community demonstrates that OHS did not follow their own founding principles. Hudson said that in the negotiations for the return of the Spalding-Allen Collection, "Unfortunately, the OHS would only respond to a market rate offer.…I find their approach to be out of character with their own mission and devastating to the tribe. Nevertheless, we are working in good faith to raise the money."[19]

One of the great challenges of the campaign was that the Nez Perce needed cash, and they needed it immediately. Hudson recommended targeting government, major corporations and foundations, and citizens. This was "no ordinary business transaction"; rather, it was a "quest," an effort that would engage all Americans. Hudson named the organization the Nez Perce Heritage Quest Alliance and developed a website that charted the progress of the fundraising efforts.[20]

The Nez Perce Tribal Executive Committee (NPTEC) quickly established a donation account with Key Bank in Lewiston. NPTEC treasurer Delia Sheeler reported that by January 8, 1996, just over $10,000 in donations had arrived, many of them $5 and $10 gifts. With these gifts and cards arriving, Bob Chenoweth reported that "it is heartening to see this community support." NPTEC staff tracked the donations and sent out thank you notes as the money came in.[21]

Bill Picard recalled how NPTEC snapped into action to meet the fundraising goals. For the six-month period allotted to come up with the funds, every NPTEC meeting had time devoted to status updates and donor discussions. Individual NPTEC members worked the phones and travelled to meet donors in Spokane, Boise, and other parts of the Northwest. Picard said that he spent considerable time "traveling to meet with people. So there was a lot of time and effort for, not only for the executive committee, but also for the staff of the Nez Perce tribe to do the same thing, help go out and help with this effort." Reflecting on the experience Picard noted, "You can't really put a dollar amount on the time that you maybe missed a graduation, or maybe missed a baseball game that you'll never be able to watch again with your children or that kind of stuff. So there was a lot of effort put into raising these funds that took people away from their homes."[22] Richard Ellenwood put it bluntly, "without help, we cannot afford to pay this price. Yet our heritage must be saved."[23]

Chapter 11

Idaho School Kids, NPR Listeners, and Grunge Bands Do Their Part

A month into the campaign, help came from Idaho schoolchildren. On February 9, 1996, the Nez Perce Tribal Executive Committee (NPTEC) issued a press release honoring fourth-grade students at Frontier Elementary School in Boise who had initiated fundraising activities in response to learning about the Tribe's campaign in the classroom. Students worked with their teachers to contact all fourth graders in the state, and a $300 grant from the school's Parent Teacher Organization provided the funds to cover the bulk mail donation requests. According to their teacher, Susan Hutchinson, after she told her students about the Spalding-Allen Collection, "their reaction was 'the Nez Perce are part of our state's heritage. We've got to do something. There's things we can do as kids.'" Student Kelsey Hawes suggested popcorn sales. Classmate Carley Packard said, "Idaho's people should keep the artifacts because the Nez Perce live here, and it is the Nez Perce Tribe that made them." Nez Perce chairman Samuel Penney recognized the initiative of the Frontier Elementary students by issuing certificates of appreciation presented by a tribal representative and sending a group of Nez Perce drummers and dancers to the school.[1]

Thousands of students contributed to the Spalding-Allen campaign. In Caldwell, Idaho, eight hundred students donated change. In Blackfoot, Idaho, they collected aluminum cans and sold cupcakes. In Boise, they made pizza bread. In Prosser, Washington, the students washed cars, sold baked goods, and hosted a dunking booth. According to history teacher Dean Smith, "The kids like the idea of being part of something. This is a tangible thing, something they can touch and feel." Marcella Gibson, a teacher at Jefferson Junior High School in Caldwell, said that sale of the collection by the Ohio Historical Society "kind of incensed me. The kids said that's not right, they (OHS) shouldn't be doing that." As of April 7, 1996, the Nez Perce Tribe had raised nearly $200,000.[2]

Anne Desaulniers and Karen Weinberg, fourth-grade teachers at Adams School in Boise wrote to Tom Hudson on May 8, 1996, that when they had learned the story of the Nez Perce artifacts they became "interested in helping." Their class started collecting change and then two "enterprising girls," Catherine Martini and Mary Pat Cunningham, made a flier about efforts to buy back the artifacts and then established a lemonade stand on a "blustery March day." Strategically placing their stand near a speed bump, they raised more than $24. A second neighborhood sale earned another $18.50. A school bake sale netted $106.07. The class counted all of their change and the teachers gave a precise count: $53 in dollar bills, $21.50 in quarters, $21.90 in dimes, $8.50 in nickels, and nearly $57 in pennies. The teachers closed their letter, "We are pleased to present this check for $283 to the Nee-mee-poo people in support of your efforts to keep the Spauld-ing-Allen [sic] collection here in Idaho with you, where it belongs. With the check comes all of our good will and friendship."[3]

Pamela Corbin, a fourth-grade teacher at Sawtooth Elementary School in Twin Falls, Idaho, wrote a week later, on May 14, sending a check for $410. Her class had read about the cause and wanted to do something. They held a bake sale during their Spring Art Show. "All of us at Sawtooth wish you success in your fund raising efforts. By studying Idaho History, we have come to appreciate the value the Nez Perce people played in the history of the northwest."[4]

Acknowledging the energy behind schools collecting money led the Heritage Quest Alliance to launch a coordinated plan to ask schools to contribute $57.90, the symbolic amount of money based on Spalding's estimate of the value of the collection in his letter to Allen. To mobilize school kids around the country, Richard Ellenwood said, "School children all over Idaho have shown their concern by helping us raise funds. We now call upon the children of America to join us and protect our past."[5] According to the Nez Perce Heritage Quest Alliance webpage, schoolchildren learned about "Nez Perce history and their rich connection to US history," while coming up with creative solutions for gathering money. Students at Jefferson Junior High in Caldwell, Idaho, contributed $1,320 through candy and cookie sales, car washes, and donations from the community. The school also competed with Jefferson Junior

High in Columbia, Missouri, to see who could collect the most money.[6] At Housel Middle School in Prosser, Washington, students raised money though bake sales, car washes, and a dunking booth. Students at Lena Whitmore Elementary School in Moscow, Idaho, recycled cans. Students from Jefferson Junior High School in Columbia, Missouri, raised money by selling privileges at school such as the right to chew gum or wear hats in class. Schoolchildren sent in pictures, cards, and letters in support of the efforts. All of the school gifts were matched up to $50,000 by an anonymous donor.[7] NPTEC chair Samuel Penney told the press, "we hope all Americans, especially our children will join us. Their reward will include the feeling of joy when someday they visit the collection here in Spalding knowing that they helped bring it home."[8]

In addition to the money donated by schoolchildren, something far more significant occurred. The students studied Nez Perce culture and saw the connection between the contemporary Nez Perce Tribe and their nineteenth-century ancestors. To NPTEC member Bill Picard, the campaign "was not only to ask for donations, but also to raise awareness of what the tribe's culture is, and…what the tribe does. And that we're not just a culture that's read about in a book. But that we're actual people. That we're here and that we do practice, continue to practice, our culture." Picard continued, "These kids felt that urgency…the tribe went out to enhance the knowledge of local people as to what the tribe is and what it does. And that continues today."[9]

National Public Radio (NPR) broadcast a story on the Spalding-Allen Collection campaign on their Morning Edition program, which flooded the Tribe with calls of support. After hearing the NPR story, listener Brian Colona mailed a donation to the Heritage Quest Alliance including the following note, "I heard of your story on NPR Radio's "Morning Edition" on 3-8-96 on KPBS, San Diego.…I was appalled at the greed of the museum in Ohio for requiring payment for your artifacts. Once again, I feel shame for being a white American. I hope my donation helps you reach your goal and deadline."[10] According to Hudson, "we're getting calls from all over the U.S. from Hoboken, N.J., to Columbia, Mo., to Missoula, Mont., to Prosser, Wash." Sentiment is strong, and not just among the Nez Perce, that the collection should remain in Idaho, said Hudson. Tribal historian Allen Slickpoo Sr. reflected, "Our people saved the Lewis and Clark expedition. It is fitting that 200 years later all Americans have the opportunity to honor this act."[11]

Major rock bands joined the schoolchildren in pledging $57.90. These included Pearl Jam, Soundgarden, Alice in Chains, Pete Droge, and the Presidents of the United States.[12] The bands also lent their support through announcements on the cable music channel MTV. Four hundred rock radio stations spread the word of the campaign.[13] The members of Alice in Chains signed drumheads, and Pearl Jam's Eddie Vedder sent a signed platinum CD to Kerri-Ann Andrews of Lewiston, who sold the items as part of a benefit auction and concert that yielded $2,960.[14] According to Tom Hudson, the bands were "all really enthusiastic about it." Hudson reflected, "I think that our younger people will hear from the celebrities that are important in their lives that this is an important cause. It's telling our country that this is a cause for everyone."[15]

Chapter 12

The Nation Rallies to the Nez Perce Side

A key element of the fundraising campaign and the Nez Perce Heritage Quest Alliance website was the sponsorship of individual items in the collection. Each of the twenty Spalding-Allen artifacts had a webpage with a photograph and further information on the item, including its appraised value, as well as information about the sponsor.

Major donors came forward. The Lillian B. Disney Foundation provided a $100,000 gift to sponsor the man's bead-and-quillwork shirt; this gift was matched by an anonymous $150,000 donation. Lillian Disney had a close connection to the region. She grew up on her family's farm in Lapwai, Idaho, near the Spalding mission, and she and Walt Disney married in nearby Lewiston in 1925. Another key donor was Tom Redmond, founder of Redmond Products Inc. and a Colorado Appaloosa horse breeder; he made a gift of $50,000 and provided a matching grant of $50,000 for money donated after April 15, 1996. Redmond told the *Denver Post*, "We ride the Nez Perce trail every year. I've been involved in re-establishing their Appaloosa herd. I gave them a stallion. They're fighting to preserve their heritage."[1] Redmond's gifts sponsored the woman's hide dress with dentalium shells.

Redmond's gift came with an admonition from his assistant Dale Ahlquist. In a letter to Tom Hudson dated April 17, 1996, Ahlquist wrote, "As I've indicated to you, Mr. Redmond takes great interest in the history of the American West and is very concerned about preserving its heritage." He continued, "although there is a strange and perhaps uncomfortable irony about the Nez Pere Tribe being put into a position of having to buy back these artifacts, the Tribe would still be well-served to speak well of Rev. Spalding and avoid making derogatory reference to his experience with the Tribe." Ahlquist concluded, "after all, it must be acknowledged that Rev. Spalding, in fact, played an important role in preserving this valuable legacy. I hope I make myself clear."[2] There is no evidence that this warning caused anyone involved in the Heritage Quest Alliance or any Niimíipuu people to speak differently of Henry Spalding. However, it demonstrates that the fundraising campaign spoke to individuals with differing views of Western history.

More Spalding-Allen Collection artifacts found sponsors. Camelita Spencer of Spencer Ranch sent a $20,000 check to sponsor the second woman's beaded dress, closing her letter with, "my family is happy to be able to help keep these wonderful artifacts here in Idaho."[3] The University of Idaho Women's Center contributed $7,000 to sponsor the woman's saddle. According to center director Betsy Thomas, more than fifty people contributed to the donation.[4] Inner Vision Bookstore of Moscow, Idaho, sent $2,000 to sponsor the beaded moccasins. Dean and Andrea Pittenger, with their friends Mike and Teresa Beiser and Mike and Debby Alperin, sponsored the dentalium shell bracelet. *High Ground Magazine* sponsored the horsehair rope for $700.

The growing support for the Nez Perce was reflected in the composition of the Heritage Quest Alliance Advisory Board. The list included important regional politicians: Phil Batt, governor of Idaho; Larry Craig and Dirk Kempthorne, US senators from Idaho; and Patty Murray, US senator from Washington. Other members of the board included Butch Alford, publisher and editor of the *Lewiston Morning Tribune*; Bill Holm, curator emeritus of the Burke Museum in Seattle; Richard West Jr., director of the National Museum of the American Indian; and, perhaps surprisingly, Joanne Spalding-Stacy, the great-granddaughter of Reverend Henry Spalding.

Joanne Spalding-Stacy sent letters to the *Seattle Post-Intelligencer*, the *Spokesman-Review*, and the *Lewiston Morning Tribune* on December 5, 1995, in which she stated, "I fervently hope the Nez Perce can somehow retain those splendid examples of their heritage there on the reservation, and in my own small way have been trying to aid in this." She continued, reflecting a common view held in the nineteenth and early twentieth century, that her ancestor Henry Spalding sent the items to Allen not in exchange for trade goods but to preserve Nez Perce heritage because "by 1846 Spalding foresaw that the long wagon trains of settlers would soon wipe out the Nez Perce culture." This prediction never came to pass, however. Nez Perce culture adapted to the tumultuous changes that occurred during and after the missionary period. As this struggle over the Spalding-Allen Collection demonstrated, far from being "wiped out," the Nez Perce have demonstrated their resiliently and tenacity.

Dear Friend,

I hope you get your artifacts back from Ohio. We had a bake sale and the $68.61 is going to the tribe so you can get the artifacts back. What things of your's are in Ohio? It has been fun to learn about the Nez Perce tribe.

Sincerly,

Dianna Dugger.

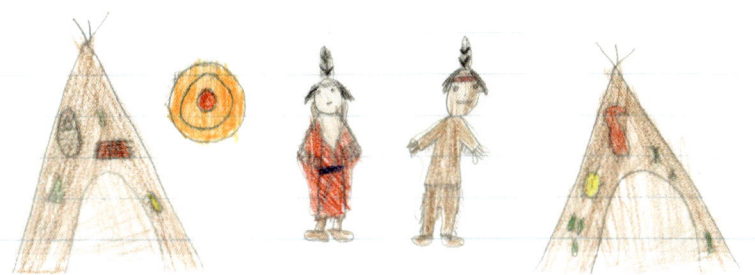

Letter from a student at Butte View Elementary School in Emmett, Idaho. Students at the school held a bake sale and sent $68.61 to the Nez Perce fundraising efforts. Schoolchildren across Idaho and beyond raised money to support the Nez Perce purchase of the Spalding-Allen Collection and at the same time learned about the Nez Perce people. Courtesy of the Nez Perce National Historical Park.

In her letter, Spalding-Stacy wrote, "It seems the Ohioans are the 'traders' and are seeking the highest bidder. Their 'ownership' comes only because a descendent of Allen didn't store them and gave them for safe keeping." Given the expense of building and staffing the National Park Service headquarters, Spalding-Stacy reasoned, "let us find the funding to save this quality display of our Northwestern heritage." She concluded, "One hundred and twenty years ago U.S. troops drove the Nez Perce off their homeland. We owe them a little help in holding on to the remnants of their culture."[5]

Members of the Nez Perce Tribe continued to make their case in the media for the cultural value of the collection. Clara Higheagle said the collection keeps her seven children in touch with the old ways. She explained, "It teaches them how to carry forward the tradition." Richard Ellenwood reminded the public of the sacred nature of the artifacts in the collection, "certain spiritual qualities went into making them." And Josiah Pinkham made the connection between the Nez Perce of the present and those ancestors who created the items in the Spalding-Allen Collection. According to Pinkham, the collection has value as "a strong representation of what our people are as well as

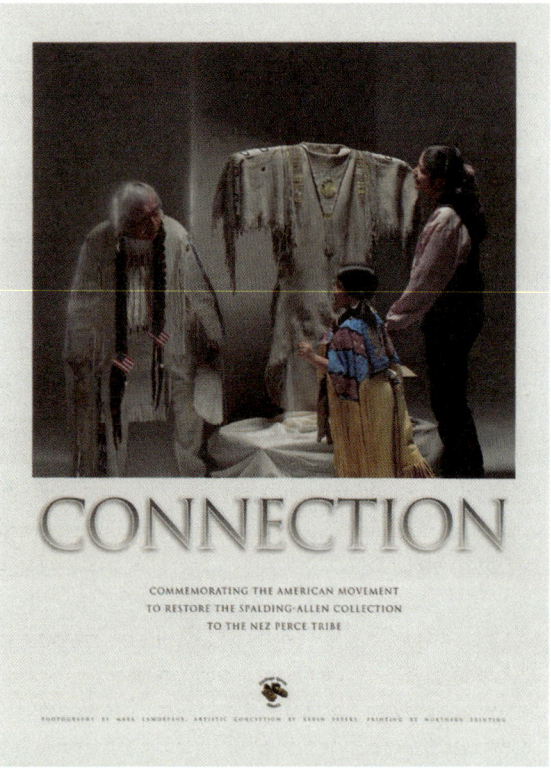

Supporters of the Nez Perce Tribe's campaign could purchase a Heritage Alliance poster for $57.90. The poster features Horace Axtell and Lynette Pinkham and her daughter, Temi Cree Meninick.

what they were."[6] Tribal elder Herman Rueben spoke of the value of the collection. "To the tribe it is priceless. They are ceremonial, what else can I say? It comes from the heart—knowing these things were once worn by tribal members, perhaps relations. The artifacts belong here."[7]

Donors across the country sent small gifts with cards and letters of encouragement. Mary and Brock St. Clair wrote, "To the Nez Perce People we are very saddened by the unwillingness of the Ohio Historical Society to return to you what is yours. We have decided to use some of the money we would have spent on Christmas presents for individuals to go instead to helping you buy back your artifacts." Their note continued, "If the historical society has a change of heart and returns the collection free of charge please use this money for something else" while the Reverend Ginny and Jim Burnett penned, "We hope this is postmarked in time for the Spalding-Allen Collection Fund payment. This act of Oberlein [sic] College and the Ohio Historical Society is one of stealing from others...which is a sin. May God change their hearts." Finally, Valerie Brace of Aloha, Oregon, echoed a common sentiment, noting, "What a rip-off!! You have to buy your belongings back that were stolen! Good luck on your fundraising."[8]

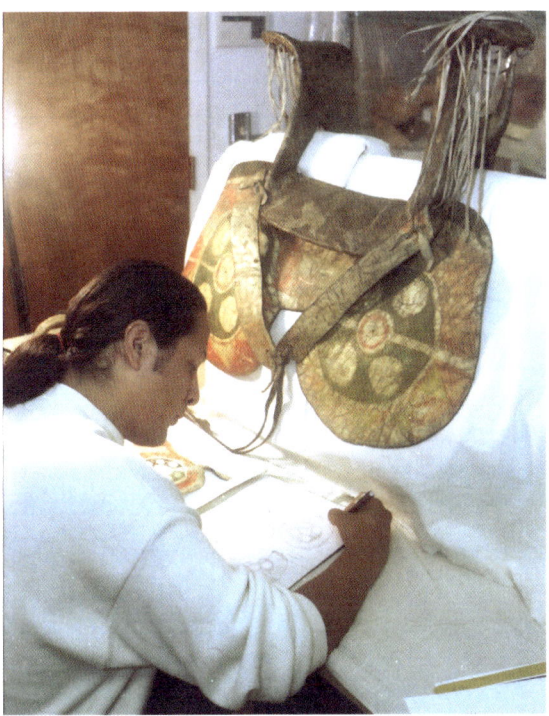

Nakia Williamson-Cloud drawing the woman's saddle in the Spalding-Allen Collection. Photograph courtesy of the *Lewiston Morning Tribune*, May 3, 1996. As NPS prepared to return the collection to the Ohio Historical Society, Nakia Williamson-Cloud, Tisa (Pinkham) Matheson, and Kevin Peters made detailed drawings of objects in the collection. Image provided by the Nez Perce National Historical Park.

Friends challenged each other to contribute to the cause. Reverends Jack and Janet Smith wrote to sixty-five of their friends starting their letter with, "I don't remember ever asking you for money—but there is a first for everything!" The Smiths explained how the collection came into the possession of Oberlin College, then the Ohio Historical Society, "the folk who now want them back." They continued, "Significant funds have been raised, but as of this date they are still short of the full purchase price (or it is highway robbery?)." They encourage their friends to send $57.90 to match their contribution. "Some of you may be able to be even more generous—that would be appreciated." They closed their appeal with the address for the Spalding-Allen Collection Fund and the reminder to "please do it promptly, to beat the June 1 deadline."[9] As of April 18, more than $450,000 in donations had been received.[10]

On the Heritage Quest Alliance website, supporters could purchase a Heritage Alliance poster for $57.90. The *Wallowa County Chieftain* newspaper also helped sell the posters for a $25 tax-deductible donation to the Spalding-Allen Collection Fund or $57.90 for a copy autographed by those pictured in the poster: Horace Axtell and Lynette Pinkham and her daughter, Temi Cree Meninick.[11] As Mindy Cameron of the *Seattle Times* reported, the Heritage Quest Alliance website included "the latest evidence of the creative inspiration behind this fund drive: an art auction that organizers believe may be the first in cyberspace." The auction featured works donated by artists around the country, including paintings, photographs, sculptures, ceramics, drums, and an atlatl.[12] Pam Palmer who helped Tom Hudson organize the auction, gushed, "This isn't just any old art auction. This is going to be visible to the world." Some of the artists who donated works for the sale included Grangeville sculptor John Geis; Moscow artists Ross Coates, Marilyn Lysohir, and Carolyn Fortney; and Ocean Park painter Nancy Lloyd. By June 1, 1996, the auction had netted $3,540.[13]

As the fundraising campaign was in full swing, Park officials and the Nez Perce knew that it was far from certain that they would succeed in raising the money to keep the Spalding-Allen Collection at the Nez Perce National Historical Park. According to NPS curator Bob Chenoweth, "we needed to document as well as we possibly could the artifacts." NPS officials invited in Nez Perce tribal members to capture all of the information possible before returning the artifacts to Ohio, where many felt the collection would remain or be sold at auction. Nakia Williamson-Cloud,

Kevin Peters, Josiah, Tisa, and Lynnette Pinkham, and many others, including elders Nancy Halfmoon and Esther McAddy, came to see the objects.[14] They recorded information on the collection and made detailed drawings of the items. As Chenoweth said, visitors included Niimíipuu people "with not only artistic ability, but also people that understood how these things were made. So we had these times set aside where we laid all the stuff out and people came and looked at it."[15] Nez Perce artist and National Park Service ranger/cultural interpreter Kevin Peters recalled examining the collection as the time approached to say goodbye to it and ship it back to OHS. Peters used a magnifying glass to examine the knots used in the construction of the men's shirts. According to Peters, "Looking at the type of knots [all of them] sinew-sewn. The quill-work is sinew-sewn. I think that even the beadwork is sinew-sewn. But what we found was interesting was when you start counting the fringes on the arms, they were all intact. And it's just amazing after almost 200 years." Peters continued, "We found out the number of fringes matched on each side. There's a couple hundred of them. They had counted them out very carefully. And they matched....They really thought about balance back then."[16]

Nez Perce cultural specialist Josiah Pinkham reflected on the labor involved in creating the regalia in the Spalding-Allen Collection. "I do bead beadwork and I can go down to Joanne Fabrics and I can buy yarn. I can buy string, I can buy thread. I can just pick that stuff up." These Nez Perce, Pinkham explained, "were twining sinew and using it. They had thread, too, available at the time. But predominantly, a lot of...[what] they were using to manufacture...was stuff that they had made. They dyed the quills. They collected them. They made the sinew to basically string those beads on. And that's a phenomenal effort."[17]

The open house for the collection went on for months, which was open to anyone in the community to come and see the objects. There was also another reason according to Chenoweth, "but you know, the other part of it, the motivational part of it was we wanted people to see potentially what we could lose."[18]

On May 3, 1996, as the documentation of the collection was underway and fundraising efforts accelerated, Jenny Ferguson, a 1993 Oberlin College graduate, wrote a letter titled "Oberlin should acknowledge rightful owners of Nez Perce artifacts" to the *Oberlin Review*. Ferguson remarked that after receiving repeated requests from Oberlin to

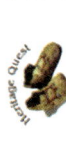

Heritage Quest Alliance

COLLECTION INDEX

Sponsor an Artifact

Help preserve this unique collection of extraordinary Nez Perce cultural materials.

For a larger view, appraised value and more information on each artifact, click on the thumbnail photos below.

Woman's Hide Dress | Woman's Saddle | Woman's Woven Hat | Bison Hair Rope | Horse Hair Rope

Elk Antler Quirt | Hemp & Cornhusk Bag | Woman's Woven Hat | Man's Beaded & Quilled Shirt | Man's Quilled Shirt

Woman's Crupper | Man's Beaded Pouch & Belt | Woman's Woven Hat | Beaded Head Pouch | Woman's Hide Dress

Quilled Moccasins | Beaded Moccasins | Dentalia Shell Bracelet | Man's Quilled Leggings | Cradle Board Photo

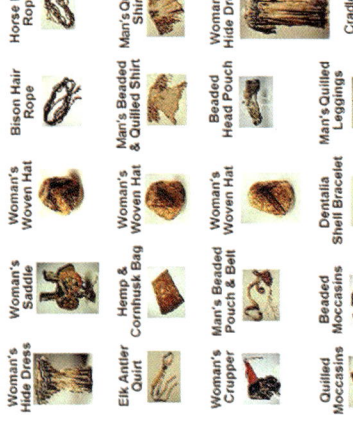

Heritage Quest Alliance

Nez Perce Tribe Seeks To Reclaim Their Past

Internet Fundraising Art Auction Extended!

New Heritage Quest Poster for Sale!

Check out the latest news on our fundraising efforts!

June 1st Deadline for Protecting Collection Approaches

After 150 years of separation the Nez Perce Tribe is poised to retrieve a unique collection of its people's artifacts. This collection includes both the oldest and most extraordinary historic representatives of Plateau Indian culture in existence. But there is a catch.

The collection is owned by the Ohio Historical Society. After loaning the collection to the Nez Perce for years, OHS recently demanded its return. In a last ditch effort to save the collection, the Tribe entered into an agreement to purchase it at the appraised value of $608,100. However, funds must be raised by June 1st, 1996, or the collection will be returned to Ohio, possibly for sale to other parties. Without prompt action, this opportunity and the collection itself may be lost forever.

We are calling upon all people who are touched by our situation to join the Heritage Quest Alliance in its fund-raising efforts. The Nez Perce people have received wide support from rock bands to Lillian B. Disney. There are many ways you can help. Artists and art collectors are particularly asked to participate in a first-of-its kind art auction on the Internet.

Please read further about our situation. Once you are convinced you should help, please contact us. We need you. This is a unique opportunity, a rare privilege, to give to a cause that will benefit many generations.

- Write your check today, and send a tax deductible donation to the Spalding-Allen Collection Fund c/o Key Bank. PO Box 1208, Lewiston, Idaho 83501.

For more information, contact Tom Hudson, Nez Perce Heritage Quest Alliance.

As part of their fundraising efforts in early 1996, the Nez Perce Heritage Quest Alliance created a website that included information on the Spalding-Allen Collection and the Nez Perce Tribe's campaign to repatriate it. Visitors to this site found many ways to contribute to the cause. Donors could sponsor individual items in the Spalding-Allen Collection by donating the appraised amount for each item. The Friends of the University of Idaho Women's Center contributed $6,000 to sponsor the woman's saddle, the Lillian B. Disney Foundation donated $100,000, and an anonymous donor from the Pacific Northwest gave $150,000 to sponsor the man's beaded and quilled shirt for its appraised value of $250,000. Tom Redmond, *High Ground Magazine*, Dean and Andrea Pittenger, Inner Vision Bookstore, and Ralph and Barbara Reed sponsored other items. Courtesy of the Internet Archive. https://web.archive.org/web/19961222033220/http:/www.uidaho.edu/nezperce/index.htm

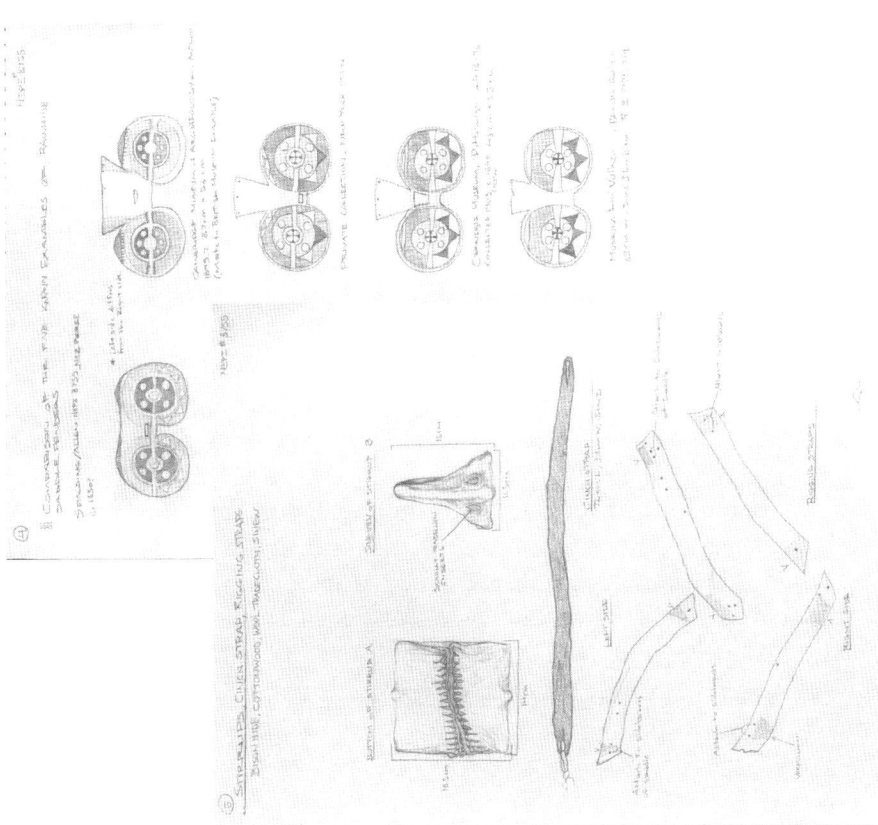

Detailed drawings of the design and construction of the woman's saddle in the Spalding-Allen Collection. Illustrations by Nakia Williamson-Cloud. Courtesy of the Nez Perce National Historical Park. These drawings are available on the Plateau Peoples' Web Portal: https://plateauportal.libraries.wsu.edu/collection/spalding-allen-collection-nez-perce

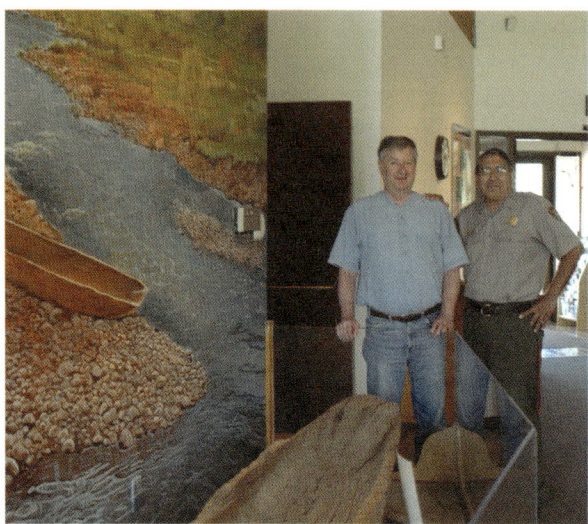

Bob Chenoweth and Kevin Peters inside the Nez Perce National Historical Park's Visitor Center next to the mural painted by Nakia Williamson-Cloud. Courtesy of the Nez Perce National Historical Park.

donate to the college, she instead "decided to give something back" by sending a check to the Nez Perce foundation's Spalding-Allen Collection Fund. Noting that she was unsure if the Nez Perce efforts to reclaim the collection had "gotten much attention on campus" Ferguson characterized the provenance of the collection as follows:

> Somehow, what was taken from Nez Perce Indians by the infamous Rev. Henry Spalding, sent to his friend Dr. Dudly [*sic*] Allen in Ohio, donated by Allen's son to Oberlin College, permanently loaned to the Ohio Historical Society (OHS) and then temporarily loaned to the Nez Perce National Historical Park became "property" of OHS to be sold back to the Nez Perce for $608,000.[19]

While some might quibble with Ferguson's description of Spalding as "infamous," her argument demonstrates why the public overwhelmingly supported the Tribe's efforts to regain the collection. It did not seem right that what was permanently loaned and then gifted to OHS should become "property" sold under difficult terms, a high price combined with a short time to make payment.

Ferguson chastised Oberlin for not taking an active role in the negotiations between the Nez Perce and Ohio Historical Society and for not insisting that "the collection should be returned, rather than sold." For this reason, she continued, "I believe Oberlin College has acted irrespon-sibly." While the Oberlin fundraising letters she received called on her to "have faith" in Oberlin, Ferguson continued, "I can have no faith in an institution which acts only on its own financial interests by protecting its relationship with the Ohio Historical Society and shows no under-standing of the ways in which its historical ties have taken a toll on other communities." As she reasoned, "Oberlin has willingly accepted gener-ous gifts from the families of missionaries and has profited greatly. The College should be just as willing to acknowledge that some of the items it has received were obtained unjustly. In addition, Oberlin College should cover the bill which has now been attached to those gifts." In the end, Oberlin did not become involved in the negotiations or financially con-tribute to the Nez Perce cause.

Native American flutist R. Carlos Nikai gave a benefit concert at Lew-iston (Idaho) High School where he raised $7,000 in ticket and CD sales. On Saturday, May 25, 1996, a final benefit concert to solicit last-minute donations included performances by Ruber Dawg, Master Poe, Roy Ball, the Lapwai Indian Hot Steppers, Nez Perce Spirit Drummers, and classi-cal guitarist Tom Armstrong. The concert drew families with young kids as well as senior citizens. The performers reminded the audience to stop by the donation table, and lines formed. Guitarist Doug Osborn of Clarkton told the audience, "Let's keep these artifacts here…if those people back East want them so bad, let 'em come out here and get 'em. They should come out here and get the whole experience, see the reservation, see the ter-rain where they [the Nez Perce] live…The Indians have been screwed with so much, they shouldn't be screwed with anymore."

In between acts, Richard Ellenwood addressed the audience. He spoke of the challenges of negotiating with OHS. "They would not sell it and they would not give it back." He reflected on the positive aspects of the campaign to retain the Spalding-Allen Collection: "A lot of people believe these items are so important to our country." Ellenwood continued, "They don't just belong to the tribe, they belong to everyone." He thanked all of those who had supported the tribe, including the national media and letter writers. Ellenwood described how an elderly woman in Massachu-setts, on a fixed income, contacted Nez Perce officials to make a dona-tion. "We're appreciative of what's going on and what's happening here today." He said, "We're all the same, we all run in the same vein…we can all live together as one people." As the concert concluded, organizer Kerri

Andrews of Lewiston asked the audience to "dig deep, way down into your pockets" for donations. Approximately $80,000 remained to be raised, she said. Ellenwood was confident that they would reach their goal. "The tide turned and turned a little more....Now you can hear the drum beat a little louder every day, till it deafens your ears and it's nearly here."[20]

After months of intense effort, the Nez Perce nearly had enough money to purchase the Spalding-Allen Collection. On May 30, they were $45,000 short of the required $608,100. According to Tom Hudson, there would be no flexibility in meeting the full price required by OHS: "We must have the full amount on time." As many small gifts continued to arrive by mail, Hudson arranged a $50,000 matching pledge from Tom Redmond. Feeling optimistic that the collection would not have to be sent back to Ohio, Hudson said, "at this point I would have to say over my dead body. I don't often say something like that, but I am absolutely convinced we will succeed."[21] On meeting the goal, Hudson said, "It's going to be right down to the wire. Yes, I do think we will make it. This is like an E ride at Disneyland."[22] On May 31, one day before the deadline imposed by OHS, the Nez Perce Tribe achieved their goal of raising the full $608,100. Potlatch Corporation donated $25,000, which, when combined with other smaller donations and a $2,500 check from Frontier Elementary School in Boise, put them over the goal.[23]

Two days before the deadline, when it was clear the asking price would be met, OHS and the Nez Perce Heritage Quest Alliance issued press releases on the completion of the collection purchase. OHS director Gary Ness attempted to put OHS in the best possible light, remarking that the sale of any collection was "an unusual activity for the society. However, we understand the tribe's interest in the collection, and in contemplating their offer we were encouraged that the Nez Perce share our desire to preserve the collection and continue to make it accessible to members of the public."[24] The *Columbus Dispatch* reported that the sale was a "windfall for the society's acquisition fund, about four times what the society typically spends each year buying artifacts and library materials."[25]

Chairman Penney framed his remarks more broadly, "This purchase officially ends a 150-year odyssey for an extraordinary part of our heritage. Our people, and supporters all over the U.S. will celebrate the homecoming of the Spalding-Allen Collection." According to the release, support came from more than two thousand donors and fifty schools that contributed the symbolic amount of $57.90. Donations also came from

Germany, Switzerland, France, Italy, and Japan.[26] At the height of the campaign, fundraiser Tom Hudson and his assistant Pam Palmer received thirty to fifty calls a day, at all hours of the day and night.[27] Penney noted, "The people of the United States have demonstrated that they value our Native American Heritage. We are deeply grateful to all those who have joined us in the spirited and successful effort."[28]

In a story the following day, Penney said, "This historic event should not be seen as an acquisition of museum artifacts. It is a restoration of an important part of the Nez Perce culture."[29] Penney remarked, "We found partners and friends when we did not expect them. And we have seen a light of respect and compassion which suggests a greater future for our United States." Though some Nez Perce faulted Rev. Spalding for his suppression of native religious culture, Spalding's great-granddaughter, Spalding-Stacy argued that "there would be nothing left if not for this collection. He [Spalding] did a great favor for the tribe without knowing it." However, she felt angry that the Nez Perce had to buy the collection back and called the price a "ransom."[30]

Deputy counsel for Nez Perce Tribal Executive Committee (NPTEC) Julie Kane celebrated the success of the fundraising effort as a great point of pride for the Nez Perce. She said, "We're going to have a party, some-time this summer, and invite everyone who has helped us in this effort."[31] Decades later she reflected, "The letters to the editor, the general take of the public is that they (the collection) should be turned over to the tribe. Those are tribal items. I think that's what most people thought. I was very grateful that they stayed here and weren't sold off to some collector."[32]

Considering the end of the campaign, Nakia Williamson-Cloud recalled that many people responded to the campaign and "realized that this is where these things belong here in this land. And so I think in that way it was a good thing. And I think our leaders that at that time, our elders that were alive at that time…were making good decisions." Williamson-Cloud continued, "I guess we're always asking ourselves what are we doing and are we doing the right thing. And ultimately, I think, you know, when we look back, even though there was probably some negative aspects and some things that probably weren't so good overall." Nevertheless Williamson-Cloud concluded, "I think we can walk away and say what was done and what was accomplished was a good thing for us. Not only for us but again, for this land and for the people that now live here."[33]

The Spalding-Allen Collection "needed to be home," according to Bill Picard with "the people who put these things together....They needed to be with the family....They were lost in Ohio." But the permanent return of the collection also signified a reunion of the collection between living Nez Perce and their lost elders. As Picard recalled, "it was like reconnecting with your elders. Reconnecting with maybe your great-great-grandfather who you've only seen in pictures. Or maybe only heard about in oral history. Only heard about in stories. But here's some items that belonged to him. So there's a reconnection between you and those that made these items." This connection had a spiritual aspect, too. According to Picard, "the importance of these items being home is because the spirituality between those that made those items, those that gave up those items, those that sacrificed, and now being brought back, the reconnection with those people. The reconnection with the owners of the items. And then also the reconnection of those items with their owners."[34]

Nez Perce artist Kevin Peters remembered that they had the boxes ready to pack up the Spalding-Allen Collection and ship it back to Ohio. He asked the question, why did we have to purchase these? Answering this question, Peters explained, "It's not necessarily 'we' [the Nez Perce Tribe]. It is the American people. Because we had people from all over. We had kids, you know, with jars of pennies. And it was an amazing, an amazing event in the end." Peters continued, "we had the boxes here, ready to put them all back in and ship them back. And I was just like, I can't believe this. When it finally came through, it was like, hurray! Now we can burn the boxes."[35]

The cause to repatriate the Spalding-Allen Collection resonated with the American public. "It became an American phenomenon," said Tom Hudson. "It became an American cause. An entire nation came forward to help a tribe. This may be unprecedented." The significance of the moment was not lost on Hudson. He told a reporter, "I thought if I failed, I would have failed a lot of people. I would have failed history." Hudson spoke of how his initial anger spurred him to act. "My motivation and the motivation of a lot of people was to right a wrong." This anger changed over time as thousands came forward to support the Nez Perce Tribe. Hudson said, "I saw the Ohio Historical Society as irrelevant. I now saw a new legacy for the collection…as a connection between the people across the United States and [the] Nez Perce Tribe."[36]

Bob Chenoweth flew to Columbus, Ohio, to hand carry the deerskin cradleboard back to Niimíipuu country. After OHS received payment for the Spalding-Allen Collection, on May 30, 1996, Chenoweth received the cradleboard. Unlike the journey to Ohio the first time, which had taken months, the cradleboard returned to Idaho after a seven-hour flight. Upon seeing the cradleboard, Chenoweth immediately noticed that it had the same design elements as one of the dresses in the Spalding-Allen Collection. Chenoweth remarked, "it was instantly clear the person who made the dress also made the cradleboard…it has a lot of touches, those extra little things you'd do for your baby to show your pride."[37] According to Tom Hudson, "there's a design of dentalia shells—white spiral shells from Vancouver Island—and very old trade beads that are identical on the woman's dress and the cradleboard." Hudson continued, "It's so unique and so ornate that it must have been family related. I'm sure they're from a mother and child."[38] At a special viewing for Nez Perce leaders and elders on May 31, 1996, Hudson said, "I can't stop smiling. I've watched elders come through and look at it with such reverence. This is truly a homecoming."[39] Reflecting on the campaign, Hudson noted, "The story is a little like the melodramas where a hero steps in at the final movement to save the day. Only the heroes were too numerous to count."[40] After the flurry of effort to secure the collection, this event was a moment of well-deserved celebration.

Seeing the cradleboard for the first time was an emotional moment for Superintendent Frank Walker. "It just got me right here," said Walker while tapping his hand over his heart. The successful return of the collection made Julia Davis cry. Describing the repatriation of the collection, "it was just an internal burning feeling for all of the tribe to say, 'yes we can do this.' We need to push ourselves that extra mile just as our ancestors did."[41]

In a ceremony of return, Henry Spalding's great-granddaughter, Joanne Spalding-Stacy, carried the cradleboard in a slow procession led by Allen Slickpoo Sr. The group included more than one hundred Nez Perce people, moving through the gymnasium at the Pi Nee Waus Community Center in Lapwai. Curator Bob Chenoweth accompanied her, carrying a pair of moccasins from the collection. Spalding-Stacy handed the cradleboard to Nancy Halfmoon, an elder in the Spalding Presbyterian Church, and Chenoweth gave the moccasins to Charles (Pete) Hayes, a Nez Perce tribal member from Kamiah. The moccasins represented a long trail, and the cradleboard symbolized the children of the Nez Perce Tribe. This exchange marked the transfer of ownership to the Nez Perce Tribe from OHS. Slickpoo said, "The Ohio Historical Society failed to recognize the sentimental and cultural value of the artifacts." As most of the artifacts were used in sacred ceremonies, Slickpoo continued, "It was kind of like buying back an altar that was taken away from us." An invited police officer kept an eye on the cradleboard during the ceremony. According to Chenoweth, "There are people who deal in the market of buying and selling other people's culture. So we're just trying to be cautious."[42]

Tom Hudson predicted that other institutions would not be so bold or greedy in the future when negotiating with Native communities. "America has come forward and set a moral standard that our Native American heritage should not be for sale, and it would be priceless." Nez Perce tribal member and federal archaeologist Sandi McFarland argued that Native cultural heritage should not be bought and sold. "They [Native artifacts] don't really belong to these people. They belong to the people who made them."[43]

Nez Perce elder Horace Axtell reflected on the repatriation of the Spalding-Allen Collection, "Our values have been reactivated you might say. You feel like you're a stronger person. We have all of our things together again." Superintendent Frank Walker admitted that he was initially skeptical of the fundraising campaign. "People were talking about bake sales and car washes, and I said this is way too much [money] to be thinking in these terms." Sandi McFarland was grateful the collection would remain in Nez Perce country. She had studied the Spalding-Allen basketry for her MA thesis. "I do a lot of bead work and corn-husk weaving. I go there [the Nez Perce National Historical Park] and look at the bags, and look at designs on the clothing, and I take them and drawn them on paper and reproduce them in my works." According to McFarland, holding onto the Spalding-Allen artifacts added significantly to the Tribe's collections, "They capture that moment of time when many artifacts were being lost, traded or gotten rid of because of assimilation." She said the quest to repatriate the collection "reunited people in the tribe and made them stronger, because they had a cause. They look inside themselves to see what it means to be Indian today. They still have pride that was lost for many years."[44]

Prior to July 2020 when the Spalding-Allen Collection came down for a conservation evaluation and a rest prior to a new exhibit installation, visitors to the Nez Perce National Historical Park's headquarters in Spalding, Idaho, could see much of the Spalding-Allen Collection in the permanent exhibit area. The Nez Perce were the focus of the exhibit with very little mention of Henry Spalding. A panel placed beside one of the woman's dresses read:

The Spalding-Allen Collection

In 1836 Henry H. Spalding established a Presbyterian mission among the Nez Perce here at the confluence of the Clearwater River and Lapwai Creek. In 1846 Spalding sent two boxes containing Nez Perce artifacts to Dr. Dudley Allen of Kinsman, Ohio. Allen donated these to Oberlin College in 1893 and by 1943 they had become part of the collection of the Ohio Historical Society (OHS) in Columbus. In 1969 the National Park Service "rediscovered" this collection and began negotiation which resulted in the collection's loan to Nez Perce National Historical Park. With the exception of the cradleboard, this collection was exhibited from 1981 to 1995. The Ohio Historical Society requested the return of the collection in 1993, but several loan extensions were granted in order to negotiate the purchase of these artifacts by the Nez Perce Tribe. In November, 1995 the collection was removed from exhibition in preparation for its return to Ohio.

In December, 1995, the Nez Perce Tribe agreed to purchase the collection after lengthy negotiations with OHS. On May 30, 1996, Tribal Chairman Samuel Penney presented a check to the OHS for the purchase of the entire Spalding-Allen Collection. At that time the cradleboard was reunited with the rest of the collection. In 2002 Oberlin College located an additional bag belonging to the collection and generously returned it to the Nez Perce Tribe. This is the oldest documented collection of Nez Perce material anywhere in the world.[45]

The text is a concise and neutral summary of the events described here. However, it obscures the contested status of the collection and the genuine struggle over negotiating a price and the terms for its repatriation to Nez Perce country. The second paragraph reveals a subtle dig at OHS. When Oberlin discovered a lost bag from the collection, unlike OHS, the college "generously returned it to the Nez Perce Tribe." OHS officials *may* have wanted to do the right thing: their actions, however, cannot be construed as "generous."

The Bailey Collection: Nez Perce Items Plundered and Eventually Returned

One consequence of the public struggle to obtain the Spalding-Allen Collection was the return of another Nez Perce collection held in Ohio. On

July 24, 1995, curator Bob Chenoweth spoke with Raymond Schuck from the Allen County Historical Society (ACHS) in Lima, Ohio. The two discussed a small but highly significant collection of Nez Perce artifacts plundered by Harry Lee Bailey, a lieutenant in the US 21st Infantry. Like the Spalding-Allen Collection, the provenance of the Bailey Collection was well documented.[46] Chenoweth described their conversation regarding the return of the items "to their homeland, either to the National Park Service or the Nez Perce Tribe." Chenoweth explained that the artifacts "had been taken from people who had not wanted war and whose descendants felt a very strong connection to them."[47] Schuck was amenable to the request and agreed to bring it before his board of directors.

The Bailey Collection is one of only a few documented examples of war loot taken during the 1877 Nez Perce War. After an attack by General Oliver Howard against a Nez Perce camp near Cottonwood Creek on July 11 and 12, 1877, the Nez Perce fled the Clearwater Battle site, leaving many personal items behind. Many US soldiers, including Bailey, took souvenirs before burning the village. These few items are the only documented objects that survived the battle, a turning point in the 1877 war. The attack by General Howard compelled the Nez Perce to move east through the Lolo Pass into the Bitteroot Valley to seek shelter with the Crow Tribe of Montana. In 1927, Harry Lee Bailey donated his collection of papers, photographs, and artifacts including a child-sized buckskin dress, a beaded sheath, and five bronze bells to the ACHS. The society displayed the objects for over twenty-five years.

Schuck replied to Chenoweth's request to return the artifacts to the Nez Perce Tribe, indicating that his society wished to donate the collection "because it was the right thing to do" but felt compelled to wait to see what happened with the OHS Spalding-Allen Collection.[48] ACHS did not want "to tip that one way or another." They waited until the sale of the Spalding-Allen Collection was finalized in part because they did not wish to jeopardize their receipt of state funds administered by the OHS. They did not want to risk retribution from the society.

In August 1998, after an exchange of letters between the Nez Perce Tribe, the Nez Perce National Historical Park, and the ACHS, NPTEC chairman Samuel Penney and Josiah Pinkham travelled to Lima, Ohio, to receive the Bailey Collection. Tom Henry, a reporter for the *Toledo Blade News,* wrote that, at the return ceremony, a white sheet was lifted, and the gathered audience saw "the dress—a vivid reminder…of the [Niimíipuu] women and children who were killed or forced to flee their village when it was invaded by the U.S. 21st infantry near Clearwater, Idaho, on July 12, 1877."[49] Josiah Pinkham spoke of ACHS's decision to return the collection, "It's a powerful thing to be here today, to be part of what's right." Unlike OHS's sale of the Spalding-Allen Collection at full appraised value, here the collection was donated. Pinkham explained, "These things represent our people. These things carry a story. I say with a good heart I'm proud to be here."[50] NPS curator Bob Chenoweth reflected that it had been three years since they had learned of the Bailey Collection, and in that time, the fundraising efforts to secure that Spalding-Allen Collection had been completed. According to Chenoweth, the saving of the Spalding-Allen Collection was a "sweet success because of the overwhelming support of the American public who contributed to this cause."

Unlike OHS, the ACHS made their decision based on an appreciation of historical context. As Chenoweth noted, the ACHS recognized "the need to have the artifacts returned to the people and place where their story resides. This may seem like a small thing, an easy thing. But in this time where many institutions choose to capitalize on a situation to their advantage," the ACHS "chose simply to give back what had been taken so many years before."[51]

Chapter 13

Chief Joseph's Shirt at Auction

Although the Nez Perce Tribe successfully repatriated the Spalding-Allen Collection and received the Baily Collection, these accomplishments did not stop the dynamics of the marketplace excluding the Niimíipuu people from retaining their cultural heritage. Indigenous communities around the world face similar pressures. These communities simply cannot (or will not) match the prices wealthy collectors are able to pay. A war shirt with well-documented provenance provides one such example.

On May 16, 2012, lot eighty-six at an American Indian art auction hosted by Sotheby's listed the fringed hide war shirt that once belonged to Chief Joseph. Similar to the shirts in the Spalding-Allen Collection, this shirt has impeccable provenance; however, the real value of the shirt was not initially realized. The shirt entered the marketplace in the 1990s as a fine example of an old Plateau-style garment. The poncho-style shirt is constructed of two skins. The skins, likely deer, were cut in two behind the front legs, and the two back halves were joined at the shoulders to form the front and back of the shirt. The two front halves of the skins were folded to make the sleeve, with the forelegs retained below the open armpits. The shirt has hair quillwork and contains fringes of white weasel and jackrabbit. The geometric designs of solid blocks of color, framed with finger-width lanes of darker colors are common with Plateau and Crow styles.[1]

In addition to the beauty of the garment, further research revealed its exceptional provenance. The shirt is unusually well documented. In 1877, John Fouch took the earliest known photograph of Joseph wearing the shirt not long after his October 5, 1877, surrender to General Oliver Howard and Colonel Nelson Miles. The US commanders ordered the surrendered captive Nez Perce to march 400 miles from Bear Paw,

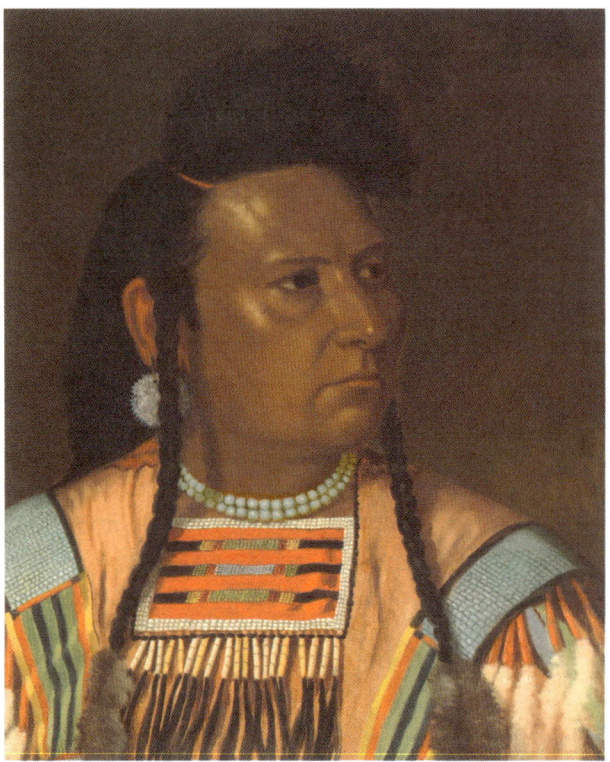

During Joseph's imprisonment at Fort Leavenworth in Kansas, artist
Cyrenius Hall created this painting of the leader. National Portrait
Gallery, Smithsonian Institution. Cyrenius Hall, March 20, 1830–1904.
NPG.68.19. Courtesy of the Smithsonian Institution.

Montana, to Fort Keogh near present-day Miles City, Montana. They
arrived on October 13, 1877, and it was here at Fort Keogh that Fouch
took the portrait of Joseph seated with his hands apparently frostbitten.
The varying lengths of the quillwork and the hair locks under the neck
flap clearly show the shirt in the photograph is the same one on auction.
Chief Joseph had saved this sacred item of regalia when so much else
had been lost. A newspaper reporter present the day of the photograph
described Joseph's shirt as including square blocks of beads "resembling
the epaulettes of an army officer and all around his shoulder and breast
were pendant long white fur tassels, presenting an elegant appearance."[2]

Two weeks after they arrived, General Sherman ordered Joseph and
his people to move from Fort Keogh to Fort Leavenworth, Kansas. The

military sent the Nez Perce by flatboat and train. Arriving on November 27, 1877, in their new surroundings the Niimíipuu people suffered from lack of sanitation, meager supplies, and poor rations. It was at Fort Leavenworth that Cyrenius Hall painted Joseph's portrait in June 1878. The painting of Joseph—wearing the same shirt—is now at the National Portrait Gallery. Hall carefully reproduced the color of the beading and other decorations of the hide shirt. An image based on this stunning portrait was used by the US Postal Service to design a postage stamp of Chief Joseph in 1968.

In 1878, the military ordered Joseph and his people to move from Fort Leavenworth to the Quapaw Indian Agency near Baxter Springs, Kansas, and then to the Ponca Reservation in Indian Territory (Oklahoma) a year later. Not until 1885 could Joseph's band return to the Northwest. Federal officials barred Joseph from returning to his beloved Wallowas or to the Nez Perce Reservation in Lapwai, Idaho, but instead ordered him and those Nez Perce who stayed with him up to the Colville Reservation in north central Washington. Joseph stayed at Nespelem on the Colville Reservation until his death on September 21, 1904. Joseph's widow hosted a potlatch after his death and gave away many of his possessions, including clothing and war bonnets. Joseph's shirt was likely dispersed with the rest of his belonging at this potlach. He had been buried immediately after his death, but in June 1905, with the erection of a white marble monument in his honor, he was reburied under it with great ceremony on June 20, 1905.[3]

Chief Joseph's shirt at the Sotheby's sale included a letter of provenance from Stephen Shawley, the first (though later disgraced) curator of the Nez Perce National Historical Park. He stated that Peopeo Tholekt received the shirt during the potlatch. PeoPeo Tholekt had passed away at the home of his nephew, Jesse Redheart, in 1935, and the shirt was last seen in Jesse's possession. Jesse participated in the 10th National Appaloosa Horse Show in 1957 in a shirt which *Sports Illustrated* reported as "attire inherited from his ancestor, Chief Joseph, leader of the Nez Perce Indians who developed the Appaloosa." Redheart died in October 2010.[4]

Public reaction to the sale of Joseph's shirt was not positive. The author of the History Blog wrote of the sale, "Today in depressing auction news, a beaded, quilled hide shirt with white weasel fur fringe and human hair decoration worn by Nez Perce leader Chief Joseph sold at the Coeur d'Alene Art Auction in Reno, Nevada on July 21st for $877,500 to yet another anonymous private collector."[5] A comment on the blog by "D. B. Cooper," posted on July 24, 2012, read, "I'm going to cross my fingers and hope that it was the Nez Perce tribe bidding through a proxy. At least I hope. I honestly have no idea how you could with a good heart and clear mind keep something like this in your house." Another comment by "livius drusus," author of the History Blog, July 24, 2012, read, "I think many of these collectors see these pieces as…aesthetic products first and foremost. The historical context enhances the value and fascination of the object, but it doesn't put any kind of moral onus on them." This "moral onus" of outbidding a source community for an example of their cultural heritage is something that collectors and the companies that sponsor auctions have not acknowledged.

The Nez Perce Tribe never had a chance to acquire Joseph's shirt. Even if they had bid on it, the community would have faced William I. Koch, one of the brothers of the billionaire family of Koch Industries and one of the wealthiest collectors in the world. Koch exhibited the shirt at the Yellowstone Art Museum located in Billings, Montana, as part of the William I. Koch Collection from December 1, 2012, through March 23, 2014. The shirt is now most likely in one of Koch's mansions, along with portions of his extensive art and wine collections—completely inaccessible to tribal members.

Chapter 14

Reflections on Spalding and the Spalding-Allen Collection

In his barter of Nez Perce goods, the missionary Henry Spalding sought to end traditional Nez Perce culture, advocating that the Nez Perce adopt Western dress, agriculture, and a stern version of Christianity. When Spalding shipped the Nez Perce goods he acquired through trade or coercion to Dudley Allen, he requested specific goods in exchange to further his missionary activities (in essence operating a shadow economy outside of the resources provided to him by his American Board of Commissioners for Foreign Missions [ABCM] overseers). Ironically, at the same time Spalding worked to "civilize" the Nez Perce by advocating the abandonment of their cultural practices, he was creating a collection of their earliest documented material culture. Spalding's collecting and the survival of his correspondence to Allen describing the objects saved this collection of Nez Perce material culture from potential obscurity and destruction.

Over the decades, the integrity of the Spalding-Allen Collection was threatened time and again. Officials at Oberlin College separated Spalding's letter from the collection, disrupting the provenance until Professor Fletcher restored the labels for much (but not all) of the collection. At OHS, the provenance was again threatened as the collection remained neglected while on "permanent" loan from Oberlin College; additionally, a group of African baskets was mistakenly added to the collection. After years on extended loan to the National Park Service (NPS), the collection's future was in jeopardy until the Nez Perce Tribe was able to purchase their own cultural heritage and return it to its original home in 1995. This journey of the Spalding-Allen Collection, started by a missionary who used his influence to loot Nez Perce material culture and barter it to keep his mission afloat, points to the importance that the origins (provenance) and subsequent care of collections. Primary sources, such as the items in the Spalding-Allen Collection and the accompanying correspondence, are critical for understanding our shared history. Yet many scholars do not consider why and how archival collections were created and preserved. The key to understanding any primary source is its provenance. Provenance is important well beyond the life history of one particular collection, no matter how significant that collection is. When the provenance of a collection is lost, such as when the collection is broken up, mixed with other items, or organized by topic, the context in which the items were created, preserved, and used is lost, and the usefulness of the collection is greatly diminished. Large collecting institutions, such as the Smithsonian, store millions of Native American objects (artifacts, papers, letters, photographs, and physical remains) with little or no provenance. As an example, a woman's dress made of elk hide, glass beads, and elk teeth by an unknown tribe sometime in the nineteenth century is much less interesting from a scholarly, cultural, and collector's view than that same dress that can be clearly identified as made by a Nez Perce, acquired by Henry Spalding at Lapwai in the Oregon Territory circa 1840, and is the earliest such dress documented. Archives, or more broadly, collections, are at the center of understanding the past. As the historian Antoinette Burton writes, "at issue in the project of interrogating archival evidence—what counts, what doesn't, where it is housed, who possess it, and who lays claim to it as a political resource—is not theory, but the very power of historical explanation itself."[1] I argue that the ownership and location of the Spalding-Allen Collection were critical issues for the Nez Perce Tribe who were—and are—seeking to revive and maintain their cultural traditions.

In questioning the provenance of archives and collections, scholars gain a richer understanding of the creation and preservation of collections. No archives are "objective" or "neutral." Rather, collections privilege some individuals and silence others. Spalding described the collection he sent to Allen to maximize the rarity and value of the items, expecting that Allen would send an equivalent value back to the mission in trade goods that Spalding could exchange for labor and supplies. Spalding, however, silenced the names of the individuals who made or traded the goods he acquired. He worked to suppress Nez Perce culture by insisting that they cease their traditional seasonal migrations to specific places when foods such as salmon, roots, or berries were available for harvest. As a missionary, he wanted them to stay in one place and take up sedentary agriculture. Spalding assigned Christian names to the Nez Perce and told them that they had to abandon their traditional religion, dress, and customs. In this coercive context, Spalding bartered and traded for examples of the Nez Perce culture that he sought to extinguish. The collection Spalding created was nearly lost on several occasions. Stuffed in barrels, it survived a two-year trip from the Oregon Country to Hawaii, then around the tip of South America to the East Coast of the United States, and finally carried overland to Ohio, being damaged in the process. After Allen's descendants gave the collection to Oberlin, the provenance was lost until Professor Fletcher reestablished the association of the artifacts with the collector. Oberlin officials loaned the collection to the Ohio Historical Society (OHS) where the items should have been better cared for; however, OHS did not steward the collection well, never investing in conservation services or research time. Only the cradleboard ever went on display. The collection was scattered across multiple locations in Ohio, and African baskets were mistakenly added to the collection. OHS established ownership only in 1979, following a formal request from the National Park Service for a loan. The initial loan terms included difficult-to-administer one-year loans and a reappraisal of the collection every five years. After the collection doubled in appraised value, OHS took steps to cash in on the collection.

The appraised price of the Spalding-Allen Collection went from $52,700 in 1980 to $104,850 in 1985 as a result of the research and the investment of $12,000 for conservation work, done at Harper's Ferry Center and paid for by the Nez Perce National Historical Park. NPS officials also had the collection appraised by an expert in Plateau materials, which led to a dramatic increase in the monetary value of the collection. In all of their negotiations over the collection, OHS avoided—whenever possible—dealing with tribal officials. OHS asserted that they first received a formal offer by the Nez Perce in December 1995; it is clear that Richard Halfmoon, the vice chair of the Nez Perce Tribe Executive Committee, sought to acquire the Spalding-Allen Collection as early as 1979. In 1995, the Nez Perce offered to buy the collection at the full appraised value, although many Nez Perce objected to paying for the collection. After taking their case to the public, it was clear that the majority of Americans supported the Nez Perce cause to keep their heritage in

Idaho. The campaign to raise the funds for the purchase reverberated well beyond the small Nez Perce Nation. Fundraiser Tom Hudson and his Nez Perce supporters took the opportunity to not only raise money to keep the important collection but also to educate the American public regarding Nez Perce history and culture. As the Nez Perce fundraising effort revealed, Americans across the country supported the return of the collection to its creators, often criticizing OHS for the high sale price. In a reversal of history of the 1877 conflict between Nez Perce and the federal government, this time a division of the federal government, the National Park Service, collaborated closely with the Nez Perce. OHS may be acknowledged for parting with the collection. Appraiser Paul Raczka noted, "It speaks to the integrity of [OHS]…to ensure the collection remained intact. The fact that it would also return to the originating tribe, to bridge a gap in historical knowledge by providing a first-hand view of the material culture of their ancestors, was also not lost on the board." He continued, "Their actions are to be highly commended."[2] Nevertheless, the high sale price required by OHS reflected poorly on their institution and demonstrated a lack of sensitivity to Native American history. OHS got their money, but they also took a battering in the public sphere.

Reflecting on the ethics of the agreement between OHS and Nez Perce, Bill Picard likened it to what would happen if he found a wallet on the street. "If I was in the streets of Coeur d'Alene and I walked up and found somebody's wallet on the ground and picked it up, it doesn't belong to me. And so I would dig in it to look, find out who it belongs to and I'd get it back to them." Picard continued, "But the Ohio [Historical] Society stumbled on some stuff that doesn't belong to them. And instead of giving it back to who it belonged to, they said, we'll sell it to you for 600 and some thousand, but we'll only give you six months to buy it, or we're going to sell it to someone else." Picard noted that this was not an isolated case, and museums and art galleries that hold American Indian collections need to ask, "who does this truly belong to and where did it come from? How did we end up with it? And then maybe look at trying to get it back to the original owners." Picard reflected, "I think a lot of the tribes don't even know that their stuff's out there in museums."[3]

For the Nez Perce Tribe, the acquisition of the collection required the attention of many individuals and the raising of significant resources. However, the process also educated the American public regarding the

Tribe and demonstrated their tremendous agency. These were not victims of history; rather, they were activists for their traditional culture, successfully arguing for social justice and utilizing the public sphere.

Nez Perce elder Horace Axtell observed that many fellow Nez Perce are making artifacts such as those in the Spalding-Allen Collection and that these items, handed down from one generation to another, "will one day be valuable, just as the 20 [Spalding-Allen] artifacts were 150 years later." For value in this tradition combines cultural value and the prices that collectors are willing to pay for Niimíipuu crafted goods. As for the Spalding-Allen Collection, Axtell said, "we really don't know who they belonged to. They belong to the tribe."[4]

While the public nature of the struggle over the Spalding-Allen Collection was noteworthy, Josiah Pinkham reflected that it was "representational of a lot of different challenges that native people face in trying to reassemble what was shattered. And I think that the Spalding-Allen Collection is representational of our efforts to basically put things back together." For Pinkham, the collection is one of many efforts underway by the Nez Perce to reassemble a culture that was disrupted by Spalding and subsequent history.[5]

In December 1996, months after the Tribe's purchase of the Spalding-Allen Collection, a small but highly significant portion of the Nez Perce homeland was returned to the tribe. The Trust for Public Lands, a national organization that purchases land to sell to governmental and public agencies to preserve natural lands and sites of historic importance, purchased a 10,300-acre ranch in the Wallowa Valley and returned the property to the Nez Perce. The Tribe agreed to convert the cattle ranch, which bordered the Hells Canyon National Recreation Area and the Wallowa-Whitman National Forest, into habitat for salmon and elk. The Bonneville Power Administration also contributed $2 million to purchase an additional 6,200 acres and another $4.5 million to develop an inventory of the lands and establish a management plan.[6] The Wallowa Valley was the traditional home of Chief Joseph's band. To mark the occasion, a group of Niimíipuu on horseback, including Nakia Williamson-Cloud, rode to meet a group of 250, including reporters from the *LA Times* and NPR. Horace Axtell said the acquisition of the land was a "good feeling like one gets when money that he had lent out a long time ago is finally returned."[7] The return of this property along with the repatriation of the Spalding-Allen Collection marked important steps forward in the restoration of Nez Perce cultural heritage.

Reflecting on the purchase of the Spalding-Allen Collection and the wider efforts of the Nez Perce Tribe to sustain their culture, Pinkham remarked, "We're involved in so many other aspects of putting things together...we were involved in a struggle to put grey wolves back out into Idaho's 'wilds.' And we also put Coho [salmon] back in the streams, even though the state of Idaho threatened to incarcerate us." Not long after the Spalding-Allen Collection returned to the Nez Perce, Pinkham recalled, "We acquired the precious lands over in Oregon. Over in [Chief] Joseph's homeland and that was a pretty cool deal. So you know, those fronts are all related in that people all over are facing the challenge of not just surviving but putting back together those things that were lost." Pinkham continued, "And so you could probably consider land acquisition, collections like this, language, you know, we're really struggling to basically put all that stuff back together, because we know that we're relying upon that as [a] people to survive."[8]

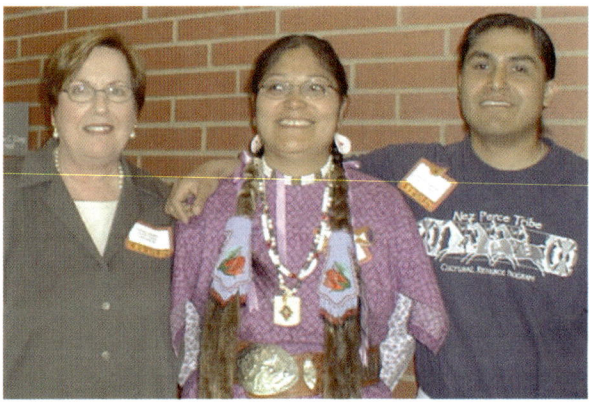

Photograph of Linda Grimm, Lynnette Pinkham, and Josiah Pinkham at a 2002 Oberlin symposium, "Closing the Circle: A Repatriation Journey." During the symposium, Lynette Pinkham gave a master class on the technique of flat-twined weaving. Her brother Josiah accepted a flat-twined woven bag on behalf of the tribe as the Nez Perce tribal ethnographer and accompanied the bag on its way home. Courtesy of Oberlin College.

The efforts to regain the Spalding-Allen Collection should not be viewed as an isolated instance of Nez Perce advocacy but rather part of a larger and longer series of actions to maintain tribal sovereignty and continue their traditional lifeways, from nineteenth-century resistance to the reservation system to contemporary efforts to manage their cultural and natural resources.

Seven years after the community's purchase of the collection, one more missing item surfaced. In April 2002, two members of the Nez Perce Tribe, Lynette Pinkham and her brother Josiah, travelled to the campus of Oberlin College to retrieve a long-lost piece of the Spalding-Allen Collection. Alerted to the possibility that items from the Spalding-Allen Collection had not all been accounted for, Oberlin students in Professor Linda Grimm's introductory anthropology class scoured the Oberlin campus for Nez Perce objects. One student in particular, Elizabeth Atack, searched diligently and eventually located a flat-twined Nez Perce bag intermixed with textiles form Southeast Asia. After subsequent research confirmed the bag's connection to Spalding, the Oberlin Anthropology Department decided to return it to the Nez Perce Tribe. Josiah Pinkham mentioned that the bag had been used to carry food, while Lynette, a skilled weaver, remarked, "Our children will learn from this. To see this, it's amazing to have this quality of work and to have it and cherish it in our possession." Unlike the previous time, no fundraising campaign was required. Oberlin College returned the bag without charge.[9]

The actions of OHS during the negotiations over the Spalding-Allen Collection damaged the reputation of the institution, but OHS was to face worse problems in the coming decade. The Ohio state legislature slashed the OHS appropriation from $13.6 million in fiscal year 2008 to $7.9 million in 2010, a 42 percent decline in two years. OHS fired more than half of its full-time employees (moving from a staff of 400 in 2001 to just 184 in 2009), closed many of its historic properties, and reduced access to the state archives from three days a week to only one.[10] As a result of the reductions, access to OHS collections and archives became more difficult for researchers. Indeed, multiple requests by the Washington State University Libraries interlibrary loan department to the OHS library went unanswered; nor could OHS staff locate the curator files of Dr. Loveday—files that Dr. Loveday suggested I consult in my research.[11]

Chapter 15

Sacred Places and a Private Golf Course

After the sale of the Spalding-Allen Collection, the Ohio Historical Society did not improve their relations with Native American communities or provide better care for their prominent Native American collections. Among their most significant holdings is the Newark Earthworks, one of the most massive construction works of the ancient world, built over a period of six hundred years by the Hopewell culture between 250 and 500 CE. Two major sections of these earthworks survive: a twenty-acre circle and a fifty-acre octagon. Native Americans consider these sites sacred. The city of Newark, Ohio, purchased the mounds from a private farmer in 1910, and then leased the land to the private Moundbuilders Country Club. In 1934, the city of Newark transferred ownership of the site to the OHS. OHS has renewed the Moundbuilding Country Club's lease since then. The club turned the mounds into an 18-hole golf course with no public access. According to Richard Shiels, a history professor at Ohio State University, "Playing golf on a Native American spiritual site is a fundamental desecration." He notes that the "mounds need to be a public site and the club needs to relocate."[1] In 2005, the Country Club owners barred non-club members from stepping on the green to view the moon's alignment with the Newark Earthworks, an event that occurs only every 18.6 years.[2] The club had cancelled a planned public viewing over concerns that the crowds, combined with recent rains, would damage the green. Nevertheless, as many as one hundred viewers covertly snuck onto the course.

Amid growing controversy over golfing on the site, in 1997, OHS renewed the lease to the Moundbuilders Country Club through 2078. According to their lease, the club "shall not mar the beauty of the mounds" and shall ensure that the public will have reasonable access to the site. Moundbuilders president Mark Walters argued, "We want to make sure everyone can see it, but we have to balance our needs too. We pay a lease." Access to the site for non-club members is by way of an observation platform next to the club parking lot. Barbara Crandell, a Cherokee elder, was arrested in 2002 for trespassing, after she refused orders to leave the grounds. Friends and supporters paid her trespassing conviction fine of $883 in Sacagawea dollar coins. Crandell explained that when the public has full access to the site "it's the day they spray the herbicide," and she continued, "I asked them if they had any smallpox blankets." Furthermore, Crandell recalled that golfers went out of their way to make visitors to the mounds feel uncomfortable.[3]

In the decades after the return of the Spalding-Allen Collection, the American public and judicial system have sided consistently with Native American communities on preventing the sale of Native American sacred objects. As Paul Raczka observed, "NAGPRA has had a strong influence on the market for Native American art. More than anything it has caused uncertainty in acquiring any piece for fear it will fall under the jurisdiction of the law." According to Raczka, it is the cultural patrimony section of the Native American Graves Protection and Repatriation Act (NAGPRA) that is the most ambiguous. He observed that in today's art market, the significance of the Spalding-Allen Collection to the Nez Perce people would likely cause the sale to fall under the cultural patrimony portion of the law. This categorization would prohibit its sale outside the Native community. Raczka continued, "This has proven to be the case with several pieces being withdrawn from the larger auction houses, one case being a Sioux shirt identified as belonging to an ancestor of a contemporary family. It was claimed the piece was integral to the culture of the group to survive."[4] However, the auction market is unpredictable, and for many communities, the period between the publication of auction notices and catalogs and the actual sale is too short to for them to prepare formal objections, as was certainly the case with the Chief Joseph shirt.

Chapter 16

The International Marketplace for Cultural Heritage

The struggle for North American Native communities to reclaim their cultural heritage has moved overseas. In 2013, the Hopi repeatedly failed in their attempts to stop a major sale of one hundred American Indian objects by the Drouot auction house in Paris. Among the sacred items up for auction were twenty-four Hopi *katsinam* considered by the Hopi (and other Pueblo peoples) to be divine, living beings. Gregory Annenberg Weingarten, vice president and director of Annenberg Foundation, lived in Paris and followed the news coverage of the Hopi's unsuccessful attempts to block the sale in French courts. He approved a budget for the Annenberg Foundation of up to $1 million to purchase twenty-seven sacred items: the twenty-four Hopi katsinam and three items sacred to the San Carlos Apache of Arizona. Working in secrecy with Pierre Servan-Schreiber, the French lawyer who had represented the Hopi in pro bono litigation prior to the auction, the Annenberg Foundation staff purchased twenty-four of the twenty-seven items, including the most expensive item of the auction: a Hopi Crow Mother headdress that sold for $130,000.

As a bidder representing the Annenberg Foundation was purchasing many of the Hopi lots anonymously over the phone, the owner of the auction house, Alain Leroy, asked his staff to investigate. His staff assured Leroy that the bids were legitimate and that the funds had been previously wired. Leroy remarked after the sale that "it's a good outcome for the Hopi but not the collectors, I suppose." His statement in part underscores Leroy's wish to keep artifacts circulating among collectors. There is no indication on his part that the sale was a good outcome for social justice—that sacred collections were returning to their home of origin.

Annenberg Foundation staff worked with the US Department of State but kept the bidding otherwise secret until after the sale. Immediately following the sale, Annenberg representatives contacted the Hopi to inform them that the katisnam would be returned and consulted on the best way to return the belongings. In the end, the Annenberg Foundation spent $530,695 and obtained all but three of the twenty-four Hopi lots and three other sacred Apache artifacts.[1]

New York Times reporter Tom Mashberg concluded his story on the Annenberg purchase by noting, "the fact that the Katsinam had to be bought and paid for, even by benefactors, was a bittersweet nod to the reality that American Indian artifacts have become highly sought, expensive commodities." Sam Tenakhongva of the Hopi, reflecting on the sale, expressed a sentiment shared by some of the Nez Perce when deliberating on whether to buy back the Spalding-Allen Collection, "no one should have to buy back their sacred property, but now at least they will be at home with us and they will go to rest."[2]

In an interview shortly after the sale, Servan-Schreiber noted that the only way to stop similar auctions "is by creating a collective perception that they are wrong. Whether through the media, or court action, people need to know why it is wrong, so that everybody thinks it is." He continued, "I hope that one day, people will realize that not everything can be bought or sold."[3]

The struggle for the return of Native collections from European museums continues. Since 1978, the Zuni have successfully repatriated more than one hundred *Ahayuda* (sacred war gods) from museums across the United States, citing NAGPRA. However, US repatriation laws do not yet apply in Europe. Octavius Seowtewa, a Zuni elder, travelled with Chip Colwell, curator of anthropology at the Denver Museum of Nature and Science, to ask for the repatriation of Ahayuda from European collections. The Zuni make two Ahayuda a year, on the winter solstice, to protect the community from harm and promote fertility. A complex set of rituals govern their manufacture.[4] According to Seowtewa, only the Zuni Bow priests are allowed to touch the Ahayuda, which are owned by the Tribe, so any found outside the community are considered by the Tribe to have been taken illegally.

During their visits to museums in Europe, the National Museum of Ethnology in Leiden, in the Netherlands, was the most receptive to the Zuni concerns. The museum removed Ahayuda from display and their curator, Pieter Hovens, indicated in an email that "he was also hopeful that the repatriation would take place."[5] Colwell found other European museums "more colonial" in their resistance to return collections to their source communities.

In December 2014, the Navajo Nation sent a delegation to Paris to buy at auction seven masks used in their winter Nightway Chant ceremony. At the same auction, several lots of Hopi katsinam were up for sale, but the Tribe did not bid, on the grounds that the seller cannot own such spiritual beings and therefore cannot sell them. Deswood Tome, Navajo Nation spokesman, told the Associated Press, "buying these masks…is a precedent that we've set." However, the sale signaled that the auction of sacred American Indian objects in France was becoming more controversial. As Navajo speaker Pro Tem LoRenzo Bates noted in a press release, "it was clear that the French people are becoming more and more aware of Navajo people's concern over the respect of Navajo human rights, and it was evident by the news agencies and organization that came out to the auction to seek Navajo Nation input.[7] These events underscore the importance of provenance and the ongoing efforts of Native peoples to retrieve their cultural heritage from collectors and museums.

Chapter 17

Conclusion

The story of the Spalding-Allen Collection took place during a shift in relations between museums and Native communities. Through the late nineteenth century into the later twentieth century, many museums collected and displayed Native American materials in ways that affirmed the superiority of Euro-American culture and implied that Native communities had essentially vanished. As Williamson-Cloud observed, for generations, Native people have been told that everything they knew has no value anymore. "The broader society can't even conceptualize what that is like. I think other minority groups understand it though, that's why things are happening the way they are right now." Museums have played a role in this, Williamson-Cloud explained, by collecting and preserving items for Indigenous cultures with no buy-in from the people they are representing.[1] However, in the 1990s, after the passage of the Native American Graves Protection and Repatriation Act (NAGPRA) and the development of the National Museum of the American Indian (NMAI), the dialog between many Native American communities and museums has changed to one of consultation. Museums such as the NMAI and the Burke Museum closely collaborate with Native American communities on exhibits that feature Native American culture. There has also been a dramatic growth in Native American cultural centers and museums. The Association of Tribal Archives, Libraries, and Museums (ATALM) has recognized excellence in museums since 2007 with institutions such as the Tamástslikt Cultural Institute, the Ziibiwing Center of Anishinabe Culture and Lifeways, the Cherokee Heritage Center, and the Makah Cultural and Research Center receiving awards.[2]

On September 14, 2016, I visited the collections center at the National Museum of the American Indian (NMAI) in Suitland, Maryland, with representatives from the California Indian Museum and the Ziibiwing Cultural Center (in Michigan). Greeting us at the door to the collections center was a statue of Chief Joseph of the Nez Perce. We then entered a unique type of museum collections facility, one built after extensive consultations with Native communities. As the curator Joe Horse Capture explained, the reception area was oriented with the cardinal directions, and windows and a skylight flooded the area in natural light. In the center of the room, four glass bricks set into the floor of the reception foyer let in light to the collections area below. When we went downstairs to see the collections, we paused in the ceremony room, a private space where Native American visitors could perform ceremonies or prepare themselves before entering the collections space. A circular sand pit provided a traditional space for smudging, and nearby bins stored materials such as sweet grass as well as implements to accommodate most tribal traditions. Another outdoor space was available for communities whose traditions required outdoor ceremonies.

Joe Horse Capture explained that he and his fellow curators at the NMAI never used the term "storage" when speaking of the area for keeping museum objects. Instead, they described the area as "collections" to acknowledge that the collections are vibrant, living items, not something dead or inert. In arranging the collections, NMAI staff changed the organization from Heye's original classification by object type (like basketry, where baskets from all Tribes would be grouped together). Instead, curators oriented the rows of compact shelving and grouped collections according to region and community, with the provenance of each piece recorded in a museum catalog record quickly accessible via a barcode placed by the item.

Another major change from Heye's earlier curation of the collections is that Native input is welcomed, and suggestions from Native communities are implemented in practice. For example, ceremonial or sacred items are shelved up high so that NMAI staff do not accidentally allow the general public to see the items. Some objects include notes regarding handling, such as instructions that Makah whale hunting objects should only be touched by men.

As the NMAI staff opened drawers of beautiful Pomo baskets, I saw that each was carefully housed and individually bar coded. Strict temperature and humidity controls ensure optimal preservation conditions.

The NMAI can consult with conservators from the other Smithsonian branches on the Suitland campus. One of their ongoing efforts is to closely monitor the collections for signs of insect infestation. This examination is part of a long-term project to cleanse the objects from earlier days when staff under Heye employed mothballs and other toxic powders to keep pests away. While certainly protecting the objects from bugs, the use of such chemicals is anathema to Native communities.

When I started this research, I was interested in the story of the Spalding-Allen Collection's purchase and the ethics of sale. During the course of writing about other collectors, including Myron Eells, Lucullus McWhorter, and Clifford Drury, I realized that where collections reside is important. I have argued that the location of collections matters so that the people who live in particular places may have access to the collections that inform that place. How can residents truly understand a place if all objects from that location are held in distant repositories?

As I considered these notions, I was challenged by one of my Washington State University (WSU) history professors to think more about why place matters. He argued that collections being kept in Washington, DC, made research more convenient for scholars. He needed to visit only one city to access vast collections. At the time, I do not think I gave a convincing reply. I said something along the lines that places mattered and that travel was expensive. This circumstance privileged elite scholars, such as himself. Having reflected on these issues for several years and having had the opportunity to visit institutions such as the Library of Congress and Smithsonian with Native colleagues, I realize that where collections are housed and cared for does matter and that the needs of Native communities vary greatly.

The large federal institutions such as the Library of Congress, the Smithsonian, and the National Park Service, for example, have the capacity to preserve collections because of their access to conservators. For some materials, it is the content rather than the format that is critical. The earliest surviving recordings of Native American songs were made using wax cylinders. This format is particularly difficult to migrate because each time the cylinder is played there is the potential for damage. The Library of Congress brings state-of-the-art audio engineering to convert these recordings to digital formats that can be widely shared by source communities. It is the content that is critical, the ancient songs or language spoken by fluent tribal elders, rather than the cylinder recorders themselves.

The resources available to devote to cultural programs vary greatly among Native communities. Some communities have state-of-the-art museum facilities and full-time professional staff, while other tribes have inadequate facilities and rely on temporary staff and volunteers. So it is often not simply a matter of giving everything back, at least in the immediate term, but rather one of developing relationships and supporting Native communities in their efforts to sustain their cultures and ensure that collections are easily accessible to their source communities. To achieve this, collecting institutions need to listen to source communities and develop collaborations based on mutual respect. These collaborations may include returning collections, arranging long-term loans, providing preservation assistance, working together on grant proposals, and other activities to sustain collections and cultures.

The model of an individual scholar travelling to collections in major metropolitan areas works well for a professional historian with institutional support for visiting collections. However, this model works less well for groups or entire communities who wish to access collections. It certainly privileges the dominant Euro-American culture over Native communities.

Native American collections are living, breathing, and intimately connected to the region in which they were fabricated. The shirts, dresses, bags, and other items in the Spalding-Allen Collection come from an identified place on the Columbia Plateau; the plant fibers, animal skins, quills, and dyes all derive from that specific place. All are aspects of how the land sustained the Niimíipuu people. For many members of the Nez Perce Tribe, these items are an enduring testament to their homeland, going back thousands of years. The dress in the Spalding-Allen Collection, according to Nakia Williamson-Cloud, is more than an heirloom or a work of handicraft. It is a living record. "The reason we carry on with, to some on the outside, outdated things and ways, is there's a value that's there in the importance of those items that were passed down by the elders." The dress relates to the first laws, "to the time when our people were placed here," Williamson-Cloud said, "when time changed from the time of the animal people to the time of the humans." He continued, "The second one to stand up for us was the deer. He would provide meat and clothing. We had nothing, nothing to protect ourselves. The deer and the other ungulates, bighorn sheep, elk that was their sacrifice to us. Something as simple as a buckskin dress reaffirms our identity, our lineage, our connection to the land and how it is connected to us. It is a reciprocal relationship to us." Therefore, items were handed down through successive generations as a representation of lineage, commitment, and responsibility, he said. Because the tribe did not have a written language, its members used these things as a way to recite and remember their family, tribal and inter-tribal relationships, and stories. They have a life of their own. Williamson-Cloud continued, "Once they're curated, filed away in a box, put on display, they lose a little of that sometimes. If they're in the area, they're in the context of all this broader understanding I'm trying to relate." This relationship with the land is Nez Perce culture, said Williamson-Cloud. This is one reason the Nez Perce have fought to protect the environment and their right to fish, hunt, and gather. "We're not trying to preserve the land and resources for the sake of doing it, we're preserving ourselves and our unique identity."[3]

The objects are not just historical curiosities but represent a deep connection to the land and are inspirational models for sustaining cultural traditions, such as weaving, curing, and beading. The collection therefore represents Nez Perce lifeways, not just beautiful objects. Language, traditional skills, trade, place, are all imbued in the Spalding-Allen Collection of Nez Perce material culture gathered by a missionary in the Oregon Country, shipped to Ohio, and, after more than a century, returned home.

According to Josiah Pinkham, "when we make things, and we make them as a Nez Perce…and a Nez Perce person will wear that, and they'll stand there and they'll look like a Nez Perce. And that sets us apart from other people in our area. Not because we're better, but because we have a unique place in this world. And part of that unique place is the visual appearance of what it means to look like a Nez Perce." He explained, "We wear particular things and that's what separates us. And it's also because we have a unique way of putting those things together because it's a reflection of our relationship with our landscape." He continued, "When our future generations come along, they see that relationship and they want to embrace that relationship in a way that ensures their survival, too. Because one of the things that I know is that the Nez Perce people have been here the longest. And it's because we have strived for generations to have a sensitive relationship with the landscape." The landscape is rich with materials and life. "That landscape includes deer. It includes elk, plants, water, fish.…We don't get there on our own. We

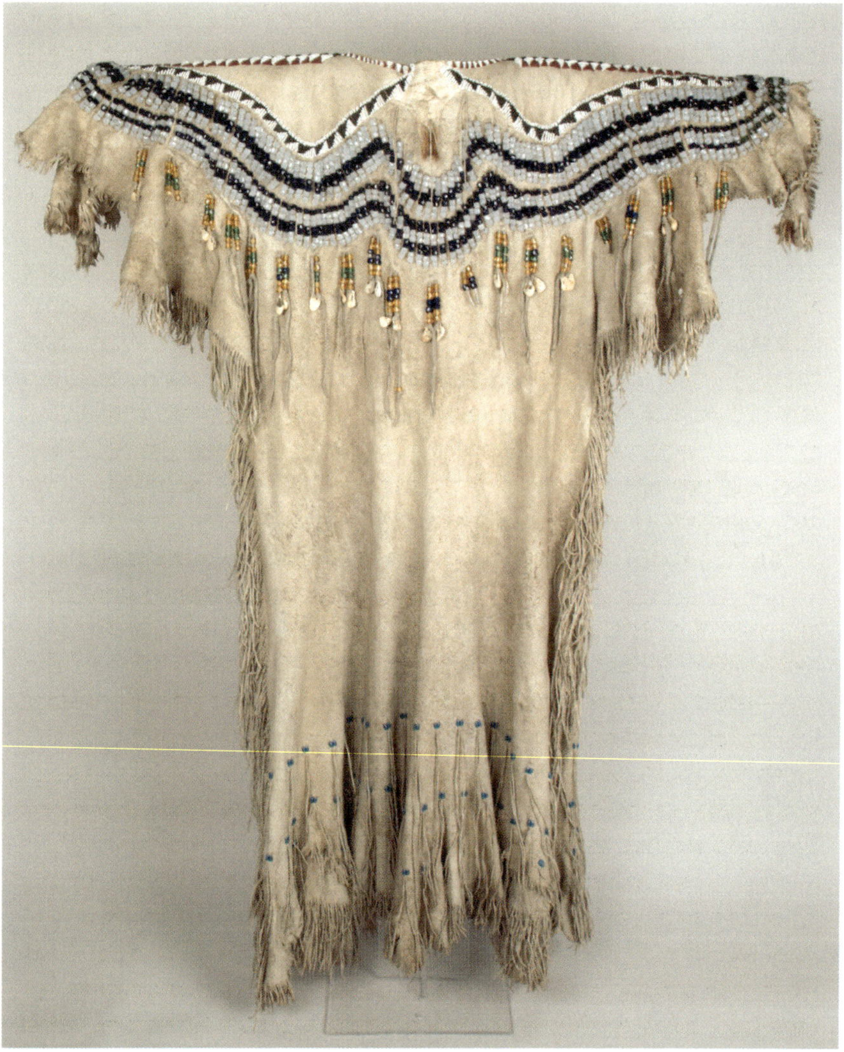

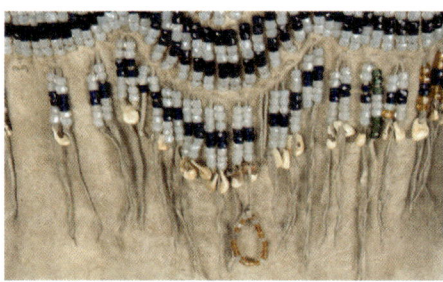

One of two dresses in the Spalding-Allen Collection. It is made of elk and deer skin and decorated with fringe, glass beads, and elk teeth. Wrinkles around the waist indicate the dress was worn with a belt. Photographs by Zach Mazur. Courtesy of the Nez Perce National Historical Park. NEPE 8757.

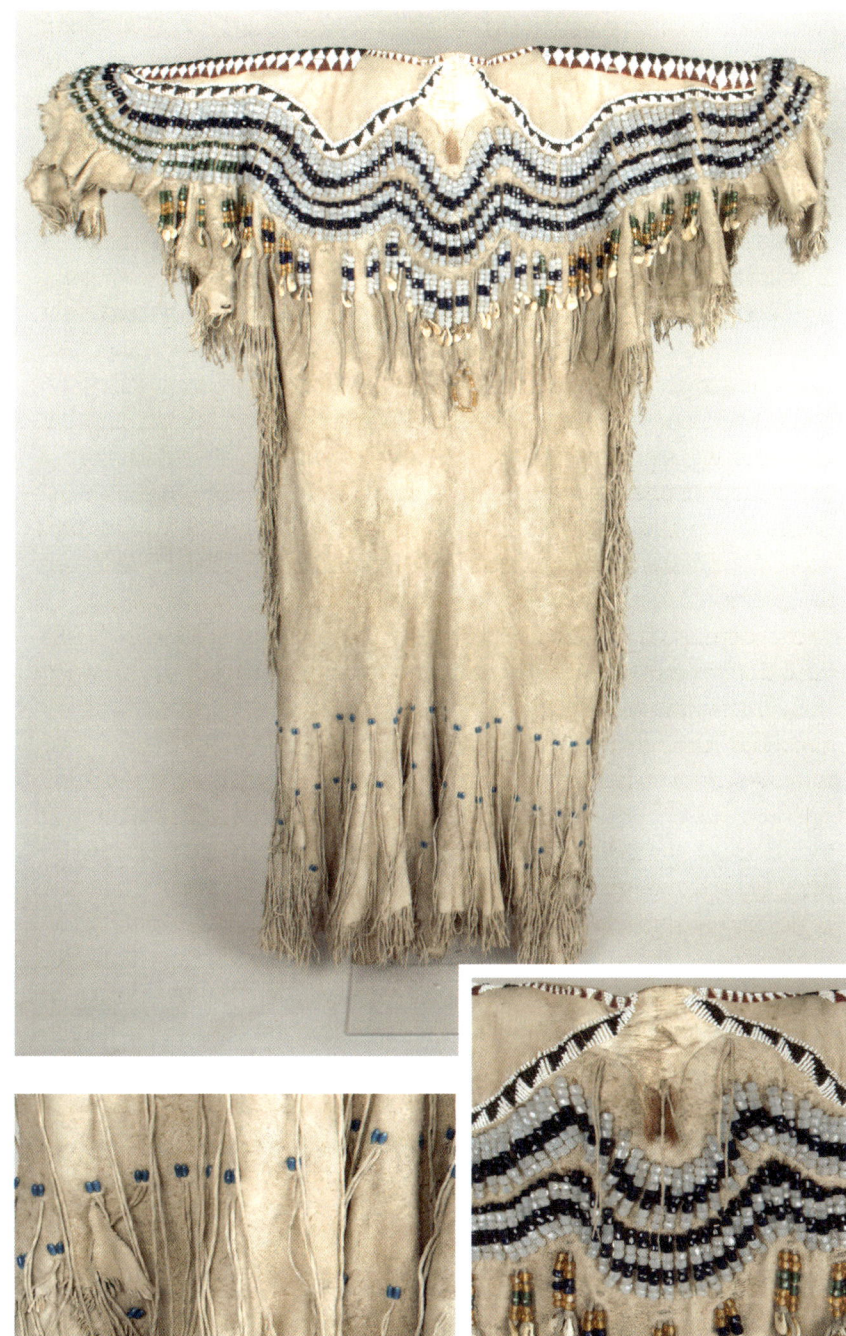

have a lot of help. We've got deer looking out for us. We've got elk help-ing us out. We've got buffalo feeding us. Salmon. All those things kind of culminate in a visual appearance that says look at the way that I am here. These are the things that take care of me. I'm not parading these things around because I'm a proud Nez Perce. I'm wearing these things as a sense of gratitude for what takes care of me."[4]

Making items according to traditional cultural practices is a form of prayer according to Pinkham, "Because you're praying that when your kids come to be and they have their grandkids, what you're praying for is hey, I really want you guys to help me take care of this, because this is spe-cial. And I want you guys to take care of this because this is going to not only ensure that your kids have as good a quality of life as I do, but that their kids will have that quality of life, too. And that's one of the things that we're losing. And that's what this stuff represents on a spiritual level is that it's really important for us to carry that on and to maintain that visual appearance. Because it's not about the striking visuals, it's about the deeper meaning that that symbolizes."[5]

In 2019, the National Park Service finalized plans to update the exhibit areas at the Nez Perce National Historical Park (NEPE). After some forty years on display—an extremely long time for garments—the Spalding-Allen Collection will rest in the temperature-controlled collec-tions area in the basement of the park headquarters. Replacing the dated and static exhibit spaces will be new displays that reflect the continuing traditions of the Niimíipuu people. Several rotating exhibit cases will provide park curators with more flexibility for future displays.

Images of the Spalding-Allen Collection are now available online on the Nez Perce Tribe's Path on the Plateau Peoples' Web Portal.[6] The indi-vidual items in the collection include extensive descriptions and tradi-tional knowledge shared by members of the Nez Perce Tribe. I collabo-rated with Nakia Williamson-Cloud to add the images and descriptions gathered from the research conducted for this book. For example, one of the men's shirts includes an extensive description by Josiah Pinkham of the traditional Niimíipuu method for preparing animal skin and details on the techniques of porcupine quillwork. There is also Allen Slick-poo Sr.'s 1995 description of the sacred qualities of the shirt.[7] Multiple detailed photographs of the shirt taken by Zach Mazur feature the horse-hair wrapped rosette and panels of quillwork on the shoulders. Sharing this research in consultation with the Nez Perce Tribe on the Plateau Peoples' Web Portal is one way I hope to honor the Nez Perce Tribe's research process.

In the decades after the purchase of the Spalding-Allen Collection, the larger, rarer pieces in the collection continued to increase in monetary value. In a 2011 appraisal to determine replacement value of the items for insurance purposes, Paul Raczka valued the man's quilled and beaded shirt at an eye-popping $2.5 million while the second man's shirt with more damage to the sleeves was listed at $1.5 million and the two women's dresses were each valued at $500,000.

While these values reflect the excellent provenance and condition of the Spalding-Allen Collection, the marketplace largely harms traditional communities and limits their access to their material culture—key for continuing lifeways. In the case of the Spalding-Allen Collection, multimillion dollar appraisals also burden the Tribe and the National Park Service, who share the expense of insuring the collections.

The next time you visit a non-Native museum and see exhibits of Native American material culture, take note. Consider the provenance of the collections. Is the collection where it should be? Are Native voices present in the curation of the objects? Does the museum fully and ethically collaborate with source communities? Acknowledging colonialist collecting traditions is an important first step. How we—as non-Natives—redress this past is critical.

We are so entrenched in the legacies of these collecting practices that sometimes it is difficult to remove ourselves. Working for so many years as a librarian and archivist, I rarely give a second thought in naming a collection—it's almost always by the creator or collector of a collection. In January 2020, in a conversation with Nakia Williamson-Cloud, prior to an art installation titled "Schaenexw (Salmon) Run," created by Lummi Nation artist Dan Friday in the WSU Terrell Library Atrium, Williamson-Cloud remarked on the problematic nature of calling the collection the Spalding-Allen Collection in the first place. Spalding never made any of the items; instead, he took them in the context of religious instruction that said traditional Nez Perce culture was evil. But, in the end, Spalding used this collection for his own benefit, to support his mission. Why then do we still call it the Spalding-Allen Collection? This made complete sense to me; however, I had not considered it in this way until he spoke. Bill Picard posed a similar question: if the regalia was evil, why did Spalding keep it? "That's the part that…always gets me is that he tells them how bad they are…it's like tricking your little brother. Telling him…'You don't want this candy. It's terrible. That's the worst kind of stuff.' And so you convince your little brother that it's bad, and then you eat his candy. You know? I mean, that's kind of what Henry Spalding did here."[8]

In March 2021, I received a letter from Julie Kane, chair of the Planning Committee for Renaming the Spalding-Allen Collection, inviting me to participate in one of a series of programs to mark the twenty-fifth anniversary of the repatriation of the Spalding-Allen Collection. Tisa Matheson spoke at the first program, providing her perspectives on how the collection has influenced her cultural practices. The next event featured Nakia Williamson-Cloud's reflections on the impact the collection has had in his life. For the next program, I joined Josiah Pinkham, Kevin Peters, Lynnette Pinkham, and Bob Chenoweth as part of a panel discussion on the legacy of the Spalding-Allen Collection. The final event of the series on June 26 included a ceremony renaming the collection in Nimipuutimt, thereby highlighting the community's role in creating and bringing the collection home. After careful deliberation, the name selected was *wetxuuwíitin'* which means "returned after period of captivity."

Acknowledgments

I owe a great debt to Dr. Tabitha (Beth) Erdey and Robert (Bob) Chenoweth at the Nez Perce National Historical Park (NEPE). Beth Erdey processed the bulk of archival records that made this research possible. She also provided access to images and put me in touch with many of my interviewees. Bob Chenoweth recorded a wonderful interview regarding the Spalding-Allen Collection, provided comments on an early draft of this manuscript, and preserved boxes of valuable documents. Linda Paisano at NEPE also kindly recorded an interview. I am thankful to Dean Jay Starratt for his support in trusting me to balance my research and other responsibilities while working full time.

This project would not have been possible without Nez Perce voices. Thanks to Nakia Williamson-Cloud and Josiah Pinkham for steering me through the Nez Perce research permit process and for recording expansive interviews. I am also deeply indebted to Bill Picard and Kevin Peters who shared their knowledge in oral histories. I appreciate Julie Kane for speaking to me of her memories of the events of the campaign.

Thanks also to Lesley Poling, registrar at the Ohio Historical Society; Amos Loveday, former curator of collections at the Ohio Historical Society; Bob Carroll, retired OHS board member; Ken Grossi, archivist at Oberlin College; and Ashley Morton, at the Fort Walla Walla Museum. Leah Pepin at the Burke Museum assisted with several details. Frank Walker and Susan Buchel, now retired from the National Park Service, graciously recorded interviews.

Melissa Sarlin and Bill Huntington at Whitman College sent the Spalding and Allen correspondence. Before revising the manuscript into the present book, it was first a dissertation. I was fortunate to have a patient and stellar committee Robert McCoy (chair), Jeff Sanders, Jennifer Thigpen, and Bob Bauman. Noriko Kawamura read an early draft as part of a writing seminar.

I want to thank the external reviewers and Washington State University Press, especially Linda Bathgate, for their careful labor to improve the manuscript. It was important to me also to work with the only academic press operating on the Nez Perce Tribe's ancestral lands.

I am fortunate to be a part of a community of scholars, notably Kimberley Christen, Will Hamlin, Debbie Lee, Alex Merrill, Roberta Paul, and Nicole Tonkovich. I am also grateful for Steven Grafe's scholarship on the Spalding-Allen Collection. Thanks to the Pettyjohn Fund in History for covering the costs of the excellent transcriptions created by Teresa Bergen and the beautiful photographs of the Spalding-Allen Collection taken by Zach Mazur. NEPE staff, including Bob Chenoweth, Beth Erdey, Linda Paisano, Kevin Peters, and Lynette Pinkham, took the collection temporarily off display and handled the items so that we could photograph them. During the long process of revising my dissertation into this book, J. Diane Pearson provided encouragement and corrected several errors. NEPE curator Kristine Leier shared updated catalog records of the collection.

My parents, James and Nancy Bond, remain a constant source of support, patiently assisting me through all of my educational endeavors. Most importantly my wonderful wife and partner, Robin Bond, encouraged me at every step, listened to my minute progress along the way, and continues to inspire me to be a better person.

Notes

Introduction

1. The Nez Perce people refer to themselves as Niimíipuu, meaning "the people." In the eighteenth century, French Canadian fur trappers mistakenly referred to the Niimíipuu as Nez Perce, French for pierced nose, although that was never a common practice in the community. In this book, I use Nez Perce and Niimíipuu interchangeably. Niimíipuu is the spelling preferred by the Niimíipuu language program.

2. Steven Grafe, "'Our Private Affairs in Way of Barter': Correspondence Between Dudley Allen and Henry Harmon Spalding, 1838–1848," *Idaho Yesterdays* 40, no. 3 (Fall 1996): 3. Spalding's original letter is held in the Oberlin College Library Archives.

3. Curtis M. Hinsley, "Collecting Cultures and Cultures of Collecting: The Lure of the American Southwest, 1880–1915," *Museum Anthropology* 16 (1992): 12.

4. Christian F. Feest, "American Indians and Ethnographic Collecting in Europe," *Museum Anthropology* 16 (1992): 7.

5. Plateau or Columbia Plateau refers to a geologic and geographic region that spans portions of the states of Washington, Oregon, and Idaho. The Plateau is bordered on the west by the Cascade Mountain Range and on the east by the Rocky Mountains. The Columbia River cuts through the region. The Plateau Indians are the Indigenous tribes that inhabit the region.

6. Lucullus V. McWhorter, *Yellow Wolf: His Own Story* (Caldwell, ID: Caxton Printers, 1940) was the first account of the 1877 war to include Nez Perce voices. His *Hear Me, My Chiefs! Nez Perce Legend & History* (Caldwell, ID: Caxton Printers, 1952), published posthumously, is an expansive work that includes early Nez Perce history and legend but ends with the aftermath of the 1877 conflict. See also Merrill D. Beal, *"I Will Fight No More Forever": Chief Joseph and the Nez Perce War* (Seattle: University of Washington Press, 1963). Alvin Josephy devotes only two pages of his magisterial *The Nez Perce Indians and the Opening of the Northwest* (New Haven and London: Yale University Press, 1965) to Nez Perce history after the death of Chief Joseph. Robert R McCoy, *Chief Joseph, Yellow Wolf, and the Creation of Nez Perce History in the Pacific Northwest* (New York: Routledge, 2004) analyzes the narratives of the 1877 war in the popular and scholarly press prior to Lucullus McWhorter. For recent treatments of the conflict, see Elliott West, *The Last Indian War: The Nez Perce Story* (New York: Oxford University Press, 2011); Kevin Carson, *The Long Journey of the Nez Perce: A Battle History from Cottonwood to the Bear Paw* (Yardley, PA: Westholme Publishers, 2011) and; Allen Pinkham and Steven Evans, *Lewis and Clark among the Nez Perce: Strangers in the Land of the Nimíipuu* (Washburn, ND: The Dakota Institute, 2015). For the aftermath of the war: J. Diane Pearson, *The Nez Perces in the Indian Territory: Nimiipuu Survival* (Norman: University of Oklahoma Press, 2008) and Willard William, Alan Marshall, and J. Diane Pearson, *Rising from the Ashes: Survival, Sovereignty, and Native America* (Lincoln: University of Nebraska Press, 2020); and three more recent works on the Nez Perce Reservation allotment: Nicole Tonkovich, *The Allotment Plot: Alice C. Fletcher, E. Jane Gay, and Nez Perce Survivance* (Lincoln: University of Nebraska Press, 2012) and *Dividing the Reservation: Alice C. Fletcher's Nez Perce Allotment Diaries and Letters 1889–1892* (Pullman: Washington State University Press, 2016), and Emily Greenwald, *Reconfiguring the Reservation: The Nez Perces, Jicarilla Apaches, and the Dawes Act* (Albuquerque: University of New Mexico Press, 2002).

7. The AAM Code of Ethics for Museums was adopted in 1993 by the AAM Board of Directors and amended in 2000. "AAM Code of Ethics for Museums," accessed December 30, 2020, https://www.aam-us.org/programs/ethics-standards-and-professional-practices/code-of -ethics-for-museums/.

8. Rand Jimerson, *Archives Power: Memory, Accountability, and Social Justice* (Chicago: Society of American Archivists, 2009), 355–358.

9. "SAA Council Endorsement of Protocols for Native American Archival Materials," Society of American Archivists, accessed September 30, 2019, https://www2.archivists.org/statements/saa-council-endorsement-of-protocols-for-native-american-archival-materials.

10. Carol Zimmer, "New Study Links Kennewick Man to Native Americans," *New York Times*, June 19, 2015.

11. Rob Hotakainen, "Skeleton of Kennewick Man Could Soon Go to Washington State Tribes," *Olympian*, September 16, 2016; Burke Museum, "The Ancient One, Kennewick Man," News & Stories, December 16, 2016, accessed January 5, 2017, http://www.burkemuseum.org/blog/kennewick-man-ancient-one.

12. Annette Cary, "Tribes Encouraged that Kennewick Man Will Be Reburied," *Tri-City Herald*, August 19, 2015.

13. Max Carocci, "Review Essay: Changing Debates in Museum Studies since NAGPRA," *Transmotion* 4, no. 1 (2018): 127.

14. Chip Colwell, "Can Repatriation Heal the Wounds of History?" *The Public Historian* 41, no. 1 (2019): 99.

15. Colwell, "Can Repatriation Heal the Wounds of History?" 90.

16. Dylan Brown, "The Spoils of Wars and Massacres: NAGPRA 25 Years Later," Indian Country Today Media Network, June 9, 2015, accessed December 30, 2020, https://indiancountrytoday.com/archive/the-spoils-of-wars-and-massacres-nagpra-25-years-later-KXYPt6NOtUSGAoo5BhnonA.

17. Brown, "The Spoils of Wars and Massacres."

18. Frank Walker, Oral History Interview, June 2, 2015.

19. Amy Margaris and Linda Grimm, "Collecting for a College Museum: Exchange Practices and the Life History of a 19th-Century Arctic Collection," *Museum Anthropology* 34, no. 2 (2011): 109, 112.

20. Christian F. Feest, "American Indians and Ethnographic Collecting in Europe," *Museum Anthropology* 16 (1992): 7.

21. Donald Ritchie, *Doing Oral History: A Practical Guide* (Oxford and New York: Oxford University Press, 2003), 40.

22. The Nez Perce Research Permit form is available online at https://www.nezperce.org/government/natural-resources.

23. For examples of their work, see Bob Chenoweth and Tabitha Erdey, *Nuunimnix: An Exhibition in Celebration of the Fiftieth Anniversary of the Nez Perce National Historical Park* (Lewiston: Confluence Press, 2015), 24–26, 35–37, 41–44.

24. Steven Ross Evans, *Voice of the Old Wolf: Lucullus Virgil McWhorter and the Nez Perce Indians* (Pullman: Washington State University Press, 1996), 2.

25. Trevor James Bond, "From Treasure Room to Archives: The McWhorter Papers and the State College of Washington," *Pacific Northwest Quarterly* 102, no. 2 (2011): 69.

26. See the foreword by Diane Mallickan, *Encounters with the People: Written and Oral Accounts of Nez Perce Life to 1858*, ed. Dennis Baird, Diane Mallickan, and William R. Swagerty (Pullman: Washington State University Press, 2015), xii.

27. Kimberly Christen, "Opening Archives: Respectful Repatriation," *American Archivist* 74, no. 1 (2011): 185–210.

28. "Spalding Allen Collection," Plateau Peoples' Web Portal, accessed April 30, 2020, https://plateauportal.libraries.wsu.edu/collection/spalding-allen-collection-nez-perce.

29. These chapters appeared as articles in the *Oregon Historical Quarterly* and the *Pacific Northwest History Quarterly*.

30. Nakia Williamson-Cloud, Oral History Interview, May 14, 2015.

31. Constance Classen and David Howes, "The Museum as Sensescape: Western Sensibilities and Indigenous Artifacts," in *Sensible Objects: Colonialism, Museums and Material Culture*, ed. Elizabeth Edwards, Chris Gosden, and Ruth Phillips (Abingdon, UK: Routledge, 2006), 199–222, 200.

Chapter 1 The Nez Perce and the Missionary Collector

1. Alvin Josephy, *The Nez Perce Indians and the Opening of the Northwest* (New Haven and London: Yale University Press, 1965), 145.

2. Josephy, *The Nez Perce Indians*, 15.

3. Deward Walker, "Nez Perce," in *Handbook of North American Indians*, vol. 12, ed. William Sturtevant (Washington, DC: Smithsonian Institution, 1998), 425, 420.

4. Deward Walker, "Nez Perce," 425.

5. Archie Phinney, *Nez Perce Texts* (New York: Columbia University Press, 1934): 27–29; Ted Catton, *Nez Perce National Historical Park Administrative History* (Missoula: Historical Research Associates, 1996), 1.

6. Josephy, *The Nez Perce Indians*, 16–17.

7. Alan Marshall and Samuel Watters, "Nimiipuu at the Edge of History," in *Rising from the Ashes: Survival, Sovereignty, and Native America*, edited by William Willard, Alan G. Marshall, and J. Diane Pearson (Lincoln: University of Nebraska Press, 2020), 10.

8. Allen Pinkham and Steven Evans, *Lewis and Clark Among the Nez Perce: Strangers in the Land of the Nimiipuu* (Washburn: The Dakota Institute, 2015), 34.

9. Pinkham and Evans, *Lewis and Clark Among the Nez Perce*, 429.

10. Dennis Baird, Diane Mallickan, and William R. Swagerty, *Encounters with the People: Written and Oral Accounts of Nez Perce Life to 1858* (Pullman: Washington State University Press, 2015), 173. See pages 173–93 for various primary sources recounting the visit in the East.

11. Albert Furtwangler, *Bringing Indians to the Book* (London and Seattle: University of Washington Press, 2005), 14–15.

12. Nakia Williamson-Cloud, Oral History Interview, May 14, 2015.

13. Jacqueline Peterson and Laura Peers, *Sacred Encounters: Father De Smet and the Indians of the Rocky Mountain West: A Catalogue of the Exhibition* (Norman and London: University of Oklahoma Press, 1993), 83.

14. Steven Grafe, "'Our Private Affairs in Way of Barter': Correspondence Between Dudley Allen and Henry Harmon Spalding, 1838–1848." *Idaho Yesterdays* 40, no. 3 (Fall 1996): 22.

15. Steven Grafe, *The Origins of Floral-Design Beadwork in the Southern Columbia River Plateau*. PhD diss. Albuquerque: University of New Mexico, 1999, 347.

16. Clifford Drury, *Pioneer of Old Oregon: Henry Harmon Spalding* (Caldwell, ID: Caxton Printers, 1936), 91–92, 144–61.

17. Baird et al., *Encounters with the People*, 211.

18. Baird et al., *Encounters with the People*, 211.

19. Williamson-Cloud, Oral History Interview.

20. Genevieve McCoy, "The Difficulties of Translating Mission Theory into Practice: The Whitman-Spalding Nez Perce Mission," *The Journal of Presbyterian History* 77, no. 3 (Fall 1999): 185.

21. Clifford Drury, *The Diaries and Letters of Henry H. Spalding and Asa Bowen Smith relating to the Nez Perce Mission 1838–1842* (Glendale, CA: Arthur H. Clark Company, 1958), 166–67.

22. Elliott West, *The Last Indian War: The Nez Perce Story* (New York: Oxford University Press, 2011), 43.

23. West, *The Last Indian War*, 43.

24. Drury, *The Diaries and Letters of Henry H. Spalding and Asa Bowen Smith*, 278.

25. Drury, *Pioneer of Old Oregon: Henry Harmon Spalding*, 167.

26. Walker, "Nez Perce," 433.

27. West, *The Last Indian War*, 45–46.

28. Chip Colwell, "Curating Secrets: Repatriation, Knowledge Flows, and Museum Power Structures," *Current Anthropology* 56, no. 12 (2015): 267, 268.

29. Jennifer K. Bauer, "How the Nez Perce Tribe Got a Valuable Collection of Artifacts Back Against All Odds," *Inland 360*, August 12, 2020.

Chapter 2 Collecting Native American Material Culture

1. Bob Chenoweth and Tabitha Erdey, *Nuunimnix: An Exhibition in Celebration of the Fiftieth Anniversary of the Nez Perce National Historical Park* (Lewiston: Confluence Press, 2015), xii.

2. Constance Classen and David Howes, "The Museum as Sensescape: Western Sensibilities and Indigenous Artifacts," in *Sensible Objects: Colonialism, Museums and Material Culture*, ed. Elizabeth Edwards, Chris Gosden, and Ruth Phillips, 199–222. (London: Routledge, 2006), 209.

3. Christian F. Feest, "American Indians and Ethnographic Collecting in Europe," *Museum Anthropology* 16 (1992): 8.

4. Feest, "American Indians and Ethnographic Collecting in Europe," 8.

5. Chenoweth and Erdey, *Nuunimnix*, xii.

6. Feest, "American Indians and Ethnographic Collecting in Europe," 8. For an overview of the European tradition of creating cabinets of curiosities, see Patrick Mauries, *Cabinet of Curiosities* (London: Thames & Hudson, 2002), 7–67.

7. Chenoweth and Erdey, *Nuunimnix*, xiii.

8. Rick Kearns, "This Aztec Headdress Came to Europe 500 Years Ago: It Can't Go Home," Indian Country Today Media Network, July 2, 2014, accessed January 6, 2021, https://indiancountrytoday.com/archive/this-aztec-headdress-came-to-europe-500-years-ago-it-can-t-go-home-9RMNgpQw7E--z6Cwdmp8Bg.

9. Robin K. Wright, "A Collection History: Washington Native Art," in *A Time of Gathering*, ed. Robin K. Wright (Seattle: Burke Museum and University of Washington Press, 1991), 32.

10. Wright, "A Collection History," 32.

11. Wright, "A Collection History," 33–34.

12. John Francis McDermott, "William Clark: Pioneer Museum Man," *Journal of the Washington Academy of Sciences* 44, no. 11 (November 1954): 370, 373.

13. Wright, "A Collection History," 33–34.

14. Wright, "A Collection History," 33–34.

15. Feest, "American Indians and Ethnographic Collecting in Europe," 10.

16. Feest, "American Indians and Ethnographic Collecting in Europe," 11.

Chapter 3 The Spaldings and the Allens

1. Steven Grafe, "'Our Private Affairs in Way of Barter': Correspondence Between Dudley Allen and Henry Harmon Spalding, 1838-1848." *Idaho Yesterdays* 40, no. 3 (Fall 1996), 6.

2. Clifford Drury, *Pioneer of Old Oregon: Henry Harmon Spalding* (Caldwell, ID: Caxton Printers, 1936), 271.

3. Clifford Drury, *The Diaries and Letters of Henry H. Spalding and Asa Bowen Smith Relating to the Nez Perce Mission 1838–1842* (Glendale, CA: Arthur H. Clark Company, 1958), 313.

4. Steven Grafe, *The Origins of Floral-Design Beadwork in the Southern Columbia River Plateau.* PhD diss. Albuquerque: University of New Mexico, 1999, 347.

5. Henry Spalding to Dudley Allen, April 29, 1843, Spalding Collection, Whitman College Archives.

6. Grafe, "Our Private Affairs in Way of Barter," 8.

7. Grafe, "Our Private Affairs in Way of Barter," 9.

8. Joan Abrams, "Tribal Members Head to Ohio: Journey Is Part of Quest to Keep Nez Perce Artifacts Near Tribe; Documents Raise New Questions About Claim to Collection," *Lewiston Tribune*, December 10, 1995.

9. Robert Fletcher, "The Spaulding-Allen Indian Collection." *The Oberlin Alumni Magazine* 26 (February 1930): 138; Grafe, "Our Private Affairs in Way of Barter," 4.

10. Grafe, "Our Private Affairs in Way of Barter," 4.

11. Grafe, "Our Private Affairs in Way of Barter," 4.

12. Grafe, "Our Private Affairs in Way of Barter," 5.

13. Jacqueline Peterson and Laura Peers, *Sacred Encounters: Father De Smet and the Indians of the Rocky Mountain West: A Catalogue of the Exhibition* (Norman and London: University of Oklahoma Press, 1993), 63.

14. Grafe, "Our Private Affairs in Way of Barter," 8.

15. Peterson and Peers, *Sacred Encounters*, 63.

16. Josiah Pinkham, Oral History Interview, May 14, 2015.

17. Grafe, "Our Private Affairs in Way of Barter," 5.

18. Bob Chenoweth, Oral History Interview, February 17, 2015.

19. Nez Perce National Historical Park, box 34 folder 9, Resource Management Records 1936–2002, NEPE-00638.

20. Drury, *The Diaries and Letters of Henry H. Spalding and Asa Bowen Smith*, 292.

21. Drury, *The Diaries and Letters of Henry H. Spalding and Asa Bowen Smith*, 330.

22. Nakia Williamson-Cloud, Oral History Interview, May 14, 2015.

23. Jennifer K. Bauer, "How the Nez Perce Tribe Got A Valuable Collection of Artifacts Back Against All Odds," *Inland 360*, August 12, 2020.

24. S. S. Kasprycki, "The Native American Collection of Friderik Baraga: The Missionary as Ethnographic Collector," *Etnolog* 8, no. 59 (1998): 335, 342.

25. Bill Picard, Oral History Interview, June 2, 2015.

26. Picard, Oral History Interview.

27. Pinkham, Oral History Interview.

28. Williamson-Cloud, Oral History Interview.

29. Fletcher, "The Spaulding-Allen Indian Collection," 138.

30. Grafe, "Our Private Affairs in Way of Barter," 11–12.

31. The catalog numbers for the hat and the baskets are NEPE 34570, 34571, 34572, 34573.

32. During their journey across the Pacific Ocean to the West Coast of the American continent, members of the Wilkes expedition visited 280 islands and charted 800 miles of the Oregon Country. They also collected 60,000 plant and bird specimens that later went to the Smithsonian Institution. Authorized by Congress in 1836 during the administration of Andrew Johnson, the United States Exploring Expedition of 1838–1842 was commanded by Navy lieutenant Charles Wilkes.

33. Jack Nisbet, "Henry and Eliza's Box of Flowers," *The North Columbia Monthly* (April 2014), 3; J. Orin Oliphant, "The Botanical Labors of the Reverend Henry H. Spalding," *Washington Historical Quarterly* 25, no. 2 (1934): 95.

34. Oliphant, "The Botanical Labors of the Reverend Henry H. Spalding," 93.

35. Henry Spalding to David Greene, June 6, 1846, quoted in Oliphant, "The Botanical Labors of the Reverend Henry H. Spalding," 98–99; Nisbet, "Henry and Eliza's Box of Flowers," 3.

36. Nisbet, "Henry and Eliza's Box of Flowers," 5.

37. Curtis M. Hinsley, "Collecting Cultures and Cultures of Collecting: The Lure of the American Southwest, 1880–1915," *Museum Anthropology* 16 (1992), 13.

38. Grafe, "Our Private Affairs in Way of Barter," 12.

39. Deward Walker, "Nez Perce." In *Handbook of North American Indians*, vol. 12, edited by William Sturtevant. (Washington DC: Smithsonian Institution, 1998), 422.

40. Chenoweth, Oral History Interview.

41. Allen Slickpoo and Deward Walker, *Noon Nee-Me-Poo (We, the Nez Perces): Culture and History of the Nez Perces* (Nez Perce Tribe of Idaho, 1973), 72.

42. Pinkham, Oral History Interview.

43. Drury, *Pioneer of Old Oregon: Henry Harmon Spalding*, 180–81; quoted in Trevor James Bond, "The Hunt for Oregon Missionary Sources: Clifford M. Drury's Enduring Archives Legacy," *Oregon Historical Quarterly* 114, no. 1, 54.

44. Picard, Oral History Interview.

45. Walker, "Nez Perce," 434.

46. Pinkham, Oral History Interview.

47. Drury, *Pioneer of Old Oregon: Henry Harmon Spalding*, 272.

48. Pinkham, Oral History Interview.

49. Richard Campen, *Architecture of the Western Reserve 1800–1900* (Cleveland and London: Press of Case Western Reserve University, 1971), 168.

Chapter 4 The Ohio Years: From an Indian Cabinet of Curiosities to Oberlin College

1. Kent Richards, *Isaac I. Stevens: Young Man in a Hurry* (Pullman: Washington State University Press, 2016), 202–211.

2. Richards, *Isaac I. Stevens*, 209.

3. Steven Evans, *Voice of the Old Wolf: Lucullus Virgil McWhorter and the Nez Perce Indians* (Pullman: Washington State University Press, 1996), 11–12.

4. J. Diane Pearson, "Nimiipuu Peoplehood, Survival, and the Indian Territory," in *Rising from the Ashes: Survival, Sovereignty, and Native America*, ed. William Willard, Alan G. Marshall, and J. Diane Pearson (Lincoln: University of Nebraska Press, 2020), 31–32.

5. Nicole Tonkovich, *Dividing the Reservation: Alice C. Fletcher's Nez Perce Allotment Diaries and Letters 1889–1892* (Pullman: Washington State University Press, 2016), 3.

6. Bob Chenoweth and Tabitha Erdey, *Nuunimníx: An Exhibition in Celebration of the Fiftieth Anniversary of the Nez Perce National Historical Park* (Lewiston: Confluence Press, 2015), xiv.

7. Nicole Tonkovich, *Dividing the Reservation*, 101–102.

8. Evans, *Voice of the Old Wolf*, 13–14.

9. "Indian Materials Taken from Accession List," folder 5, box 34, Oberlin College Department of Zoology Resource Management Records 1936–2002, NEPE-00638, Nez Perce National Historical Park, Lapwai, Idaho.

10. Mary Jane Lenz, "George Gustav Heye: The Museum of the American Indian," in *Spirit of a Native Place: Building the National Museum of the American Indian*, ed. Duane Blue Spruce (Washington, DC: National Museum of the American Indian, Smithsonian Institution, in association with National Geographic, 2004), 87–89.

11. Lenz, "George Gustav Heye," 89–95.

12. Robert Fletcher, "The Spaulding-Allen Indian Collection." *The Oberlin Alumni Magazine* 26 (February 1930): 139.

13. Clifford Drury letter to E. O. Holland, August 15, 1935, box 1, folder 2, cage 144, Drury Papers, Washington State University Libraries, Manuscripts, Archives, and Special Collections, Pullman.

Chapter 5 A Return to Self-Governance

1. James Patterson, *Grand Expectations: The United States, 1945–1974* (New York and Oxford: Oxford University Press, 1996), 376.

2. Patterson, *Grand Expectations*, 376; Bob Chenoweth and Tabitha Erdey, *Nuunimníx: An Exhibition in Celebration of the Fiftieth Anniversary of the Nez Perce National Historical Park* (Lewiston: Confluence Press, 2015), xiv.

3. Revised Constitution and Bylaws of the Nez Perce Tribe of Idaho, box 2, folder 10, cage 515, Theodor Little Papers, Washington State University Libraries, Manuscripts, Archives, and Special Collections, Pullman.

4. Ted Catton, *Nez Perce National Historical Park Administrative History* (Missoula: Historical Research Associates, 1996), 9.

5. The committee approved the loan on September 21, 1942. Oberlin College Archives, Oberlin, Ohio.

6. Carl Wittke letter to Harry Shetrone, October 22, 1942, box 34, folder 5, Resource Management Records 1936–2002, NEPE-00638, Nez Perce National Historical Park, Lapwai, Idaho.

Chapter 6 Asserting Their Rights

1. List of the materials transferred between the Oberlin Zoological Museum and the Dudley Allen Art Museum, 1958, box 34, folder 5, Resource Management Records 1936–2002, NEPE-00638, Nez Perce National Historical Park, Lapwai, Idaho.

2. Untitled speech delivered by Theodore Little, Nez Perce tribal attorney, Clarkston, Washington, July 6, 1962, cage 515, Theodore Little Papers, Washington State University Libraries, Manuscripts, Archives, and Special Collections, Pullman.

3. Theodore Little Papers, Untitled Speech.

4. "Indian Is Upheld in Fishing Case," *Lewiston Morning Tribune*, December 15, 1967.

5. "Nets Above Dam Get Approval," *The Dalles Chronicle*, December 15, 1967.

6. "Spalding-Allen Collection Revisited," July 27, 1993, box 34, folder 5, Resource Management Records 1936–2002, NEPE-00638, Nez Perce National Historical Park, Lapwai, Idaho.

7. "Spalding-Allen Collection Revisited."

Chapter 7 Raising Their Voices: A Portrait of Two Institutions

1. Bob Chenoweth, "The Spalding-Allen Collection," Bob Chenoweth Papers, Unprocessed, Nez Perce National Historical Park, Lapwai, Idaho.

2. Mark Papworth to Jack Williams, March 23, 1970, box 12, folder 11, Resource Management Records 1936–2002, NEPE-00638, Nez Perce National Historical Park, Lapwai, Idaho.

3. George Purdy, son of Doris Purdy, posted the film on YouTube: *Occupation of Alcatraz, 11-29-1969*, accessed November 13, 2016, https://www.youtube.com/watch?v=1md5YYKl-9g.

4. James Patterson, *Grand Expectations: The United States, 1945–1974* (New York and Oxford: Oxford University Press, 1996), 722.

5. George Horse Capture, "Introduction: The Way of the People," in *Spirit of a Native Place: Building the National Museum of the American Indian*, ed. Duane Blue Spruce (Washington, DC: National Museum of the American Indian, Smithsonian Institution, in association with National Geographic, 2004), 36.

6. Bob Chenoweth and Tabitha Erdey, *Nuunimnix: An Exhibition in Celebration of the Fiftieth Anniversary of the Nez Perce National Historical Park* (Lewiston, ID: Confluence Press, 2015), xvi.

7. Brad Baker to Roderick Sprague, September 23, 1978, box 12, folder 11, Resource Management Records 1936–2002, NEPE-00638, Nez Perce National Historical Park, Lapwai, Idaho.

8. Chenoweth, "The Spalding-Allen Collection"; OHS Director to OHS Curator of Archaeology, October 20, 1978, Allen Memorial Art Museum, Oberlin.

9. Chenoweth, "The Spalding-Allen Collection"; Superintendent to OHS Director, January 10, 1979, Nez Perce National Historical Park, Lapwai, Idaho.

10. Richard Spear to Raymond Baby, October 20, 1978, box 12, folder 11, Resource Management Records 1936–2002, NEPE-00638, Nez Perce National Historical Park, Lapwai, Idaho.

11. Martha Potter Otto to Emil Daneberg, May 10, 1979, box 9, Ohio Historical Society 1979, external organizations folder, Emil C. Daneberg Series X, Record Group 2/11, Oberlin College Archives.

12. Emil Daneberg to Leslie H. Fishel, May 26, 1979, box 9, Ohio Historical Society 1979, external organizations folder, Emil C. Daneberg Series X, Record Group 2/11, Oberlin College Archives.

13. Russell Dickenson to Thomas Smith, July 18, 1979, box 12, folder 11, Resource Management Records 1936–2002, NEPE-00638, Nez Perce National Historical Park, Lapwai, Idaho.

14. Richard Halfmoon to Amos Loveday, November 13, 1979, box 34, folder 4, Resource Management Records 1936–2002, NEPE-00638, Nez Perce National Historical Park, Lapwai, Idaho.

15. Christopher Maag, "Vanishing History," *Monthly Columbus Magazine* (November 2009), accessed December 31, 2020, https://www.columbusmonthly.com/article/20140206/NEWS/302068650.

16. Ohio Historical Society, *Annual Report: Fiscal Year 2004*, 5.

17. Ted Catton, *Nez Perce National Historical Park Administrative History* (Missoula: Historical Research Associates, 1996), 5.

18. Catton, *Nez Perce National Historical Park Administrative History*, 45.

19. Chenoweth, "The Spalding-Allen Collection."

20. Chenoweth, "The Spalding-Allen Collection."

21. Bob Chenoweth, Oral History Interview, February 17, 2015.

22. Chenoweth, "The Spalding-Allen Collection."

23. Park officials did invest in fire and burglar alarms as well as heaters and humidifiers for the structure. Catton, *Nez Perce National Historical Park Administrative History*, 91.

24. Susan Buchel, Oral History Interview, October 22, 2015.

25. Catton, *Nez Perce National Historical Park Administrative History*, 91–93.

26. Buchel, Oral History Interview.

27. Buchel, Oral History Interview.

28. Elin Woodger and David Burg, *The 1980s* (New York: Facts on File, 2006), 14–15.

29. Douglas Evelyn, "'A Most Beautiful Sight Presented Itself to My View': The Long Return to a Native Place on the Mall," in *Spirit of a Native Place: Building the National Museum of the American Indian*, ed. Duane Blue Spruce (Washington, DC: National Museum of the American Indian, Smithsonian Institution, in association with National Geographic, 2004), 182–83.

30. Evelyn, "'A Most Beautiful Sight Presented Itself to My View,'" 183.

31. Evelyn, "'A Most Beautiful Sight Presented Itself to My View,'" 183.

Chapter 8 From Loan to Recall

1. Frank Walker, Oral History Interview, June 2, 2015.

2. Public Law L. 101-601, 16 November 1990, accessed December 31, 2020, https://www.govinfo.gov/content/pkg/STATUTE-104/pdf/STATUTE-104-Pg3048.pdf.

3. Rita Reif, "3 Masks to Stay in Auction," *New York Times*, May 21, 1991.

4. W. Richard West Jr., "As Long as We Keep Dancing: A Brief Personal History," in *Spirit of a Native Place: Building the National Museum of the American Indian*, ed. Duane Blue Spruce (Washington, DC: National Museum of the American Indian, Smithsonian Institution, in association with National Geographic, 2004), 55–56.

5. Moshin Askari, "Indian Culture Treasured Remnants of the Nez Perces: Artifacts at Spalding In Jeopardy Unless Deal Is Struck with Ohio Society That Owns Them," *Lewiston Morning Tribune*, September 19, 1993.

6. Ted Catton, *Nez Perce National Historical Park Administrative History* (Missoula: Historical Research Associates, 1996), 94.

7. Susan Buchel, Oral History Interview, October 22, 2015.

8. Amos Loveday, email to author, February 19, 2015.

9. Houser, Admx., Appellee v. Ohio Historical Society, Appellant no. 79-988.

10. Robin Wright to Gary Ness, July 25, 1988, Administrative Records, Burke Museum, Seattle, Washington.

11. Robin Wright to Gary Ness, July 25, 1988.

12. Buchel, Oral History Interview.

13. Buchel, Oral History Interview.

14. Jacqueline Peterson and Laura Peers, *Sacred Encounters: Father De Smet and the Indians of the Rocky Mountain West* (Norman and London: University of Oklahoma Press, 1993).

15. Jacqueline Peterson to Melinda Knapp, April 6, 1990, box 5, Jacqueline Peterson Papers, MS2012.03, Washington State University Libraries, Manuscripts, Archives, and Special Collections, Pullman.

16. Melinda Knapp to Jeffrey Pavelka, May 17, 1992, exhibition coordinator, box 5, Washington State University Libraries, Manuscripts, Archives, and Special Collections, Pullman.

17. Pierre Jean De Smet was a Jesuit missionary and a key part of the Sacred Encounters exhibit; Buchel, Oral History Interview.

18. Jeffery Pavelka fax to Jacqueline Peterson, May 12, 1992, box 5, Washington State University Libraries, Manuscripts, Archives, and Special Collections, Pullman.

19. Frank Walker and Amos Loveday, record of telephone conversation, June 9, 1992, box 34, folder 4, Resource Management Records 1936–2002, NEPE-00638, Nez Perce National Historical Park, Lapwai, Idaho.

20. Frank Walker, Oral History Interview, June 2, 2015.

21. Frank Walker to Gary Ness, June 10, 1992, box 34, folder 4, Resource Management Records 1936–2002, NEPE-00638, Nez Perce National Historical Park, Lapwai, Idaho.

22. Frank Walker and Gary Ness, record of telephone conversation, June 12, 1992, box 34, folder 4, Resource Management Records 1936–2002, NEPE-00638, Nez Perce National Historical Park, Lapwai, Idaho.

23. Walker memorandum, October 20, 1992, box 34, folder 4, Resource Management Records 1936–2002, NEPE-00638, Nez Perce National Historical Park, Lapwai, Idaho.

24. Dr. George Carroll conversation with author, February 27, 2015.

25. Amos Loveday, email to the author, February 19, 2015.

26. Walker, Oral History Interview.

27. Jennifer K. Bauer, "How the Nez Perce Tribe Got a Valuable Collection of Artifacts Back against All Odds," *Inland 360*, August 12, 2020.

28. Buchel, Oral History Interview.

29. Frank Walker, email to regional director Charles Odegaard, March 16, 1993, box 34, folder 5, Resource Management Records 1936–2002, NEPE-00638, Nez Perce National Historical Park, Lapwai, Idaho.

30. Susan Buchel, email to Bill Walters, Kent Bush, and Stephanie Toothman, March 15, 1993, box 34, folder 5, Resource Management Records 1936–2002, NEPE-00638, Nez Perce National Historical Park, Lapwai, Idaho.

31. Buchel, Oral History Interview.

32. Moshin Askari, "Nez Perce Tribal General Council Committee to Focus on Threatened Artifacts: Negotiations to Keep Spalding Collection Rile Several Council Members," *Lewiston Tribune*, September 25, 1993.

33. Askari, "Nez Perce Tribal General Council Committee to Focus on Threatened Artifacts."

34. Memorandum of understanding between Nez Perce Tribe and Department of the Interior National Park Service Nez Perce National Historical Park to bring about the acquisition of the Spalding-Allen Collection of Plateau Materials by the Nez Perce Tribe and ensure their long-term care. December 14, 1993, box 34, folder 5, Resource Management Records 1936–2002, NEPE-00638, Nez Perce National Historical Park, Lapwai, Idaho.

35. Agenda, joint meeting Ohio Historical Society, Nez Perce Tribe, National Park Service, May 3, 1994, box 34, folder 6, Resource Management Records 1936–2002, NEPE-00638, Nez Perce National Historical Park, Lapwai, Idaho.

36. Arthur Hathaway to Gary Ness, February 28, 1995, box 34, folder 7, Resource Management Records 1936–2002, NEPE-00638, Nez Perce National Historical Park, Lapwai, Idaho.

37. Gary Ness to Bill Walters, March 3, 1995, box 34, folder 7, Resource Management Records 1936–2002, NEPE-00638, Nez Perce National Historical Park, Lapwai, Idaho.

Chapter 9 Appraisals and Greed

1. Appraisal provided to the author by OHS registrar Leslie Pohling.

2. Paul Raczka, email to author, December 18, 2016.

3. Kevin Peters, Oral History Interview, July 12, 2015.

4. Josiah Pinkham, Oral History Interview, May 14, 2015.

5. Pinkham, Oral History Interview.

6. National Congress of American Indians "Support of the Nez Perce Tribe to Recover the Spaulding-Allen [*sic*] Collection," June 6–8, 1995, box 34, folder 5, Resource Management Records 1936–2002, NEPE-00638, Nez Perce National Historical Park, Lapwai, Idaho.

7. Samuel Penney to Gary Ness, June 1, 1995, box 34, folder 7, Resource Management Records 1936–2002, NEPE-00638, Nez Perce National Historical Park, Lapwai, Idaho.

8. Gary Ness to Samuel Penney, June 23, 1995, box 34, folder 7, Resource Management Records 1936–2002, NEPE-00638, Nez Perce National Historical Park, Lapwai, Idaho.

9. Frank Walker, Oral History Interview, June 2, 2015.

10. Gary Ness to Samuel Penney, June 23, 1995, box 34, folder 7, Resource Management Records 1936–2002, NEPE-00638, Nez Perce National Historical Park, Lapwai, Idaho.

11. Samuel Penney to Gary Ness, June 27, 1995, box 34, folder 7, Resource Management Records 1936–2002, NEPE-00638, Nez Perce National Historical Park, Lapwai, Idaho.

12. Associated Press, "Ohioans Recall Loan of Indian Artifacts," *Plain Dealer*, June 9, 1995, provided to the author by OHS registrar Leslie Pohling.

13. Joan Abrams, "Tribe Will Seek Help from Presbyterian Church to Purchase Museum Artifacts," *Lewiston Morning Tribune*, June 1, 1995.

14. Associated Press, "Historical Society Wants Artifacts Back," *Xenia Daily Gazette*, May 30, 1995.

15. Joan Abrams, "Tribe Will Seek Help from Presbyterian Church."

16. Associated Press, "Ohioans Recall Loan of Indian Artifacts," *Plain Dealer*, June 9, 1995.

17. Joan Abrams, "Spalding-Allen Collection: Tribe Ready to Make Offer," *Lewiston Morning Tribune*, July 30, 1995, box 34, folder 7, Resource Management Records 1936–2002, NEPE-00638, Nez Perce National Historical Park, Lapwai, Idaho.

18. Penney to Governor Batt and Governor Voinovic, October 12, 1995, box 34, folder 7, Resource Management Records 1936–2002, NEPE-00638, Nez Perce National Historical Park, Lapwai, Idaho.

19. Memorandum to Samuel N. Penney, NPTEC chairman, from Julie Kane, deputy counsel, Office of Legal Counsel, "Spalding-Allen Collection—Legal Analysis for Possible Repatriation Under NAGPRA," November 1, 1995, box 34, folder 7, Resource Management Records 1936–2002, NEPE-00638, Nez Perce National Historical Park, Lapwai, Idaho.

20. Bob Chenoweth Papers, Unprocessed, Nez Perce National Historical Park, Lapwai, Idaho.

21. Nakia Williamson-Cloud, Oral History Interview, May 14, 2015.

22. Bill Picard, Oral History Interview, June 2, 2015.

23. Email from Bob Chenoweth to NPTEC chairman Art Hathaway, August 16, 1995, box 69, folder 4, Resource Management Records 1936–2002, NEPE-00638, Nez Perce National Historical Park, Lapwai, Idaho.

24. National Park Service, "Spalding-Allen Collection Returns to Ohio," November 20, 1995, box 34, folder 9, Resource Management Records 1936–2002, NEPE-00638, Nez Perce National Historical Park, Lapwai, Idaho.

25. Joan Abrams, "Tribe to Request Restraining Order," *Lewiston Morning Tribune*, November 23, 1995.

26. Picard, Oral History Interview.

27. Jennifer K. Bauer, "How the Nez Perce Tribe Got a Valuable Collection of Artifacts Back Against All Odds," *Inland 360*, August 12, 2020.

28. "Nov. 27, 1995: A DAY OF SHAME," box 34, folder 9, Resource Management Records 1936–2002, NEPE-00638, Nez Perce National Historical Park, Lapwai, Idaho.

29. Allen Slickpoo Sr. "Insensitivity to the Native Religious, and Cultural Values," November 27, 1995, box 34, folder 9, Resource Management Records 1936–2002, NEPE-00638, Nez Perce National Historical Park, Lapwai, Idaho.

30. Allen Slickpoo Sr., "Insensitivity to the Native Religious, and Cultural Values."

31. Allen Slickpoo Sr. "Nez Perce Cultural Values of Spalding-Allen Artifact Collection," box 34, folder 9, Resource Management Records 1936–2002, NEPE-00638, Nez Perce National Historical Park, Lapwai, Idaho.

32. Allen Slickpoo Sr., "Nez Perce Cultural Values of Spalding-Allen Artifact Collection."

33. Allen Slickpoo Sr., "Nez Perce Cultural Values of Spalding-Allen Artifact Collection."

34. Amos Loveday, email to author, February 19, 2015.

35. Pinkham, Oral History Interview.

36. Frank Walker, email to Bill Waters, November 21, 1995, box 34, folder 9, Resource Management Records 1936–2002, NEPE-00638, Nez Perce National Historical Park, Lapwai, Idaho.

37. Joan Abrams, "Nez Perces Say Farewell; Tribe Holds Ceremony to Say Goodbye to Artifacts," *Lewiston Morning Tribune*, November 28, 1995.

38. "Artifacts belong to Ohio; Their Display Belongs Here," *Lewiston Morning Tribune*, November 29, 1995, box 34, folder 9, Resource Management Records 1936–2002, NEPE-00638, Nez Perce National Historical Park, Lapwai, Idaho.

39. "For Immediate Release: Time Is Slipping Away from the Nez Perce Indian Tribe, as They Strive to Retain Sacred and Historical Artifacts on Loan from the Ohio Historical Society," November 29, 1995, box 34, folder 9, Resource Management Records 1936–2002, NEPE-00638, Nez Perce National Historical Park, Lapwai, Idaho.

40. Samuel Penney to Gary Ness, November 29, 1995, provided to the author by OHS registrar Leslie Pohling.

41. Memorandum re: Nez Perce Collection to Gary Ness from Amos Loveday, December 1, 1995, provided to the author by OHS registrar Leslie Pohling.

42. Roberta Ulrich, "Nez Perce Tribe Fights to Keep Artifact Collection," *Oregonian*, December 4, 1995.

43. Louise Barber to Gary Ness, December 5, 1995, box 34, folder 9, Resource Management Records 1936–2002, NEPE-00638, Nez Perce National Historical Park, Lapwai, Idaho.

44. Roberta Ulrich, "Nez Perce Tribe Fights to Keep Artifact Collection," *Oregonian*, December 4, 1995.

45. Joan Abrams, "Letter May Help Keep Spalding-Allen Collection in Idaho," *Lewiston Morning Tribune*, December 6, 1995.

46. Tom Kenworthy, "Fragile Links to the Past: Nez Perce Tribe Battle for Artifacts Taken in 1840s," *Washington Post*, December 10, 1995.

47. Douglas Cole, "Tricks of the Trade: Some Reflections on Anthropological Collecting," *Arctic Anthropology* 28, no. 1 (1991): 50.

48. Associated Press, "Tribe Aims to Keep Collection of 19 Artifacts in Idaho," *Deseret News*, December 10, 1995.

49. Joel Connelly, "Historical Group, Tribe Battle over Artifacts' Rightful Home," *Dallas Morning News*, December 17, 1995.

50. Connelly, "Historical Group, Tribe Battle over Artifacts' Rightful Home."

51. Connelly, "Historical Group, Tribe Battle over Artifacts' Rightful Home."

52. Joan Abrams, "Spalding Display: Deal Made to Keep Indian Artifacts in Idaho: Nez Perce Tribe Reaches Agreement with Ohio Group," *Lewiston Morning Tribune*, December 13, 1995.

53. Joel Connelly, "Artifacts to Stay in Northwest—Nez Perce Will Pay a Hefty Price to Keep the Collection in Idaho," *Seattle Post-Intelligencer*, December 14, 1995.

54. Agreement to sell the Spalding-Allen Collection, provided to the author by OHS registrar Leslie Pohling.

55. Picard, Oral History Interview.

56. Tom Kenworthy, "Nez Perce Tribe Battling for History: Culture: Native Americans Dispute Ohio Historical Society's Ownership of Artifacts," *Washington Post*, December 17, 1995.

57. Julie Kane, conversation with the author, September 11, 2020.

58. Jim Carrier, "MTV, Web Aids Indians," *Denver Post*, Sunday, July 7, 1996.

59. Picard, Oral History Interview.

60. Roberta Ulrich, "Tribe Needs $600,000 for Artifacts," *Oregonian*, December 17, 1995.

Chapter 10 Securing the Collection

1. "A Better Resolution for the Nez Perce Artifacts?" *Seattle Times*, January 3, 1996, box 34, folder 8, Resource Management Records 1936–2002, NEPE-00638, Nez Perce National Historical Park, Lapwai, Idaho.

2. "A Better Resolution for the Nez Perce Artifacts?" *Seattle Times*.

3. "Batt Asks Ohio to Cut the Nez Perce a Deal on Artifacts," *Idaho Statesman*, January 10, 1996; Chenoweth Papers, Unprocessed, Nez Perce National Historical Park, Lapwai, Idaho.

4. Tom Savage to Gary Ness, March 8, 1996, box 34, folder 14, Resource Management Records 1936–2002, NEPE-00638, Nez Perce National Historical Park, Lapwai, Idaho.

5. Dr. George Carroll, conversation with the author, February 27, 2015.

6. Carroll, conversation with the author.

7. Paul Raczka, email to author, December 18, 2016.

8. The purchasing power of $608,100 in 1993 in inflation-adjusted dollars would be more than a million dollars ($1,104,905) in 2020. See the United States Department of Labor Statistics Consumer Price Index inflation calculator, http://www.bls.gov/data/inflation_calculator.htm, accessed August 22, 2020.

9. Bill Picard, Oral History Interview, June 2, 2015.

10. Picard, Oral History Interview.

11. S. S. Kasprycki, "The Native American Collection of Friderik Baraga: The Missionary as Ethnographic Collector," *Etnolog* 8, no. 59 (1998): 331–32.

12. Mindy Cameron, "Tribe's History in Hand of Creative, Giving Friends," *Seattle Times*, April 28, 1996.

13. Julie Kane, conversation with the author, September 11, 2020.

14. Addie Rolnick, "Ohio Historical Society Player in Controversy," *Oberlin Review* 124, no. 16, (March 1996), Oberlin College Archives, Oberlin, Ohio.

15. Chenoweth, Oral History Interview.

16. Tom Hudson, "Proposal Fund-Raising Coordinator Spalding-Allen Collection Fund," box 34, folder 8, Resource Management Records 1936–2002, NEPE-00638, Nez Perce National Historical Park, Lapwai, Idaho.

17. Joan Abrams, "He Gladly Shares the Credit," *Lewiston Morning Tribune*, June 14, 1996.

18. Pages from the Ohio Historical Society website, Bob Chenoweth Papers Unprocessed, Nez Perce National Historical Park, Lapwai, Idaho.

19. Addie Rolnick, "Ohio Historical Society Player in Controversy."

20. Pages from the (1996) Nez Perce Heritage Quest Alliance website, May 29, 1996, Bob Chenoweth Papers, Unprocessed, Nez Perce National Historical Park, Lapwai, Idaho.

21. Bob Chenoweth, email to multiple recipients, "Spalding-Allen Collection update," January 8, 1996, box 34, folder 8, Resource Management Records 1936–2002, NEPE-00638, Nez Perce National Historical Park, Lapwai, Idaho.

22. Picard, Oral History Interview.

23. David Melmer, "Nez Perce Plan to Buy Back Ancestral Articles," *Indian Country Today*, April 23, 1996.

Chapter 11 Idaho School Kids, NPR Listeners, and Grunge Bands Do Their Part

1. Nez Perce Tribal Executive Committee, "Nez Perce Tribe Honors Boise Fourth Graders," February 9, 1996, box 34, folder 8, Resource Management Records 1936–2002, NEPE-00638, Nez Perce National Historical Park, Lapwai, Idaho.

2. Rich Roesler, "Children Come to Aid of Indian Tribe: Money Needed to Maintain Possession of Precious Artifacts," *Spokesman-Review*, April 7, 1996.

3. Anne Desaulniers and Karen Weinberg to Tom Hudson, May 8, 1996, box 35, folder 3, Resource Management Records 1936–2002, NEPE-00638, Nez Perce National Historical Park, Lapwai, Idaho.

4. Pamela Corbin to Dear sir or madam, May 14, 1996, box 35, folder 3, Resource Management Records 1936–2002, NEPE-00638, Nez Perce National Historical Park, Lapwai, Idaho.

5. David Melmer, "Nez Perce Plan to Buy Back Ancestral Articles," *Indian Country Today*, April 23, 1996.

6. Joan Abrams, "School Children Helping Tribe Buy Back Artifacts: Pennies Could Play Role in Purchasing Nez Perce Indian Collection from Ohio," *Lewiston Morning Tribune*, April 3, 1996.

7. Spalding-Allen Collection Fundraising Update: June 1, 1996, Nez Perce Heritage Quest Alliance website, Bob Chenoweth Papers, Unprocessed, Nez Perce National Historical Park, Lapwai, Idaho.

8. Joan Abrams, "School Children Helping Tribe Buy Back Artifacts."

9. Bill Picard, Oral History Interview, June 2, 2015.

10. Brian Colona to collection fund administrator, March 15, 1996, box 34, folder 12, Resource Management Records 1936–2002, NEPE-00638, Nez Perce National Historical Park, Lapwai, Idaho.

11. Joan Abrams, "School Children Helping Tribe Buy Back Artifacts."

12. Printed pages from the Nez Perce Heritage Quest Alliance website, May 29, 1996, Bob Chenoweth Papers, Unprocessed, Nez Perce National Historical Park, Lapwai, Idaho.

13. Jerry Todd, "Tribe Uses Technology to Win Back Artifacts," *Denver Post*, July 7, 1996.

14. Unfortunately for area residents, Alice in Chains and Pearl Jam did not play in the benefit concert. Joan Abrams, "Benefit Concert Organizer Sorts through the Rumors," *Lewiston Morning Tribune*, May 22, 1996; "Benefit Raises $2,960 to Buy Artifacts," *Lewiston Morning Tribune*, May 29, 1996; Bob Chenoweth Papers, Unprocessed, Nez Perce National Historical Park, Lapwai, Idaho.

15. Joan Abrams, "Rock Groups, MTV, Jump on Spalding-Allen Bandwagon: As Deadline Approaches, Superstar Rockers Join Tribe's Push to Buy Back Collection of Nez Perce Artifacts," *Lewiston Morning Tribune*, May 29, 1996.

Chapter 12 The Nation Rallies to the Nez Perce Side

1. Jerry Todd, "Tribe Uses Technology to Win Back Artifacts," *Denver Post*, July 7, 1996.

2. Dale Ahlquist to Tom Hudson, April 17, 1996, box 35, folder 3, Resource Management Records 1936–2002, NEPE-00638, Nez Perce National Historical Park, Lapwai, Idaho.

3. Camelita Spencer to whom it may concern, box 35, folder 3, Resource Management Records 1936–2002, NEPE-00638, Nez Perce National Historical Park, Lapwai, Idaho.

4. "UI Women's Center Donates Money to Tribe for Artifacts," *Lewiston Morning Tribune*, April 18, 1996.

5. Joanne Spalding-Stacy, letter to the editor, December 5, 1995, box 34, folder 9, Resource Management Records 1936–2002, NEPE-00638, Nez Perce National Historical Park, Lapwai, Idaho.

6. Gary Fletcher, "Only Two Weeks Left: Poster Available to Help Nez Perce Retrieve Spalding Allen Artifacts," *Wallowa Country Chieftain*, May 16, 1996.

7. Dan Popkey, "Americans Pitch In to Help Tribe," *Idaho Statesman*, April 9, 1996, box 34, folder 9, Resource Management Records 1936–2002, NEPE-00638, Nez Perce National Historical Park, Lapwai, Idaho.

8. Mary and Brock St. Clair (undated); Ginny and Jim Burnett, May 30, 1996; and Valerie Brace (undated) notes accompanying donation, box 35, folder 3, Resource Management Records 1936–2002, NEPE-00638, Nez Perce National Historical Park, Lapwai, Idaho.

9. Jack and Janet Smith to dear friends, May 15, 1996, box 35, folder 3, Resource Management Records 1936–2002, NEPE-00638, Nez Perce National Historical Park, Lapwai, Idaho.

10. "UI Women's Center Donates Money to Tribe for Artifacts."

11. Fletcher, "Only Two Weeks Left."

12. Mindy Cameron, "Tribe's History in Hand of Creative, Giving Friends," *Seattle Times*, April 28, 1996.

13. Rebecca Huntington, "Use the New to Save the Old: Spalding-Allen Fund-Raiser Art Auction Conducted on Internet," *Lewiston Morning Tribune*, April 19, 1996.

14. Nakia Williamson-Cloud, Oral History Interview, May 14, 2015.

15. Bob Chenoweth, Oral History Interview, February 17, 2015.

16. Kevin Peters, Oral History Interview, July 12, 2015.

17. Josiah Pinkham, Oral History Interview, May 14, 2015.

18. Chenoweth, Oral History Interview.

19. Jenny Ferguson, "Oberlin Should Acknowledge Rightful Owners of Nez Perce Artifacts," *Oberlin Review*, May 3, 1996.

20. Anne Vasser, "Young Rockers Work to Save Some Idaho History: Lewiston Concert Raises Money to Buy Back Indian Artifacts," *Lewiston Morning Tribune*, May 26, 1996.

21. Sandra Lee, "Nez Perce Near Goal: Tribe Confident It Will Keep Collection of Artifacts, Though It's $45,000 Short," *Lewiston Morning Tribune*, May 30, 1996.

22. "Benefit Raises $2,960 to Buy Artifacts," *Lewiston Morning Tribune*, May 29, 1996.

23. Sandra Lee, "Buying a Legacy," *Lewiston Morning Tribune*, May 31, 1996; Chenoweth Papers, NEPE.

24. Ohio Historical Society, "Nez Perce Indian Tribe Completes Purchase of Spalding-Allen Collection," May 30, 1996, box 34, folder 8, Resource Management Records 1936–2002, NEPE-00638, Nez Perce National Historical Park, Lapwai, Idaho.

25. Randall Edwards, "Nez Perce Have Cash to Buy Artifacts," *Columbus Dispatch*, May 30, 1996; Chenoweth Papers, NEPE.

26. "Benefit Raises $2,960 to Buy Artifacts."

27. Joan Abrams, "He Gladly Shares the Credit," *Lewiston Morning Tribune*, June 14, 1996.

28. Nez Perce Heritage Quest Alliance, "Two Inserts for Ohio Historical Society Release Dateline May 30, 1996," box 34, folder 8, Resource Management Records 1936–2002, NEPE-00638, Nez Perce National Historical Park, Lapwai, Idaho.

29. Rich Roeslser, "Tribe Regains Articles of History," *Spokesman-Review*, May 31, 1996; Chenoweth Papers, NEPE.

30. Roeslser, "Tribe Regains Articles of History."

31. Edwards, "Nez Perce Have Cash to Buy Artifacts"; Bob Chenoweth Papers, Unprocessed, Nez Perce National Historical Park, Lapwai, Idaho.

32. Julie Kane, conversation with the author, September 11, 2020.

33. Williamson-Cloud, Oral History Interview.

34. Picard, Oral History Interview.

35. Peters, Oral History Interview.

36. Abrams, "He Gladly Shares the Credit."

37. "Cradleboard Comes Home After 150 Year Hiatus," *Tots Tatoken*, June, 1996; Bob Chenoweth Papers, Unprocessed, Nez Perce National Historical Park, Lapwai, Idaho.

38. Roeslser, "Tribe Regains Articles of History"; Bob Chenoweth Papers, Unprocessed, Nez Perce National Historical Park, Lapwai, Idaho.

39. "Cradleboard Comes Home After 150 Year Hiatus"; Bob Chenoweth Papers, Unprocessed, Nez Perce National Historical Park, Lapwai, Idaho.

40. "Nez Perce Buy Back Prized Artifacts," *Fort Apache Scout*, June 7, 1996.

41. Rebecca Huntington. "Precious Cradleboard Is Home at Last: Nez Perce Artifact Is Transported from Ohio to Spalding," *Lewiston Morning Tribune*, June 1, 1996.

42. Elaine Williams, "Back to the Tribe: Nez Perces Celebrate the Return of Spalding-Allen Collection Artifacts," *Lewiston Morning Tribune*, June 16, 1996.

43. Jim Carrier, "Native American Art Collecting Not Stylish for Everyone," *Denver Post Empire Magazine of the West*, July 14, 1996.

44. Jerry Todd, "Tribe Uses Technology to Win Back Artifacts," *Denver Post*, July 7, 1996.

45. Interpretive panel at the Nez Perce National Historical Park.

46. Accession no. 517, Nez Perce National Historical Park.

47. Bob Chenoweth, "Clearwater Battle Artifacts Returned," *CRM: The Journal of Heritage Stewardship* 9 (1999): 51.

48. Chenoweth, "Clearwater Battle Artifacts Returned."

49. Tom Henry, "Museum Returns Artifacts to Nez Perce Tribe," *Toledo Blade News*, August 20, 1998.

50. Henry, "Museum Returns Artifacts to Nez Perce Tribe."

51. Chenoweth, "Clearwater Battle Artifacts Returned."

Chapter 13 Chief Joseph's Shirt at Auction

1. "Chief Joseph's War Shirt Fetches Nearly $900,000 at Auction," *Indian Country Today*, July 24, 2012.

2. "Chief Joseph: The Captured Nez Perces Banqueted at Bismark, the Walk and Appearance of Josephy to Pass Through St. Paul Tomorrow en Route to Fort Leavenworth," *St. Paul Dispatch*, November 23, 1877; quoted in J. Diane Pearson, "Nimiipuu Peoplehood, Survival, and Relocation," in *Rising from the Ashes: Survival, Sovereignty, and Native America*, ed. by William Willard, Alan G. Marshall, and J. Diane Pearson (Lincoln: University of Nebraska Press, 2020), 70.

3. Meghan Saar, "A Tale of Two Shirts: Nez Perce Collectors Get the Chance to Own a Shirt Off Chief Joseph's Back," *True West Magazine*, July 10, 2012.

4. Saar, "A Tale of Two Shirts."

5. The History Blog, "Chief Joseph War Shirt Sells for $877,500," Archives, July 23, 2012, accessed July 19, 2018, http://www.thehistoryblog.com/archives/18392.

Chapter 14 Reflections on Spalding and the Spalding-Allen Collection

1. Antoinette Burton, *Dwelling in the Archive: Women Writing House, Home, and History in Late Colonial India* (New York: Oxford University Press, 2003), 138.

2. Paul Raczka, email to author, December 18, 2016.

3. Bill Picard, Oral History Interview, June 2, 2015.

4. Jim Carrier, "Native American Art Collecting Not Stylish for Everyone," *Denver Post Empire Magazine of the West*, July 14, 1996.

5. Josiah Pinkham, Oral History Interview, May 14, 2015.

6. Susan Arreola, "Ancestral Wallowa Valley Returned to Nez Perce Tribe," *Indian Country Today*, December 9, 1996.

7. Gary Fletcher, "Nez Perce Celebrate a Homecoming and a Healing," *Wallowa County Chieftain*, June 19, 1997.

8. Pinkham, Oral History Interview.

9. Jeff Mohram, "A Long Strange Trip," *Chronicle Telegram*, April 20, 2002; Bob Chenoweth Papers, Unprocessed, Nez Perce National Historical Park, Lapwai, Idaho.

10. Christopher Maag, "Vanishing History," *Monthly Columbus Magazine* (November 2009), accessed January 7, 2021, https://www.columbusmonthly.com/article/20140206/NEWS/302068650.

11. Certainly not all of OHS's departments provided such poor research services. Leslie Pohling, the OHS registrar, promptly responded to all of my questions, provided documents, and put me in touch with Dr. Loveday and Dr. Carroll.

Chapter 15 Sacred Places and a Private Golf Course

1. Archaeological Institute of America, "Insider: Unfair Fairways," *Archaeology* 59, no. 6 (November/December 2006), https://archive.archaeology.org/0611/news/insider.html.

2. Christopher Maag, "Ohio Indian Mounds: Hallowed Ground and a Nice Par 3," *New York Times Magazine*, November 28, 2005; Archaeological Institute of America, "Insider: Unfair Fairways."

3. "Earthworks: Last Remains of the Hopewell People," *Newsweek*, October 15, 2009, accessed January 2, 2021, https://www.newsweek.com/earthworks-last-remains-hopewell-people-80953.

4. Paul Raczka, email to author, December 18, 2016.

Chapter 16 The International Marketplace for Cultural Heritage

1. Tom Mashberg, "Secret Bids Guide Hopi Indians' Spirits Home," *New York Times*, December 16, 2013.

2. Mashberg, "Secret Bids Guide Hopi Indians' Spirits Home."

3. Dominique Godreche, "Lawyer Has Hope that Auctions of Sacred Items Will Someday Stop," *Indian Country Today Media Network*, December 22, 2014.

4. C. Colwell, *Plundered Skulls and Stolen Spirits* (Chicago and London: University of Chicago Press, 2017), 21–22.

5. Rachel Donadio, "Zuni Ask Europe to Return Sacred Art," *New York Times*, April 9, 2014.

6. Donadio, "Zuni Ask Europe to Return Sacred Art."

7. "Masks" is the term used in the Navajo press release. "Navajo Nation Buys Back 7 Sacred Masks at Controversial Parisian Auction," *Indian Country Today Media Network*, December 16, 2014.

Chapter 17 Conclusion

1. Jennifer K. Bauer, "How the Nez Perce Tribe Got a Valuable Collection of Artifacts Back Against All Odds," *Inland 360*, August 12, 2020.

2. For a complete list, see the Association of Tribal Archives, Libraries, and Museums, Guardian Award Winners, accessed April 15, 2020, https://www.atalm.org/node/369.

3. Jennifer K. Bauer, "How the Nez Perce Tribe Got a Valuable Collection of Artifacts Back Against All Odds."

4. Josiah Pinkham, Oral History Interview, May 14, 2015.

5. Pinkham, Oral History Interview.

6. Plateau People's Web Portal, Spalding-Allen Collection (Nez Perce), accessed September 14, 2020, https://plateauportal.libraries.wsu.edu/collection/spalding-allen-collection-nez-perce.

7. Plateau People's Web Portal, Spalding-Allen Collection (Nez Perce), Man's Shirt, Nez Perce, accessed September 14, 2020, https://plateauportal.libraries.wsu.edu/digital-heritage/mans-shirt-nez-perce.

8. Bill Picard, Oral History Interview, June 2, 2015.

Works Cited

Archives and Manuscript Collections

Administrative Records, Burke Museum, Seattle, Washington.

Roderick Sprague Papers, Fort Walla Walla Museum Archives, Walla Walla, Washington.

Record Group 2/11, Emil C. Daneberg, Oberlin College Archives, Oberlin, Ohio.

Registrar's Papers, Ohio Historical Society, Columbus, Ohio.

Accession Records, Nez Perce National Historical Park, Lapwai, Idaho.

Resource Management Records 1936–2002, NEPE-00638, Nez Perce National Historical Park, Lapwai, Idaho.

Bob Chenoweth Papers, Unprocessed, Nez Perce National Historical Park, Lapwai, Idaho. Once organized, these papers will be incorporated in the Nez Perce National Historical Park Resource Management Records, NEPE 33871.

Clifford Drury Papers, Cage 144, Washington State University Libraries, Manuscripts, Archives, and Special Collections, Pullman, Washington.

Theodore Little Papers, Cage 515, Washington State University Libraries, Manuscripts, Archives, and Special Collections, Pullman, Washington.

Jacqueline Peterson Papers, Unprocessed, MS 2012.03, Washington State University Libraries, Manuscripts, Archives, and Special Collections, Pullman, Washington.

Interviews

Susan Buchel, Oral History Interview, October 22, 2015.

Bob Chenoweth, Oral History Interview, February 17, 2015.

Kevin Peters, Oral History Interview, July 12, 2015.

Bill Picard, Oral History Interview, June 2, 2015.

Josiah Pinkham, Oral History Interview, May 14, 2015.

Frank Walker, Oral History Interview, June 2, 2015.

Nakia Williamson-Cloud, Oral History Interview, May 14, 2015.

Newspapers

Columbus Dispatch

Chronicle Telegram

The Dalles Chronicle

Dallas Morning News

Denver Post

Deseret News

Fort Apache Scout

Idaho Statesman

Indian Country Today Media Network.com

Inland 360

New York Times

Lewiston Morning Tribune

Los Angeles Times

Oberlin Review

Olympian

Oregonian

Plain Dealer

Seattle Times

Spokesman-Review

Toledo Blade News

Tri-City Herald

Tots Tatoken

Wallowa County Chieftain

Washington Post

Xenia Daily Gazette

Published Works

Archaeological Institute of America. "Insider: Unfair Fairways." *Archaeology* 59, no. 6 (November/ December 2006).

Beal, Merrill D. *"I Will Fight No More Forever": Chief Joseph and the Nez Perce War*. Seattle: University of Washington Press, 1963.

Bond, Trevor James. "From Treasure Room to Archives: The McWhorter Papers and the State College of Washington." *Pacific Northwest Quarterly* 102, no. 2. (2011): 67–78.

———. "The Hunt for Oregon Missionary Sources: Clifford M. Drury's Enduring Archives Legacy." *Oregon Historical Quarterly* 114, no. 1. (2013): 38–63.

Burton, Antoinette. *Dwelling in the Archive: Women Writing House, Home, and History in Late Colonial India*. New York: Oxford University Press, 2003.

Campen, Richard. *Architecture of the Western Reserve 1800–1900*. Cleveland and London: The Press of Case Western Reserve University, 1971.

Carocci, Max. "Review Essay: Changing Debates in Museum Studies since NAGPRA." *Transmotion* 4, no. 1 (2018): 127–32.

Carson, Kevin. *The Long Journey of the Nez Perce: A Battle History from Cottonwood to the Bear Paw*. Yardley, PA: Westholme Publishers, 2011.

Catton, Ted. *Nez Perce National Historical Park Administrative History*. Missoula: Historical Research Associates, 1996.

Chenoweth, Bob. "Clearwater Battle Artifacts Returned." *CRM: The Journal of Heritage Stewardship* 22, no. 9 (1999): 51–52.

Chenoweth, Bob, and Tabitha Erdey. *Nuunimnix: An Exhibition in Celebration of the Fiftieth Anniversary of the Nez Perce National Historical Park*. Lewiston: Confluence Press, 2015.

Christen, Kimberly. "Opening Archives: Respectful Repatriation." *American Archivist* 74, no. 1 (2011): 185–210.

Classen, Constance, and David Howes. "The Museum as Sensescape: Western Sensibilities and Indigenous Artifacts." In *Sensible Objects: Colonialism, Museums and Material Culture*, ed. Elizabeth Edwards, Chris Gosden, and Ruth Phillips, 199–222. London: Routledge, 2006.

Cole, Douglas. "Tricks of the Trade: Some Reflections on Anthropological Collecting." *Arctic Anthropology* 28, no. 1 (1991): 48–52.

Colwell, Chip. "Can Repatriation Heal the Wounds of History?" *The Public Historian* 41, no. 1 (2019): 90–110.

———. "Curating Secrets: Repatriation, Knowledge Flows, and Museum Power Structures." *Current Anthropology* 56, no. 12 (2015): 263–75.

———. *Plundered Skulls and Stolen Spirits*. Chicago and London: University of Chicago Press, 2017.

Drury, Clifford. *The Diaries and Letters of Henry H. Spalding and Asa Bowen Smith Relating to the Nez Perce Mission 1838–1842*. Glendale, CA: Arthur H. Clark Company, 1958.

———. *Pioneer of Old Oregon: Henry Harmon Spalding*. Caldwell, ID: Caxton Printers, 1936.

Evans, Steven Ross. *Voice of the Old Wolf: Lucullus Virgil McWhorter and the Nez Perce Indians*. Pullman: Washington State University Press, 1996.

Feest, Christian F. "American Indians and Ethnographic Collecting in Europe." *Museum Anthropology* 16 (1992): 7–11.

Fletcher, Robert. "The Spaulding-Allen Indian Collection." *The Oberlin Alumni Magazine* 26 (February 1930): 136–39.

Furtwangler, Albert. *Bringing Indians to the Book*. London and Seattle: University of Washington Press, 2005.

Grafe, Steven. "'Our Private Affairs in Way Of Barter': Correspondence Between Dudley Allen and Henry Harmon Spalding, 1838–1848." *Idaho Yesterdays* 40, no. 3 (Fall 1996): 2–12.

———. "Still They Look Handsome: the Spalding-Allen Collection." *American Indian Art Magazine* 22, no. 3 (Summer 1997): 35–43.

———. *The Origins of Floral-Design Beadwork in the Southern Columbia River Plateau*. PhD diss. Albuquerque: University of New Mexico, 1999.

Greenwald, Emily. *Reconfiguring the Reservation: The Nez Perces, Jicarilla Apaches, and the Dawes Act*. Albuquerque: University of New Mexico Press, 2002.

Hinsley, Curtis M. "Collecting Cultures and Cultures of Collecting: The Lure of the American Southwest, 1880–1915." *Museum Anthropology* 16 (1992): 12–20.

Jimerson, Rand. *Archives Power: Memory, Accountability, and Social Justice*. Chicago: Society of American Archivists, 2009.

Josephy, Alvin. *The Nez Perce Indians and the Opening of the Northwest*. New Haven and London: Yale University Press, 1965.

Kasprycki, S. S. "The Native American Collection of Friderik Baraga: The Missionary as Ethnographic Collector." *Etnolog* 8, no. 59 (1998): 331–55.

Maag, Christopher. "Vanishing History." *Monthly Columbus Magazine* (November 2009).

———. "Ohio Indian Mounds: Hallowed Ground and a Nice Par 3." *New York Times Magazine*, November 28, 2005.

Margaris, Amy, and Linda Grimm. "Collecting for a College Museum: Exchange Practices and the Life History of a 19th-Century Arctic Collection." *Museum Anthropology* 34, no. 2 (2011): 109–27.

Mauries, Patrick. *Cabinet of Curiosities*. London: Thames & Hudson, 2002.

McCoy, Genevieve. "The Difficulties of Translating Mission Theory into Practice: The Whitman-Spalding Nez Perce Mission." *The Journal of Presbyterian History* 77, no. 3 (Fall 1999): 181–94.

McCoy, Robert R. *Chief Joseph, Yellow Wolf, and the Creation of Nez Perce History in the Pacific Northwest*. New York: Routledge, 2004.

McDermott, John Francis. "William Clark: Pioneer Museum Man." *Journal of the Washington Academy of Sciences* 44, no. 11 (November 1954): 370–73.

McWhorter, Lucullus V. *Yellow Wolf: His Own Story*. Caldwell, ID: Caxton Printers, 1940.

———. *Hear Me, My Chiefs! Nez Perce Legend & History*. Caldwell, ID: Caxton Printers, 1952.

Nisbet, Jack. "Henry and Eliza's Box of Flowers." *The North Columbia Monthly* (April 2014).

Ohio Historical Society. *Annual Report: Fiscal Year 2004*. https://www.ohiohistory.org/OHC/media/OHC-Media/Documents/OHC_AnnualReport_Web.pdf.

Oliphant, J. Orin. "The Botanical Labors of the Reverend Henry H. Spalding." *Washington Historical Quarterly* 25, no. 2 (1934): 93–102.

Patterson, James. *Grand Expectations: The United States, 1945–1974*. New York and Oxford: Oxford University Press, 1996.

Pearson, J. Diane. *The Nez Perces in the Indian Territory: Nimíipuu Survival*. Norman: University of Oklahoma Press, 2008.

———. "Nimíipuu Peoplehood, Survival, and the Indian Territory." In *Rising from the Ashes: Survival, Sovereignty, and Native America,* edited by William Willard, Alan G. Marshall, and J. Diane Pearson, 31–61. Lincoln: University of Nebraska Press, 2020.

———. "Nimíipuu Peoplehood, Survival, and Relocation." In *Rising from the Ashes: Survival, Sovereignty, and Native America*, edited by William Willard, Alan G. Marshall, and J. Diane Pearson, 63–90. Lincoln: University of Nebraska Press, 2020.

Peterson, Jacqueline, and Laura Peers. *Sacred Encounters: Father De Smet and the Indians of the Rocky Mountain West*. Norman and London: University of Oklahoma Press, 1993.

Phinney, Archie. *Nez Perce Texts*. New York: Columbia University Press, 1934.

Pinkham, Allen, and Steven Evans. *Lewis and Clark Among the Nez Perce: Strangers in the Land of the Nimíipuu*. Washburn: Dakota Institute, 2015.

Richards, Kent. *Isaac I. Stevens: Young Man in a Hurry*. Pullman: Washington State University Press, 2016.

Ritchie, Donald. *Doing Oral History: A Practical Guide*. Oxford and New York: Oxford University Press, 2003.

Slickpoo, Allen, Sr., and Deward Walker. *Noon Nee-Me-Poo (We, the Nez Perces): Culture and History of the Nez Perces*. Lapwai: Nez Perce Tribe of Idaho, 1973.

Spruce, Duane Blue, ed. *Spirit of a Native Place: Building the National Museum of the American Indian*. Washington, DC: National Museum of the American Indian, Smithsonian Institution, in association with National Geographic, 2004.

Tonkovich, Nicole. *The Allotment Plot: Alice C. Fletcher, E. Jane Gay, and Nez Perce Survivance*. Lincoln: University of Nebraska Press, 2012.

———. *Dividing the Reservation: Alice C. Fletcher's Nez Perce Allotment Diaries and Letters 1889–1892*. Pullman: Washington State University Press, 2016.

Walker, Deward. "Nez Perce." In *Handbook of North American Indians*, vol. 12, edited by William Sturtevant. Washington, DC: Smithsonian Institution, 1998.

West, Elliott. *The Last Indian War: The Nez Perce Story*. New York: Oxford University Press, 2011.

Willard, William, Alan Marshall, and J. Diane Pearson. *Rising from the Ashes: Survival, Sovereignty, and Native America*. Lincoln: University of Nebraska Press, 2020.

Woodger, Elin, and David Burg. *Eyewitness History: The 1980s*. New York: Facts on File, 2006.

Wright, Robin K. "A Collection History: Washington Native Art." In *A Time of Gathering*, edited by Robin K. Wright. Seattle: Burke Museum and University of Washington Press, 1991.

Index

Italicized page numbers represent images and photographs

Also Available from WSU Press

BE BRAVE, TAH-HY!
The Journey of Chief Joseph's Daughter
Jack R. Williams
Illustrations by Jo Proferes

Exquisitely illustrated and rich with depictions of Nimiipuu Dreamer culture, Tah-hy's young voice narrates this novel about the harrowing 1877 flight of the Nez Perce.

2012 Idaho Book Award Honorable Mention, Idaho Library Association

"*Be Brave, Tah-hy!* is a gripping tale, and truly a story for Americans of all ages." —*Bellingham Herald*

ISBN 978-0-87422-313-2 / $29.95 / Paperback

TEACHING NATIVE PRIDE
Upward Bound and the Legacy of Isabel Bond
Tony Tekaroniake Evans

Native and non-Native voices convey the inspiring story of Upward Bound—a federal program designed to help low-income and at-risk students attend college—at the University of Idaho. Director Isabel Bond developed a unique curriculum celebrating the region's Native American heritage, and her dedication helped many break cycles of poverty, isolation, and disenfranchisement.

ISBN 978-0-87422-379-8 / $27.95 / Paperback

FINDING CHIEF KAMIAKIN
The Life and Legacy of a Northwest Patriot
Richard D. Scheuerman and Michael O. Finley
Photographs by John Clement

A mid-1800s surge of immigrants incited a cataclysmic upheaval that jeopardized the very existence of the Plateau's native people. Chief Kamiakin, a prominent Yakama leader, resolved to resist threats to their lands and traditional way of life. This is his story.

Finalist, 2009 Washington State Book Award

"Engrossing...The images and narrative are precise, easy to read, and above all; interesting." —*Public Library Association*

"Kamiakin's legacy is meaningful for all of us." —*Columbia Magazine*

"Anyone who picks up this highly readable volume will learn a lot about the history and culture of Interior Northwest Indians." —*Oregon Historical Quarterly*

ISBN 978-0-87422-379-8 / $27.95 / Paperback

THE SNAKE RIVER-PALOUSE AND THE INVASION OF THE INLAND NORTHWEST
Clifford E. Trafzer and Richard D. Scheuerman

Originally released in 1993 as *Renegade Tribe*, this award-winning title sensitively retells the compelling saga of western expansion and Indian-white conflict from a Native American perspective and offers a new foreword by Chief Tilcoax descendent Wilson Wewah.

"Trafzer's and Scheuerman's book, in a solid and sometimes eloquent fashion, allows us to know this politically vulnerable people." —*American Indian Quarterly*

ISBN 978-0-87422-337-8 / $24.95 / Paperback

DIVIDING THE RESERVATION
Alice C. Fletcher's Nez Perce Allotment Diaries and Letters, 1889-1892
Nicole Tonkovich

Ethnologist Alice C. Fletcher helped conceptualize the Dawes General Allotment Act of 1887 and became one of the first female federal Indian agents. Her writing offers insight into how she and others applied, resisted, and amended federal policy, as well as her internal conflicts over dividing the reservation.

"The strength of Dividing the Reservation is the level of detail Tonkovich provides on Fletcher's ideas and actions on allotment." —*Oregon Historical Quarterly*

ISBN 978-0-87422-344-6 / $29.95 / Paperback